PENGUIN BOOKS

MURDER MOST FOUL

MAX HAINES was born in Antigonish, Nova Scotia. His "Crime Flashback" column made its debut in *The Toronto Sun* in 1972. Since that time, he has researched more than two thousand murder cases around the world.

Today, "Crime Flashback" appears weekly in *The Toronto Sun* and is syndicated in more than forty newspapers across Canada. Also syndicated in Central and South America, the column has a weekly readership of more than three million and has been translated into Spanish, French, and Chinese.

Max is a member of ACTRA, Crime Writers of Canada, and the Writers' Union of Canada. He resides in Etobicoke, Ontario, with his wife Marilyn.

Other works by Max Haines

The Collected Works of Max Haines Vol. 4 (2000)
Canadian Crimes (1998)
Murders Strange But True (1997)
Celebrity Murders (1996)
The Collected Works of Max Haines Vol. 3 (1996)
Multiple Murderers II (1995)
Multiple Murderers (1994)
Doctors Who Kill (1993)
True Crime Stories Book V (1992)
The Collected Works of Max Haines Vol. 2 (1991)
True Crime Stories Book IV (1990)
True Crime Stories Book III (1989)
True Crime Stories Book II (1988)
True Crime Stories (1987)
That's Life (1986)
The Collected Works of Max Haines Vol. 1 (1985)
Murder & Mayhem (1984)
The Murderous Kind (1983)
Crime Flashback #3 (1982)
Crime Flashback #2 (1981)
Crime Flashback #1 (1980)
Calendar of Criminal Capers (1977)
Bothersome Bodies (1977)

MURDER most foul

CRIMES FROM CANADA AND AROUND THE WORLD

MAX HAINES

A SIGNET BOOK
NEW AMERICAN LIBRARY
Published in Canada by
Penguin Books Canada Limited, Toronto, Ontario

SIGNET
Published by the Penguin Group
Penguin Books Canada Ltd, 10 Alcorn Avenue, Toronto, Ontario, Canada M4V 3B2
Penguin Books Ltd, 27 Wrights Lane, London W8 5TZ, England
Penguin Putnam Inc., 375 Hudson Street, New York, New York 10014, U.S.A.
Penguin Books Australia Ltd, Ringwood, Victoria, Australia
Penguin Books (NZ) Ltd, cnr Rosedale and Airborne Roads, Albany,
Auckland 1310, New Zealand

Penguin Books Ltd, Registered Offices: Harmondsworth, Middlesex, England

First published in Viking by Penguin Books Canada Limited, 1999
Published in Signet by Penguin Books
First Printing, November 2000

10 9 8 7 6 5 4 3 2 1

Manufactured in Canada

CANADIAN CATALOGUING IN PUBLICATION DATA

Haines, Max
Murder most foul: crimes from Canada and around the world

ISBN 0-451-20047-0

1. Murder. 2. Criminals. I. Title.

HV6515.H3584 2000 364.15'23 C00-931634-5

To the Memory of
Enid Holtzman

Acknowledgments

WHILE GATHERING material for this collection of stories, I consulted many organizations and individuals.

The RCMP were most co-operative in providing information concerning the tragic death of Constable Dennis Onofrey.

Police forces in England, the United States, France, Ireland, New Zealand, Germany, Belgium and Italy generously shared details about murders that took place in their countries.

The News Research Department of the *Toronto Sun* was extremely helpful. Special thanks to manager Julie Kirsh and assistant manager Katherine Webb Nelson.

The staff at Penguin Books was, as always, tremendously supportive and encouraging, particularly Cynthia Good, Jackie Kaiser and J.C. Kennedy. The final product would not have been possible without the creative efforts of copy editor Liba Berry.

Others who assisted me and without whose constructive criticism this book would not have become a reality are my daughters, Susan, Maureen and Eleanor.

Legal advice was most generously provided by Fayth Star. As usual, a wife named Marilyn had the final word on everything.

M.H.

Contents

MURDER

most foul

Rene Ackerman

(Switzerland)

WHEN 47-YEAR-OLD Rene Ackerman was questioned by Swiss police, he told them a straightforward story. According to Rene, on Wednesday, May 12, 1982, he had dinner with his wife, Erika, after she completed her workday at a Lucerne department store. They had dined at a fashionable restaurant and had lingered until shortly after 11 p.m. Erika had driven away in her Austin Mini, supposedly to their apartment in the town of Kriens, about a mile south of Lucerne. Rene had visited with a friend. You might ask why police were so interested in Rene's activities on that particular evening. Well, I'll tell you. His wife never made it home. Folks in the tiny Swiss village of Seelisberg were startled when wild sounds attracted them to the edge of the village, where they saw a screaming woman engulfed by flames flailing about in the middle of the road. Down the road, a vehicle exploded. All in all, it was an exciting night in Seelisberg.

Villagers rushed to the burning woman's aid, using clothing and blankets to extinguish the flames. The unconscious, horribly burned woman was rushed by ambulance to Lucerne, where she died seven days later. During the week, while the woman lay in a coma, police launched an extensive investigation into the incident. The Austin Mini that had exploded was traced through its licence to Erika Ackerman, hence the questioning of her husband, Rene.

Rene proved to be quite a lad. He had divorced his first

wife four years earlier and had only been married to Erika for three months. Detectives were interested in the friend Rene had visited on the night of his wife's terrible ordeal. The friend turned out to be beautiful 34-year-old blonde Cornelia Riffel. When interrogated, she swore that Rene had been with her from a little after 11 p.m. until 4 a.m., which encompassed the time that Erika and her Austin Mini went up in flames.

Folks, even the slickest rascal does not generally spend the night with a blonde after only three months of marriage. Rene had a ready explanation. He told authorities that Cornelia was his mistress and had held that position since 1976. They had been doing what comes naturally before he married Erika and simply continued their boudoir gymnastics after he was legally wed. What can I tell you? Rene was just that kind of guy.

Cornelia was married when she met Rene, who was also married at the time. Their chance meeting broke up both marriages when the pair became lovers. What's more, they had the loot to openly enjoy themselves. Cornelia's papa had passed away, leaving her a wad of cash to squander. She and Rene did an excellent job spending it. They dined at the most expensive restaurants and owned three homes with accompanying sports cars. They even owned a racehorse, which didn't run fast, but had an enormous appetite.

Detectives were stymied. They were certain that in some way Rene was responsible for his wife's death, but given Cornelia's statement that he had been with her when the incident occurred, they couldn't get a handle on the case. True enough, Rene had a slight burn on the back of his right hand, but he came up with a convenient explanation for that. He claimed he had burned his hand putting a dish in the oven.

Meanwhile, an autopsy revealed that Erika had been doused with gasoline. Moreover, an examination of the Austin Mini indicated that someone had set the vehicle and Erika on fire. Judging from the position of the Austin, police believed the car had been pushed off the road before being torched.

It was a difficult one to figure out. Why would a man who was living high off the hog, complete with a beautiful mistress, decide to kill his wife of only three months? Why had he married Erika in the first place? There had to be a reason, and there was a good one.

It was left to forensic accountants to come up with the motive. Cornelia and Rene had been living so extravagantly they had slowly exhausted their funds. They had mortgaged the houses and other assets to keep a supply of cash flowing in. Faced with the demise of their luxurious lifestyle, they had come up with a diabolical scheme. Rene would marry someone and insure her life. Erika was picked because she was not wealthy. If he married a rich woman, Rene reasoned, he would be suspected of killing her for her money. Accountants found that Erika had two life insurance policies, one for a value of £30,000 pounds and one for £60,000. Rene was the beneficiary of both policies.

It was a tough case, but Swiss detectives kept digging away. They questioned employees at the restaurant where Erika and Rene had dined on the night in question. They learned that Erika had complained of a headache and Rene had given her some pills. A search of Rene's BMW uncovered an empty five-gallon gas can and a pair of men's gloves. The right glove had a hole burned in the back, which matched perfectly the burn on Rene's right hand.

Rene was arrested and charged with his wife's murder. Cornelia, who stuck to her story that Rene had been with her all night, was charged with being an accomplice to homicide.

In 1985, Rene stood trial. The prosecution contended that Rene had plied his wife with wine and sleeping pills at the restaurant. He then drove her to Seelisberg, where he doused both Erika and the Austin Mini with gasoline; Cornelia had followed the pair in the BMW and picked up Rene. The lovers drove back home, where they spent the remainder of the night.

Rene never confessed. Cornelia finally admitted she had picked up Rene outside Seelisburg, but claimed she had had no knowledge of the murder. The Swiss jury didn't believe either of the accused. Rene Ackerman was found guilty of murdering his wife and was sentenced to life imprisonment, while Cornelia was found guilty of being an accomplice to murder. She received a sentence of 17 years in prison.

Jim Allison
(Canada)

EVERYONE HAS heard one of those ribald stories about the farmer's daughter. Too few of us, however, have been fortunate enough to know one in the flesh, so to speak. But a real honest-to-goodness "farmer's daughter" did exist in southern Ontario.

Her name was Emma Borland, and she lived about five miles south of Galt, just before the turn of the 20th century. Mr. and Mrs. Borland knew they had a handful when Emma romanced her way through her teens. She was good-looking, had a figure to match anda yen for action. All those virile young males of Waterloo County provided the action, and Emma provided everything else.

Emma was only 21 when she married John Arnott, a wealthy merchant from Innerkip, who was quite a bit older than she was. Emma turned over a new leaf and was a good and faithful wife to John for two years, and then he passed on to his great reward. There were those around Galt who said she'd been too much for the poor soul in the bedroom. Be that as it may, at 23 Emma found herself completely free and wealthy to boot. So Emma took up where she left off when she married John. She had a barrel of fun for three full years before she turned respectable again.

This time she married Tony Orr, a successful farmer. The entire Orr family was well known socially throughout Waterloo County. Despite Emma's past reputation, she fit, or was pushed gracefully, into the social whirl of rural life.

Again Emma settled down, and really was a good wife until she was about 35. Then she simply ran away with the hired hand, just like they do in the stories. A real handsome character named Tim Mulholland had been making love to Emma while Tony was busy tending the fields or whatever. Tony traced the couple to a hotel in Niagara Falls.

Tony really loved his wife. He took her back and this time hired an unattractive, pimply-faced youngster named Jim Allison as his hired hand. Once bitten, twice shy, as they say. Anyway, they all lived happily for three more years, until all of a sudden Emma disappeared.

Tony and young Jim hitched the horses and drove into Galt to Sheriff Maynard Gould's office to report Emma missing. Alex Allison, Jim's father, was a municipal official who worked in the same building as the sheriff. The youngster took the opportunity to go down the hall to see his father. In the meantime, Tony informed the sheriff that both he and Jim had hunted for Emma all morning. He said a neighbour had heard a gunshot earlier, so Tony had looked for his own shotgun, and found that it was missing. The sheriff sympathized with Tony, but suspected that Emma was up to her old tricks again. Sheriff Gould agreed to go out to the farm with Tony. Young Jim was through visiting his father, and joined Tony and Sheriff Gould in the hall. While Tony attended to the horses, the sheriff asked Jim a pointed question: Did Emma have a boyfriend that Tony didn't know anything about? Jim informed him that there were at least two that he knew of, Weldon Trevelyan and Harry Blair.

Telling Tony he would join him at the farm later, the sheriff went looking for Trevelyan and Blair. Trevelyan readily admitted meeting with Emma. In fact, he thought it was a damn shame she was missing. He claimed he would miss her, too. Some stories just ring true; the sheriff believed Trevelyan. Then the sheriff questioned Blair. Upon being interrogated, Blair admitted making love to Emma, but denied any knowledge of her disappearance. The sheriff shook his head. He believed Blair, too.

Gould proceeded to Tony's farm. By the time he arrived, Tony and Jim had already found the missing shotgun. It smelled of cordite, and had obviously been fired recently. At this point the sheriff realized he had a possible murder on his hands. He wired John Murray, head detective of the Ontario police. Word came back that Detective Murray would arrive by train at nine the next morning. The sheriff accepted the invitation to spend the night on the farm. When he awoke at daybreak the next morning and looked out his window, he thought he saw a light go out in a grove of trees on the other side of a cornfield. Being half-asleep, he dismissed it from his mind, deciding he'd probably seen a firefly.

Tony, Jim and the sheriff drove to Galt and met Detective Murray at the train. After being briefed, the detective questioned the two main suspects, Trevelyan and Blair. However, he wasn't as convinced of their innocence as the sheriff was. In fact, Murray thought that possibly Tony had had enough of Emma and had decided to do away with her.

Once at the farm, Detective Murray quickly discovered a patch of grass that was discoloured. The discoloration, which was obviously caused by blood, led down to the cornfield. Detective Murray followed the bent foliage across the meadow to a grove of trees. There he and the sheriff found a shallow half-dug grave with no body in it. Close by, under some leaves, lay the body of poor Emma. She had been killed by a shotgun blast. Detective Murray figured that the murderer had come back after dark to dig the grave. The job wasn't finished. Then Gould remembered the light he had seen when he woke up. It must have been the murderer finishing his work for the night.

Would the killer complete the grave the following night?

In true Hitchcock fashion, the sheriff and the detective hid in the bushes that night and waited for the murderer to show up. At around midnight a lantern came bobbing through the cornfield and up to the grove of trees. The officers grabbed the man with the lantern. To their utter amazement, it was Alex Allison, Jim's father.

Alex told a tragic story. His son Jim had killed Emma, but did not have the courage to conceal the body. Jim had confessed to his father when he and Tony had come to the municipal building to report the woman's disappearance to the sheriff. Alex had dug all the previous night, but had had to stop at daybreak.

They put handcuffs on Alex, and once his son saw him, he broke down and admitted killing Emma. Jim said that he knew about the other men Emma was playing around with and thought he would try his luck with her. Emma laughed at him, and called him ugly. She said she would tell Tony to fire him. In a rage, Jim took the shotgun and killed her.

No charges were ever laid against Alex Allison, but his son Jim was hanged on February 4, 1898, in what was then called Berlin, now known as Kitchener.

Beverley Allitt
(England)

I AM OFTEN asked why England has spawned such strange and unusual murders. There is no answer to this question, but it is a fact that the tidy little isle has given rise, pound for pound, to the weirdest group of killers in the world.

Let's take a look at Nurse Beverly Allitt, who was born in the quaint Lincolnshire village of Corby Glen. At school, Beverly was bright and attentive. But when she enrolled at nearby Grantham College with an eye toward a nursing career, her scholastic endeavours took a turn for the worse. Her personality seemed to change as well. She became a shy, introverted, somewhat overweight young woman. Beverly was also plagued by a tendency toward illness, which was to continue throughout her life. She missed classes regularly due to colds, fatigue and a variety of ailments that always seemed to cure themselves. In time, she had to drop out of college, but shortly there-after she enrolled in a two-year course at the South Lincolnshire School of Nursing.

During her stay at nursing school, Beverly suffered from a series of sicknesses, but she managed to complete the course and obtain employment on a trial basis at Grantham Hospital. It had not been easy for Beverly. At various times she had blurred vision, headaches, back problems and swollen breasts. She also had been afflicted with injuries to her feet, arms, legs and fingers. In addition, she suffered from gallbladder pains, ulcers and various infections.

No one even mildly suspected that Beverly suffered from Munchausen's syndrome, a condition in which the patient strives for attention by inflicting wounds or inventing symptoms. It is rare for such individuals to exhibit signs of both Munchausen's syndrome and Munchausen's syndrome by proxy. This latter condition involves inflicting others with injuries or inducing diseases in others so that they themselves will receive reflected attention.

Beverly Allitt had both conditions, but no one knew it. What her superiors and colleagues saw in 1991 was a neat, hardworking, 24-year-old nurse taking care of the children on Ward 4 of Grantham General Hospital.

On February 21, a young woman rushed into Grantham General with her 7-week-old son in her arms. X-rays indicated little Liam Taylor had pneumonia. Liam's dad soon joined his wife and son. The parents were comforted by the spick-and-span caring nurse who kept them informed of their son's condition. She assured them that Liam was doing fine and told them to go home and get some rest.

Two hours later, at 6 p.m., the Taylors returned to the hospital. Beverly greeted them with the distressing news that Liam's condition had worsened. She explained that she had looked in on him and found he was barely breathing. The baby was rushed to a treatment room, where doctors managed to revive him.

That night, the Taylors slept in the hospital. They were relieved the next day when their son opened his eyes and seemed to be much better. Still anxious, though, they decided to sleep at the hospital that night as well. In the wee hours, Beverly called a colleague to look at Liam. The baby was chalk-white.

Beverly called for the crash team. Within minutes doctors were working frantically to save the baby's life. At 6 a.m. they concluded that Liam had suffered massive brain damage due to lack of oxygen.

While the action was taking place in Ward 4, Beverly Allitt took a back seat as more highly trained nurses and doctors took over. She smiled, washed up and went home. When she came back on duty later that day, she learned that Liam Taylor had died. Death was attributed to a muscle around the baby's heart ceasing to function. Beverly was never suspected of wrongdoing. In fact, she was never even questioned about the death. She had enjoyed the entire episode immensely.

Two weeks later, on March 5, Timothy Hardwick, a helpless 11-year-old cerebral palsy patient, who also suffered from epilepsy, was admitted to Ward 4. Timothy could not walk, talk or see, and had just had a severe epileptic seizure. In due course, he settled down and was resting comfortably.

Beverly was alone with the boy for only a few minutes before she appeared on the floor, shouting, "Quick, cardiac arrest!" A doctor rushed to the area. He was too late. A postmortem failed to ascertain a definite cause of death. Ultimately, it was attributed to epilepsy and cerebral palsy. No one suspected foul play.

March was a bad month at Grantham General. In quick succession, three babies with minor ailments had cardiac arrests. All recovered, but the frequency of these serious incidents caused authorities some concern, particularly when the three youngsters were found to have extraordinarily high levels of insulin in their blood. The only thing the cases had in common was their nurse—Beverly Allitt.

The Phillipses were overjoyed with their identical twin girls, Becky and Katie. Although very tiny, the babies were sent home 33 days after their birth. On April 1, Becky, suffering from what doctors suspected was gastroenteritis, was admitted to Ward 4 at Grantham General. Beverly Allitt spent a lot of time with the little girl. Two days later, Beverly told another nurse that Becky seemed to be in distress. Her colleague disagreed. She felt Becky was doing fine.

Next day, after Beverly fed Becky, the baby was taken home. Her parents were so pleased at her recovery they had her sleep in their bed. At 3 a.m. they awoke to look at Becky. She was dead. A postmortem failed to reveal the cause of death. It was attributed to crib death. Later, blood taken from Becky's heart would show high levels of insulin.

Doctors were concerned about Becky's twin, Katie. They decided to hospitalize her as a precaution. She was placed under the care of Beverly Allitt. That night, Beverly ran down the hall carrying Katie and shouting, "Cardiac arrest, cardiac arrest!" Doctors succeeded in saving Katie's life. Someone remarked that the automatic alarm had failed to go off when Katie stopped breathing. It must have malfunctioned. Katie Phillips was left severely brain-damaged, her right side paralyzed, her hearing impaired and partially blind.

Katie's mother, however, was most appreciative of Nurse Allitt and told staff members the conscientious nurse had saved her daughter's life. She asked Beverly to be Katie's godmother. Humbly, Beverly accepted, saying she was honoured.

Over the next eleven days, four more children unexpectedly suffered cardiac arrests. All four were saved, but some were severely brain-damaged. All of them had the same nurse—Beverly Allitt.

The fourth youngster to die at Beverly's hands was 15-month-old Claire Peck, an asthma patient. Claire was to be outfitted with an intravenous drip and receive nebulizing treatment to help her breathe. For a few minutes, the nurse and doctor attending Claire left her room. Beverly was alone with the child. In less than two minutes Beverly was shouting, "Cardiac arrest!" The doctor and nurse were at the child's side almost instantaneously, administering oxygen. Claire responded immediately. Once again, the nurse and doctor momentarily left the room. As if programmed, the words echoed through the halls once more, "Cardiac arrest, cardiac arrest!" This time the child couldn't be saved. Claire was dead.

It was all too much. Hospital authorities believed a mysterious virus might have swept through the ward. When a postmortem failed to establish the cause of Claire's death, police were called. A poisons expert, conducting tests on materials taken from Claire's body, found traces of lignocaine, a powerful anaesthetic used on patients who have suffered cardiac arrest. Since Claire was asthmatic, there was no reason she would have been given this drug. To police, this was a clear sign that the child had been poisoned.

Investigators reviewed 25 incidents involving 13 children. One nurse, Beverly Allitt, had been present at each of the 25 incidents. Three weeks after the investigation began, Beverly was arrested. She was charged with four murders, three attempted murders and six counts of causing bodily harm.

At her trial, Beverly's history revealed her years of self-maiming to bring attention to herself. Her attacks on the children in her care came about when she graduated from the condition known as Munchausen's syndrome to Munchausen's syndrome by proxy. At the end of her trial, Beverly was sentenced to 13 terms of life imprisonment, the harshest sentence given a woman by a British court in the modern era.

Since her imprisonment, Beverly Allitt has confessed that she killed three children and injured six others.

Doris Andrist & Andre Bodmer

(Switzerland)

OVER THE years, I have delved into some strange and unusual murder plots. You might remember Donald Hume, who dropped his victim's body parts from an airplane as his co-pilot, a dog, looked on; or Bob James, who inserted his wife's foot in a box containing a poisonous rattlesnake. Well, folks, Andre Bodmer and Doris Andrist rank right up there with originators of the weirdest murder plots in the vile and checkered history of homicide.

When Andre was only 15 years old, he was madly in love with his 14-year-old girlfriend, Isabella. No puppy love here; this was mature sexual love in every sense of the word. Both sets of parents, strict, affluent and religious Swiss, were aghast at the obvious sexual attraction between their children. When the parents objected too strongly, the teenagers ran away from the Swiss town of Schwyz and lived off the land in the Buednerland Forest.

In due course, they were brought back to town, but the reunion with their parents was less than jovial. Isabella was pregnant. To the delight of the young couple, their parents insisted they marry. After the nuptials, however, they left the newlyweds to fend for themselves.

Andre and Isabella made their way to Gasel, where Andre apprenticed as a butcher and Isabella attended school, her tummy showing the effects of her woodsy escapade.

After Isabella had her baby, times were rough. The Bodmers lived from hand to mouth. Sometimes they went hungry. This desperate state of affairs couldn't continue indefinitely. A solution to their dilemma was agreed upon: the attractive Isabella would become a prostitute.

And that's how it began. Soon Isabella was entertaining men in their apartment while Andre walked the baby. Their lucrative business was interrupted for a short while when Isabella found herself once again pregnant. The Bodmers' second child came into this troubled world, but as soon as Isabella regained her figure, she was back turning tricks.

The lifestyle Isabella had adopted was rather hectic, with two children and business obligations constantly overlapping. She had a tête-à-tête with hubby Andre, who agreed it was time for him to seek gainful employment. He was accepted as a journeyman butcher with the Denner Wholesale Meat Products Co. in Zurich.

The Bodmers moved to the town of Dielsdorf, about three kilometres outside Zurich. For the first time since they were little more than children, Andre, now 29, and Isabella, 28, were leading normal, productive lives. It would be most pleasant to relate that the Bodmers and their two offspring settled down to a happy, peaceful existence, but such was not to be the case.

At this point, Doris Andrist, a salesgirl in the sausage department at Denner's, enters our story. It began innocently enough. Andre gave the luscious brunette a lift home one day. A few days later, they checked into a hotel room and we can only assume they felt no great compulsion to sleep.

Doris was a knockout in the looks department and a real manipulator in the gray-matter department. Being a single girl, she longed to marry Andre, but that was impossible, as Andre was already well married to Isabella. To Doris, the solution was crystal clear. Isabella had to go.

Doris initially thought divorce might be a solution, but Andre pointed out that he was expecting to inherit his parents' restaurant; the mere mention of divorce would cut him off from this potential windfall.

Doris scratched her pretty cranium and took the giant leap to premeditated murder. She suggested they kill the woman who stood in the way of their happiness. Andre agreed this latter step would certainly achieve the desired result.

Shooting was discussed, but dismissed as being too technical. Neither knew how to fire a gun. After mulling over the problem, they agreed strangulation would suit their purposes perfectly.

Doris suggested that Andre lure Isabella into the woods, where she would strangle her. Andre disagreed. He and Isabella had not been getting along, and it was doubtful that she would be receptive to the idea of a romantic walk in the woods. Besides, he would be an immediate suspect, as is so often the case when wives bite the dust. In addition, inquisitive police might discover the relationship between him and Doris. No, there simply had to be a better plan than that.

It took a few weeks for the diabolical duo to come up with their unbelievable plot, which would divert suspicion from Andre. He would lure Isabella into the forest on the pretense that they were entering a reality contest called Game of Courage. If they won, they would be the recipients of a large sum of money. The game involved entering the woods, where Andre would blindfold Isabella and tie her to a tree. She would be released by an official of the game. There was no risk involved and they stood to win a tidy sum.

It boggles the imagination to believe that anyone would be taken in by such a scheme, but we must remember that although the spark between Isabella and Andre had diminished, he was still the father of her two children and her constant companion for most of her life. Besides, she had no knowledge of Doris's existence.

Meanwhile, Doris was a busy girl. She knew Andre's blood type was AB. If Andre had intercourse with Isabella and they attempted to simulate a rape at the time of her murder, semen left at the scene would be matched to Andre's. It was Doris's intention to leave semen from a different blood type at the site of the murder.

Doris had thought up a way to accomplish this rather difficult task. Posing as a prostitute, she had no difficulty getting picked up in vehicles by cruising males. Eventually, Doris found a gentleman with type O blood. She paid him a fee and collected his semen in a condom, which she carefully stored in her refrigerator.

On September 14, 1985, the unsuspecting Isabella was blindfolded, gagged and tied to a tree in the forest, where the two conspirators took turns throttling her until she was dead. Doris then tore off Isabella's slacks and underwear. She scratched Isabella's face and even broke some of her fingernails. Doris then spread the contents of the condom over Isabella's thighs and legs.

Next day, Andre reported to police that his wife was missing. He told them she had wanted to attend a dance, but because he hadn't wanted to go, they'd argued. Isabella had stormed out of the house and had not returned home. Later that same afternoon, a couple strolling through the woods came across her body.

The physician who performed the autopsy felt that certain aspects of the case were suspicious. There was something unnatural about the crime scene and the condition of the body. Rapists do not usually tie their victims to a tree while raping them. In addition, Isabella had not actually been raped, as her attacker had obviously ejaculated prematurely. From the semen, it was ascertained that the attempted rape had been initiated by someone with type O blood, which eliminated Andre as a suspect.

The pair of killers would have been home free had it not been for one unforeseen circumstance. They both suffered pangs of remorse and fell into a deep depression. Some five weeks after Isabella's murder, they were found unconscious in Buednerland Forest and rushed to hospital, where their stomachs were pumped. Both survived. They had taken massive doses of barbiturates.

Detectives investigating the unsolved murder of Isabella Bodmer questioned Andre. Eventually, he and Doris admitted to the murder, but would disclose no details. It was almost a year later, after Doris's photograph appeared in Swiss newspapers, that the sperm donor came forward with his strange story. Only then did Andre and Doris reveal their diabolical plot.

Andre Bodmer and Doris Andrist stood trial for murder and were found guilty. On January 8, 1988, each received a sentence of 20 years' imprisonment.

Herb & Dorothy Archer

(Canada)

YOU DON'T hear much about the tiny town of Oak Lake, Manitoba, these days, but back in the winter of 1978, it was the most talked-about community in Canada. Dr. Markus Scherz, 64, was the only medic in town. The beloved doctor and his wife, Stephanie, knew all 350 souls who called Oak Lake home.

A loud knock on the door of the Scherz home in the middle of a cold January night awoke the occupants from a deep sleep. For the first time, Dr. Scherz laid eyes on Herbert Bruce Archer and his wife, Dorothy. They were accompanied by farmer Dave Penny from nearby Routledge.

That Sunday, January 22, 1978, had been quite a night for the three visitors to the Scherz home. The saga that was to follow had started earlier when a man and woman registered as Mr. and Mrs. Maurice Crystal at the Countryside Inn Motel in Virden. Their van was parked beside the motel and had come to the attention of the RCMP. A man named Archer had rented the vehicle weeks earlier in Vancouver. The rental vehicle was supposed to be returned in two days. After several weeks passed, the van was considered to have been stolen.

Four RCMP officers, Corporal Russell Hornseth, and Constables John O'Ray, Dennis Onofrey and Candace

Smith, arrived at the motel in two police cruisers to check out the van. They knocked on the door of room 20 and identified themselves as police officers.

The motel room door opened slowly. Apprehensive, Constable Onofrey drew his gun. As soon as Archer saw the weapon, he opened fire. Onofrey was shot dead. Constable Smith, who had just finished her basic training six weeks earlier, ran for cover and drew her weapon. She fired twice and missed. Archer was more accurate. Constable Smith was hit twice, in the hip and stomach.

Archer kept firing. Corporal Hornseth was shot in the head. O'Ray ran for cover, lost his glasses and fell to the ground. He saw the desperate pair make a run toward one of the police cruisers. Archer, realizing the van was low on fuel, decided to take off with his wife in the police car. O'Ray fired several shots. One struck Dorothy Archer, wounding her severely. Speeding away in the police cruiser, Archer realized two things: he needed weapons and ammunition; and it was imperative that his wife receive medical attention.

Archer chose a farmhouse at random. Dave Penny answered the door. He was soon made aware of the situation. The Archers wanted weapons and medical help for Dorothy. Dave told Archer he didn't have any guns, but could accompany his wife to Oak Lake, which had a doctor. Archer and Dorothy proceeded to tie up Mrs. Penny and her daughter. Dorothy was directed to stand guard while her husband took off to procure weapons.

Dave drove while Archer kept him covered. They pulled into Lloyd Hatch's farm. Lloyd and Wilma Hatch were apprised of the circumstances and turned over guns to

Herb Archer. With Dave driving, the pair returned to Penny's farm. Dave's family was as he had left them, with badly wounded Dorothy Archer standing guard.

Once again, Dave found himself driving the police cruiser. This time he was heading for Oak Lake and the medical attention Dorothy Archer required.

Dr. Scherz had been practising in the town for a quarter of a century. He had been awakened in the night many times. The doctor calmly examined the patient and advised Archer that she needed surgery, which he was ill-equipped to perform. He suggested they go to Brandon, about an hour's drive away. Archer wouldn't hear of it. Instead, he had the doctor call an ambulance, which soon arrived and whisked Dorothy to hospital.

Herbert Archer had three hostages: Dr. Scherz, his wife, Stephanie, and Dave Penny. Once Dorothy was taken care of, he relaxed. It was now daylight, Monday, January 23. Archer loved to talk, and told his captives his life story. He portrayed himself as not a bad fellow, but one who had done some wrong things in his life. He admitted killing a Mountie and told his prisoners he had nothing to lose. He explained that he must not fall asleep and demanded something from Dr. Scherz to keep him awake. The doctor gave him amphetamines.

The phone rang. The RCMP was making contact with Archer. They assured him that his wife was out of danger. The desperate man demanded $100,000 cash and safe passage by air out of Canada. He also wanted a guarantee that once he was out of the country, the authorities would make no effort to bring him back. Archer advised the Mounties that his three hostages were alive and well.

Although the Archers would never be brought to trial for the murder of Maurice Crystal, the Calgary businessman was found strangled to death in his office that Sunday night. It was Crystal's credit card that Archer had used to register at the motel in Virden, where the shootout with the RCMP had occurred. When he and Dorothy fled in the police cruiser, they left the credit card behind in room 20.

Another day and night passed. Archer nodded off occasionally, but the slightest noise made him clutch his weapon and wake up. He had no idea that investigators had connected the Calgary murder with the assault on the RCMP.

The RCMP had evacuated the homes close to Dr. Scherz's house. Stores closed. School was suspended. Life in the tiny hamlet had abruptly changed. Only reporters and police were allowed in the general area of the Scherz home.

The individuals in the house had been held captive for more than eighty hours. Constable Dennis Onofrey was buried in Virden. The wait continued. The situation was tense. Archer often said during the course of the siege that he would go down fighting and save the last bullet for himself.

Despite his bravado, Archer's determination to fight it out commenced to wane. On Thursday night, he discussed his options with his captives. They told him he had a better chance if he gave himself up rather than attempt to make a deal. Police don't deal with someone who has killed one of their own. Archer listened and reluctantly agreed. He would only ask for fair treatment.

When the RCMP phoned again, Archer asked that fraud charges against him in Ontario and British Columbia be dropped, that he be provided with competent counsel and have one hour with his wife. The Mounties consented to his terms. Archer then replied, "Come and get me." After five days, the ordeal was over.

In his wake, Archer had left one officer dead and two seriously hurt. Although she recovered from her wounds, Constable Candace Smith is unable to have children. Corporal Russell Hornseth lost the sight of one eye. And an entire community was traumatized.

On November 15, 1978, Herbert and Dorothy Archer stood trial for the murder of Constable Dennis Onofrey. After 20 days of listening to the testimony of witnesses and the summations of lawyers, the jury found the defendants guilty of murder in the first degree.

Herbert and Dorothy Archer were sentenced to life imprisonment with no possibility of parole for 25 years. Herbert Archer died of a heart attack in 1990 while still in prison. Dorothy Archer was released in 1993, after serving 15 years.

Dick Bakonyi
(Canada)

IT HAS BEEN said that the perfect murder is one where murder is not even suspected. The tragic accident that takes place so logically and unavoidably, the missing person who walks away from family and friends, never to be seen or heard of again—all these could very well be homicides. We cannot discuss these cases, for they have never been recognized as anything other than what they appeared to be on the surface.

But the near misses are intriguing.

Raymond Slemko was an electrician employed with the Baldwin Electric Co. in Toronto. On a cool September afternoon, in 1960, Slemko had to check some wiring in a trench beside an artificial rink in Dufferin Grove Park. Raymond thought he detected a slight odour, and asked Moses Spurrel, an employee of the A.J. Martin Excavation Co., to give him a hand. Both men started to dig. Raymond would later tell the Supreme Court how he discovered the body of Eva Blumberger. "The electrical cord binding the blanket broke when I put my shovel under it, and I saw a foot."

Later that very day, cement was to be poured into the trench and the body of Eva Blumberger would never have been discovered. She had been reported missing several days earlier by her family, and most probably would have been missing forever had it not been for the curiosity of Raymond Slemko.

The cause of death was a fractured skull, inflicted by vicious blows to the head. Eva had not been sexually molested in any way. The day after the body was uncovered, two private investigators who had been employed by the dead girl's family to find her turned over their file on the case to the police. The main information in the file contained the results of an interview with one Deszo (Dick) Bakonyi. The police picked up Bakonyi for questioning. After hours of interrogation, he was charged with murder.

Due to marriages between members of Eva's and Dick's families, their relationship to each other was rather complicated. Eva's father had died some years earlier, and her father's brother, who was Bakonyi's father, married her mother. Eva, therefore, was Dick's stepsister, as well as his cousin.

According to Bakonyi, on September 12, Eva asked him if he would let her into his room for a meeting with her boyfriend. When Dick and Eva entered the room, Bakonyi claimed, someone placed a chloroform rag over his mouth from behind. Upon regaining consciousness he realized that Eva was gone and there was blood on his bed. Dick said he had not seen Eva since the time of this attack.

The police came up with a somewhat different set of circumstances and events. Bakonyi's landlady, Mrs. Eugenia Rudski, identified the blanket that was wrapped around the body as her own. It had been used on Bakonyi's bed. She described the evening of September 12, when she thought she heard a dull thud emanate from Dick's room. She yelled through the door, inquiring what was going on, but didn't receive any reply. Next morning she washed some dark stains off Bakonyi's bedroom floor. Other bloodstains were found on the dresser, and on Bakonyi's trousers and shoes. All the bloodstains were the same type as Eva Blumberger's. The electric wire was the same type that Bakonyi used on his hi-fi equipment. Dick was a classical music fan, who owned extensive hi-fi equipment and over $1,000 worth of classical records.

Mrs. Ilene Fraser of St. Clarence Avenue happened to be in Dufferin Grove Park the day before the body was uncovered, and swore she saw Dick Bakonyi in the trench where Eva's body was later discovered. Mrs. Fraser thought nothing of it at the time, but the next day, when the body was found, she came forward with her information. Later she identified Dick from a lineup at police headquarters as the man in the trench.

On December 3, 1960, Bakonyi stood trial for the murder of his stepsister. The evidence against him was all circumstantial, but it spun a tight web of guilt. During the trial it was brought out that Eva thought she was pregnant. She feared exposure, and possibly tried to induce an abortion. An autopsy indicated that she was not pregnant. The day Eva vanished, she left a note in Bakonyi's room, which read: *Dear Dan,* (she sometimes called Bakonyi that) *I was here . . . you were not here. Get the medicine or there will be troubles. I will call. Eva.*

The prosecution proposed that the motive for the killing could have been that Eva had accused Dick of being responsible for her imagined pregnancy. Even Bakonyi's story of being chloroformed was ridiculed. It was proved that Dick had been with members of his family later on the night of September 12, and hadn't even mentioned the alleged incident to anyone. If you are forcefully chloroformed and your stepsister has been abducted, it would seem quite natural that you would, at the very least, tell your family, if not report the incident to the police.

In Bakonyi's defence, his sister gave evidence that he was in her home at approximately the time Mrs. Rudski heard the dull thud from Dick's room.

After two hours of deliberation, the jury found Bakonyi guilty of murder. When asked if he had anything to say before sentence was passed, the accused said, "I think I have, My Lord. Eva Blumberger was my cousin. Before her death she was in trouble. I wanted to help her. That is the only reason I came to be entangled in this case. Probably because of this, I am going to lose my life. I am not afraid to die."

Bakonyi was sentenced to be hanged on May 23, 1961. On May 19, just four days before the execution was to be carried out, his sentence was commuted by the federal cabinet to life imprisonment in Kingston Penitentiary. Dick Bakonyi has since been released. His present whereabouts are unknown.

Tyrone Borglund & Eric Peever

(Canada)

THE MURDERS were atrocious, cold-blooded acts committed by boys not old enough to vote.

In January 1988, seven individuals were living in a three-bedroom bungalow on Fourteenth Avenue in Mission, British Columbia. The inhabitants had experienced diverse upheavals en route to the small town located about sixty-five kilometres east of Vancouver.

Karsten Madsen met Leny van Rikoort in 1977 in Vancouver. Karsten, at 27, had been married, divorced and deeply involved with another woman before meeting Leny. Karsten's marriage to Sharon Peever had brought two children into the world, Eric and Michael, who remained with their mother after the divorce. By the time he met Leny, Karsten was also the father of Jason, a bouncing 8-month-old baby, the result of his last involvement.

Leny and Karsten married in 1978. Their daughter, Michelle, was born that same year. Little Jason was also a part of their family. The Madsens relocated often in the following seven years, eventually settling in Mission. Like many Canadian families with young children, they required two incomes to keep a roof over their heads. Karsten made a precarious living as a drywall installer. Despite the ever-present need for more money, the Madsens appeared to be happy. They were outgoing and well-liked. The family consisted of four individuals living in the bungalow on Fourteenth Avenue. They would all become victims.

In 1985 the Madsens applied to become foster parents. Their motives came under close scrutiny. Certainly the $500 a month they would receive from the B.C. Ministry of Social Services was a factor. There is some evidence that the money enabled them to purchase a new car. Whatever the motivation, 14-year-old Tyrone Borglund moved into the Madsen home. The addition of Tyrone brought the number of residents in the bungalow on Fourteenth Avenue to five.

Initially things went well, but it wasn't long before Tyrone became a disruptive force around the house. From time to time, Leny reported his behaviour to the ministry. On more than one occasion, Tyrone was removed and placed in another home, but was taken back by the Madsens when he promised to mend his ways.

Eric and Michael, who were living with their mother, Sharon Peever, grew to be teenagers. Caught stealing from the house, Eric, the older of the two boys, was thrown out of his home by his mother's common-law husband. He contacted Karsten, his biological father, and moved in with the Madsens in Mission.

Eric and Tyrone seemed to get along well. They were approximately the same age and soon became close friends. The sixth player in the tragedy that was to follow was now onstage. One more player was required to complete the cast. Eric's younger brother, Michael, contacted Karsten and moved into the bungalow in Mission. The full cast of seven individuals was now gathered.

Karsten and Leny knew they had problems. Michelle

and Jason behaved like normal youngsters, but the three older boys were a handful. On more than one occasion, the police contacted Leny. The boys had become petty thieves. They even stole from their own home. Karsten had to keep a careful eye on his liquor. Small items often went missing. Leny gave the boys severe tongue-lashings, which seemed to sink in for a while but had little lasting effect.

Tyrone and Michael shared sleeping quarters in the basement and it was there that the three boys planned the murder of the other four members of the family. They'd decided: Karsten, Leny, Michelle and Jason would all be murdered. The boys would take money from the master bedroom, steal Leny's Toyota and take off for Fort St. John.

On the night of January 17, 1988, the stage was set. Tyrone suggested the axes. They were weapons of opportunity, just lying there in the house. The boys practised swinging the axes down in the basement. Upstairs, the house was quiet. Everyone was asleep. Eric sneaked upstairs and returned with some wine and pear brandy. The boys took long swigs from the bottles. Tyrone and Eric, equipped with the axes, slowly climbed the stairs. Michael carried a maul. He would later testify that when the reality of what they were about to do came to him; he couldn't go through with the plan. He left his co-conspirators and returned to the basement.

Tyrone and Eric continued to the master bedroom. Karsten and Leny were sleeping soundly. The moves had been well planned. Tyrone would kill Karsten while Eric took care of Leny. Tyrone lifted the large axe above his head and brought it down with all his might on the sleeping man's skull. The force of the blow split open Karsten's head.

Leny awoke with a start. She screamed, her hands instinctively shielding her head, but there was no escape. Eric brought the axe down. Her arms may have deflected the initial blow so that the first swing didn't render her unconscious. We will never know how many times Eric swung that axe, but at some time in the midst of the blood and the passion, he dropped the weapon and ran to the refuge of the basement. Tyrone finished the gruesome task in the bedroom.

Eleven-year-old Jason was awakened by the noise. Rubbing sleep from his eyes, he strolled into the master bedroom. Only half-awake, he likely couldn't quite absorb the scene he was witnessing. He said, "What are you doing to my mum?" Three vicious swings from Tyrone's axe and the little boy lay dead on the bedroom floor.

The next to wake up was 9-year-old Michelle. She too was drawn to the source of the noise. Tyrone intercepted her at the doorway. She met the same fate as Jason. There was no more noise from upstairs in the house on Fourteenth Avenue in Mission, British Columbia.

Down in the basement, there was plenty of excitement. They had actually done it. True, Tyrone was the ringleader, but they had all been involved in one way or another. Now that it was over, Eric felt he owed Tyrone an explanation. After all, he had retreated during the height of the attack. Tyrone assured him there were no hard feelings. In the end they had accomplished what they had set out to do.

The three boys entered the room of carnage. Their plan was working. In minutes they removed all the bills from Karsten's wallet and Leny's purse. The keys to the Toyota were there in Leny's purse, just as they had expected. It didn't take long for them to get out of the house, leaving behind four bodies hacked to death in the bedroom. The teenagers wheeled the Toyota out of the driveway and headed toward Fort St. John, 790 kilometres to the north-east. Good times lay ahead. Only then did Tyrone and Eric notice that their clothing was spattered with blood.

Once in Fort St. John, the boys purchased booze, called friends and partied. Two days after the killing spree, Tyrone was picked up for drunk driving. The Toyota was soon traced to Mission, the bodies discovered and the bloody multiple murders exposed.

What had triggered the vicious attack that had taken four lives? According to Tyrone, they were angry at Leny because she had given them another one of her patented tongue-lashings and had forbidden them to watch television.

All charges against 15-year-old Michael Peever were dropped in exchange for his testimony. After the murder trial, in which he appeared as the Crown's star witness, he was placed, anonymously, in a group home somewhere in British Columbia.

Tyrone and Eric stood trial for murder in adult court. The jury did not believe their claim that they had taken the axes into the Madsens' bedroom solely to frighten the Madsens. It took only three hours' deliberation to find both boys guilty of murder.

Tyrone Borglund, 16, and Eric Peever, 17, were sentenced to life imprisonment with no possibility of parole for 25 years. They are presently serving their sentences.

Ian Brady & Myra Hindley

(England)

FOR SHEER horror, the Murders on the Moors rank right up there with the worst. If the retelling of this true tale alerts just one parent to the dangers of allowing a child to accompany not only strange men, but strange women, then this effort will have been worthwhile.

Ian Brady was not your average child. While still in his preteens, he threw cats off buildings to prove that they didn't have nine lives. Once he crucified a frog and relished the sheer agony he caused the helpless creature. Between the ages of 12 and 15, he was caught breaking into several shops and houses. Each time he was apprehended, he was put on probation so that he could continue his schooling.

When Ian was 15, he left school and was promptly charged with nine counts of housebreaking. He was given one more chance by another lenient magistrate and left Glasgow to live in Manchester. Ian drank, couldn't keep a job and continued to break into houses. Apprehended again in the act, he finally met a magistrate who sentenced him to two years in Borstal. On June 9, 1958, Ian, at age 20, was released from prison.

In February 1959, Ian obtained a clerical position at Millwards Merchandise Ltd., a chemical supply company in

West Gorton, Manchester. At night he read about Adolf Hitler and the Marquis de Sade.

Myra Hindley was born in 1942 in the slums of Manchester. When she was four, her mother gave birth to a second daughter, Maureen. As a result of the overcrowding at Eaton Street, Myra moved in with her grandmother a block down the street.

Although her IQ was slightly above average, Myra was not a good student. She left school while in her teens and drifted from job to job before securing a position as a shorthand typist with Millwards in West Gorton. Much of her typing was for a lean, pale, rather eccentric young man who fascinated Myra. His name was Ian Brady.

Ian introduced Myra to his library of witchcraft, sadism and genocide. She was a quick learner. What Ian said was law; Myra never argued. The pair became inseparable. Myra purchased a minivan and, since Ian didn't drive, it was she who chauffeured them to and from work.

Through the years, Myra had remained friendly with her younger sister, Maureen, who joined Millwards in 1963. Myra confided to Maureen that she was having an affair with Ian Brady. When Myra and her grandmother moved to Wardle Brook Avenue in Hattesley, Ian moved in with them. The elderly grandmother kept to herself and never interfered with the machinations of Myra and her live-in boyfriend. Their evenings were spent experimenting with sexual perversions, drinking cheap wine and wandering the countryside in the minivan. On their days off, Ian would indulge in his hobby of photography. Myra was a willing model, posing in the nude in every conceivable position or stance that Ian suggested.

Mrs. Sheila Kilbride gave her 12-year-old son, John, a peck on the cheek before he scampered off with a friend to go to the movies. After the two lads left the movie theatre at 5 p.m., John's friend caught a bus home. He last saw John talking to a friendly blonde lady. The lady was Myra Hindley. Little John Kilbride never returned home. Police were notified of the boy's disappearance, and a comprehensive search followed, but no trace of the boy was found.

Ten-year-old Lesley Downey was excited on Boxing Day of 1964. Her mother had given her permission to attend a fair being held only two hundred yards from her residence. By 5 p.m., Mrs. Jean Downey became apprehensive when Lesley failed to return home.

A minivan circled the fairgrounds before coming to an abrupt stop. A blonde woman approached Lesley and volunteered to pay for another ride on the merry-go-round. What 10-year-old could resist such good fortune? The little girl jumped on the wooden pony. When the woman offered her a lift home, Lesley knew everything would be all right. Her mother had told her never to accept a ride with a strange man, but she hadn't said anything about taking a ride with a friendly, kind lady. Even though her house was nearby, Lesley climbed into the van beside Myra Hindley. Crouched in the shadows behind the unsuspecting child lurked Ian Brady. Lesley Downey was never seen again.

When Myra's sister, Maureen, married David Smith, it was natural for the two couples to become close friends, especially since the Smiths lived within walking distance of Myra and Ian. David Smith had been in several scrapes with the law and had been convicted of assault. He welcomed

Ian's hospitality. The two men were accustomed to staying up half the night drinking cheap wine.

The strange double life of Ian Brady and Myra Hindley came to light on the night of October 6, 1965. On that night, Myra's 77-year-old grandmother took a sleeping pill at 8:30 p.m. and went to bed. Myra and Ian cruised the streets of Manchester in her minivan. Myra parked the vehicle while Ian took a stroll. He returned with 17-year-old Edward Evans, a homosexual who had eagerly accepted an invitation to return to Ian's home for a drink.

Once back at Wardle Brook Avenue, Ian and Edward engaged in conversation while Myra called on her brother-in-law, David Smith. She convinced David to accompany her back home on the pretext that Ian had some miniature bottles he wanted to give away. As David admired the miniature bottles in the kitchen, a blood-chilling scream echoed through the house. Myra shouted, "Dave, Dave, come and help Ian." Smith ran from the kitchen to the living room and into hell.

In the eerie glow of the television set, David saw Edward Evans, whom he didn't know, lying half on the floor and half on a couch. Blood was cascading from Edward's head onto the floor. Ian stood over the fallen youngster with a bloody hatchet in his hand. As David watched in terror, Ian brought the hatchet down on Edward's head over and over again. Edward tried in vain to crawl away from his attacker.

Ian interrupted his murderous frenzy to say, "This one's taking a while to go." Then he wrapped an electric cord around Evans's neck and pulled until his victim was dead. Ian was soaked in blood. Myra's clothing had been spattered with blood as well. David Smith had been an audience to a murder that had been orchestrated just for him. Ian commented, "It's the messiest one yet. Normally one blow is enough."

Myra cleaned up the room while Ian changed clothes. Upstairs, Myra's grandmother slept through it all. Ian solicited David's help in carrying the body upstairs to a bedroom. Myra put on a pot of tea. At about 3 a.m., David suggested that he should head home. He was surprised when his companions said good night and let him leave. David felt as if he had lived through a nightmare. He ran all the way home. He was so terrified of Ian and Myra that he waited three hours before daring to sneak out of the house to call police.

When detectives arrived at 16 Wardle Brook Avenue, they were let in by Myra. A search of the back bedroom revealed the horribly mutilated body of Edward Evans trussed up in a plastic bag. Three bloodstained carpets and the murder weapon were taken from the house by police. A postmortem revealed that Evans had received 14 blows to the skull.

At the police station, Ian confessed to murder and attempted to implicate David Smith. As detectives interrogated Ian and Myra, it appeared that the murderous pair had timed the killing of Edward Evans to coincide with David Smith's arrival so that he would be a witness to murder.

The house on Wardle Brook Avenue was practically dismantled in a search for clues. The investigating officers found Ian Brady's diary. On one page they came across the name of John Kilbride, the little boy who had been missing for almost two years. They also discovered that Ian had checked two suitcases at Manchester's Central Station. The suitcases contained pornographic pictures of Myra, as well as weird photographs of the lonesome moors outside Manchester, showing Myra staring straight down, as if standing over a grave. Police located the sites depicted in the photographs and dug up the bodies of John Kilbride and Lesley Downey.

Myra Hindley and Ian Brady stood trial at historic Chester Castle on April 19, 1966. The pornographic pictures, the photos of the grave-sites of the two children and Brady's diary left little doubt as to the guilt of the accused pair.

One piece of evidence was so horrifying that hardened homicide detectives left the courtroom when it was presented. Myra and Ian had recorded Lesley Downey's last moments on tape as they sexually abused and tortured her to death. The 16-minute, 21-second tape had been discovered intact by police.

The jury took only 2 hours and 22 minutes to find Ian Brady guilty of three separate counts of murder. He received three life sentences, while Myra received two life sentences for the murders of Lesley Downey and Edward Evans. She was sentenced to a further seven years for harbouring Brady in the case of John Kilbride. Ironically, Ian Brady and Myra Hindley escaped the hangman's noose. A few months prior to their trial, capital punishment had been abolished in England.

As recently as 1987, Myra Hindley resurfaced when she assisted police in recovering the body of 16-year-old Pauline Reade, another victim of the infamous pair.

Myra Hindley remains incarcerated, while Ian Brady is presently confined in a mental institution.

Betty Broderick
(United States)

THIS IS A tale about two attractive, wealthy people who, unfortunately, were unable to settle their marital difficulties without the aid of a nickel-plated .38-calibre revolver.

Dan Broderick met Betty Bisceglia while both were university students. Dan had just been accepted at Cornell Medical School in Ithaca, New York. Betty attended the Catholic College of Mount St. Vincent in the same city. The two young people dated, fell in love, and married in April 1969, after Betty graduated and obtained a teaching job.

Following a Caribbean honeymoon, the newlyweds settled into a dormitory room at Cornell. Both realized there would be some rough times in the years ahead. Dan's immediate future would be devoted mainly to study. Betty would teach to assist her husband financially in gaining his medical degree. With student loans they would make out just fine.

They didn't.

A month after the wedding, Betty learned she was pregnant. Nine months later, she gave birth to their first child, a daughter, Kim. After the baby was born, she and Dan obtained part-time jobs to make ends meet. It was rough sledding, but the years passed and eventually Dan obtained his medical degree.

Dan had ambitions that would not be denied. He noted

that huge settlements were being dispensed in malpractice suits. What a coup it would be to be a lawyer with a medical degree. Certainly, he would have a leg up on lawyers who would have to depend on medical knowledge and expertise from an outside source. Dan decided to become a lawyer. He applied to, and was accepted by, Harvard Law School.

This time around, however, Betty objected. If Dan had to pursue a legal career, she told him, he could attend night school. Betty let Dan know that another loan on top of his medical school loan would take years to repay. Dan insisted on Harvard. The Brodericks picked up their sparse belongings and moved to Boston. It was a struggle, but once again the years passed and Dr. Dan Broderick graduated as a lawyer.

Dan and Betty moved to San Diego, California. This was it—the good times, the big money. It only took a few years. The student loans were paid off. A large home was purchased in 1976 in posh La Jolla. Little Danny junior was a welcome addition to the family.

It should have been perfect, but it wasn't. Dan threw himself into his work. He became one of the city's leading attorneys. Soon his income exceeded a million dollars a year. Dan was something of a human dynamo. Maybe it was the many years of doing without while he studied that drove him to acquire more and more wealth.

Meanwhile, two more children blessed the Broderick household. Betty hated being neglected. True, she belonged to all the right clubs, socialized with all the right people and wore designer clothing, but at the same time she was sharing her life with a man who was in love with his career and the recognition it brought him. The Brodericks argued constantly.

In 1983, two things occurred in Betty Broderick's life. Dan made it very clear that he was not happy with their marriage. Around the time that Dan revealed his disenchantment, Betty learned that he was having an affair with his tall, attractive receptionist, Linda Kolkena. Betty accused Dan of involvement with Linda, but he vehemently asserted that his relationship with the woman was purely professional. Now Dan did more than neglect his wife. He ignored her. Betty seethed. Her world was crumbling. She complained to friends and attempted to turn her children against their father. Everyone knew the Brodericks were carrying on their own private war.

In February 1985, Dan moved out and filed for divorce. He cited myriad irrational acts committed by Betty, such as destroying household effects, throwing small appliances and breaking windows. Betty defended herself legally as best she could, but Dan held all the cards. Being a lawyer, it was not difficult for him to inundate his wife with legal documents on an almost weekly basis. Betty, on the other hand, had to hire lawyers, at great expense, to ward off her husband's many legal ploys. All the while, friends kept her well informed of Dan and Linda's romance. Throughout the messy, well-publicized divorce, Dan provided Betty with a liberal allowance of $16,000 per month. Betty constantly pressed the courts for an increase.

The Brodericks were finally divorced. Now the battle advanced to the question of custody of their four children and the available funds to support them. The legal skirmishes continued unabated. During this rather hectic period, Dan married Linda Kolkena. Betty went crazy with rage. She phoned Linda, cursing and threatening like a madwoman. She often stalked their home. Dan obtained a restraining order keeping his ex-wife from coming within 100 yards of their residence.

Was Betty driven to the brink by a callous husband who thought only of himself? Many think so. Others believe that with her liberal allowance, Betty could have built a new life for herself without resorting to revenge.

On November 5, 1989, Betty Broderick went over the edge. At approximately 5 a.m., she drove up to her ex-husband's home in Marston Hills. Inside, Dan lay asleep in bed beside his wife of seven months. We will never know exactly what went through Betty's mind as she silently made her way through the well-appointed home while her 44-year-old ex-husband slept with his 28-year-old wife.

Betty climbed the stairs to the master bedroom. She was carrying her .38-calibre revolver. There in bed reposed the two individuals who had ruined her life. Later, Betty would say she remembered her finger closing on the trigger and the weapon firing once. Her account is inaccurate. She shot five times.

Linda never knew what hit her. One slug tore into her chest, while another entered her head. From the position of Dan's body, it was evident that he made some attempt to reach the telephone on the night table. A bullet entered his lung. He died within a couple of minutes. Betty crossed the room and replaced the phone. She ran from the house and sped away, stopping at a pay phone to call and tell a friend what she had done. The friend phoned acquaintances who, in turn, gained entrance to the house and discovered the bodies. That same day, Betty surrendered to police. In her purse was her .38-calibre revolver.

Betty Broderick's trial caused a sensation in California and, indeed, throughout the United States and the world. Three books and two screenplays have been written about her case. Was Betty a woman scorned or a cold-blooded killer? The California jury couldn't decide. After deliberating for four days, they reported that they were hopelessly deadlocked. The presiding judge was forced to order a mistrial.

Betty's second trial was more conclusive. She was found guilty of two counts of second-degree murder. In February 1992, she was sentenced to 15 years' to life imprisonment for each murder, and two years for possession of a gun, the sentences to run consecutively. Betty Broderick will be eligible for parole in the year 2010.

Susan Christie
(Ireland)

WHEN LIEUTENANT Duncan McAllister first laid eyes on Penny Squire, he thought she was the most beautiful girl he had ever seen. Sure enough, Penny was a knockout and looked far older than her 16 years. Age didn't matter that much to 21-year-old Duncan. He dated Penny and discovered that they both enjoyed the same outdoor sports.

Penny's dad was an English teacher employed in Lippstadt, Germany, where Duncan was posted with the British army. It was here that the young couple met. Soon they were inseparable, and for a full year spent every spare moment together.

When Duncan was posted back to England in 1983, he and Penny discussed marriage. It was a touchy subject, mainly because of Penny's tender age. The 17-year-old Penny talked it over with her parents. They had planned on a university education for their daughter, but consented to the marriage when they realized that her mind was made up.

Duncan and Penny married. For six years their union was an ideal one. Duncan, a career army man, earned an engineering degree and was promoted to captain. Everything was coming up roses for the happy couple until June 1989. That's when Duncan was posted to Northern Ireland. To British army personnel, a posting to Northern Ireland was akin to a stint in purgatory.

Despite his disappointment with the unpopular assignment, Duncan, a product of the stiff-upper-lip school, decided to make the best of a less-than-pleasant situation. Always athletic, he formed a scuba diving club, enlisting divers from members of the armed forces. One member was a cute young thing, Private Susan Christie. Right from their first dive together, it was obvious to Duncan that Susan was infatuated with him. As her instructor, he could either resist her advances or encourage them. Duncan chose to encourage them.

And now, folks, as so often occurs in affairs of the heart, there are two versions of what transpired between Duncan and Susan. Let's review Duncan's version first. He claims that although he was flattered by Susan's advances, he was fair and square with her. He told her to turn off the charm unless she intended to go all the way. Susan responded favourably, suggesting that she would be most amenable to a romp in the hay.

Stout fellow that he was, Duncan pointed out the inherent pitfalls in having the aforementioned romp with a married man who would under no circumstances leave his wife. According to Duncan, after mulling over his negative lecture for a few days, Susan was not deterred in the least. She agreed not only to a one-night romp, but to an on-going affair. As an added incentive, she revealed that she was a virgin. Duncan succumbed and the pair made love in the great outdoors beside one of those romantic lakes.

So much for Duncan's gallant tale.

Susan admitted that she was a virgin at the time of their tryst, but, according to her, that was the only truthful statement in Duncan's version of their liaison. She claimed that she desired to retain her virginity but that Duncan implored, coaxed and pressured her until one day he lured her to his home and seduced her on his own bed. We can only assume that Penny was not at home.

One thing we do know is that Duncan and Susan were doing it all the time. On a scuba-diving expedition in the South Atlantic, Susan told Duncan that she wanted to have sex in a novel manner, something that he and Penny had never done. They decided that making love underwater would be different. The pair made love twenty metres under the chilly waters off Ascension Island.

Despite the obvious thrills the extramarital sex afforded Duncan, he began to tire of his lover. When he suggested they terminate their affair, Susan went into a rage. How dare he cast her aside after he had taken her virginity! She loved him and had no intention of giving him up. Duncan attempted to explain that it had all been great fun, but he loved his wife. He even made the mistake of telling Susan that she wasn't as attractive as Penny.

Susan was furious. As so often happens in the triangle business, she blamed the blameless Penny for all her problems. On March 27, 1990, Susan, who was acquainted with Penny, arranged to take a stroll through Drumkeeragh Forest with the unsuspecting wife of her lover. When Duncan heard of the chummy walk, he was definitely less than pleased. There is a real danger in having one's mistress meet one's wife. A wrong word here or a slip of the tongue there and all hell could break loose.

As it turned out, Duncan had good reason to be concerned. On the afternoon of the infamous walk, Duncan was enjoying a Scotch and soda in the officers' mess when his commanding officer informed him that a terrible tragedy had taken place. A man had attacked Susan and Penny with a knife. Susan was in hospital with several cuts and bruises. Unfortunately, Penny hadn't survived the attack. Her throat had been slashed.

Within minutes, the full resources of the British army were employed scouring Drumkeeragh Forest. Despite their best efforts, however, no suspect was found. Detectives questioned Susan, who could offer only the vaguest description of her attacker. Evidently, one slash had taken Penny's life. The whole thing had happened so quickly that Susan had hardly been able to look at the man.

Duncan was also questioned, but he could shed no light on why anyone would want to harm his wife. As time passed, Duncan realized that the one piece of information that would put an entirely different perspective on the murder was his affair with Susan. He decided to inform police not only of the affair, but of his attempt to terminate it and Susan's reaction to his suggestion.

Now armed with the information that Penny had taken her last walk with her husband's mistress, detectives immediately uncovered clues pointing to Susan's guilt. Police discovered that Susan had been to the location of the attack a week earlier. She also had access to butcher knives, one of which could have inflicted the stab wound to Penny's throat. During her interrogation, Susan described gloves worn by her attacker; similar gloves were found in her possession. Moreover, Susan had received combat training and knew exactly how to slit an adversary's throat from behind. She also had the guts and ability to inflict superficial cuts and bruises to her arms without seriously injuring herself.

In time, Susan confessed to her affair with Duncan and her hatred of his wife. She insisted that although she wanted Penny dead, she had no recollection of the actual act of taking her life.

Susan Christie stood trial for murder. She was found guilty of manslaughter and sentenced to five years' imprisonment. The Crown appealed the light term and was successful in having the sentence increased to nine years.

Rev. D.L. Clark

(United States)

THE GOOD folks of Greencastle, Pennsylvania, were concerned when Rev. Donald Lewis Clark's wife, Phyllis, took ill. It was in the fall of 1981 that 54-year-old Phyllis complained of stomach trouble. Nothing really serious at first, just recurring stomach cramps. But the discomfort didn't go away.

Rev. Clark and most of the parishioners at the Macedonia United Brethren Church were shocked when Phyllis, obviously in considerable pain, fell down the cellar stairs of the church parsonage. Rushed to Chambersburg Hospital, approximately 15 kilometres from Greencastle, Phyllis didn't respond to treatment. On October 23, she was transferred to the Hershey Medical Centre, where she died the next day.

When asked if he wanted an autopsy performed on his dear wife, Clark suggested it wasn't necessary. He felt his wife of 29 blissful years should be laid to rest intact. Those involved tended to agree. The funeral was a solemn affair, attended by most of the minister's flock.

Clark appeared to be beside himself with grief. No doubt, as he watched the casket being lowered into its final resting place, he thought how different all this was from the breakup of his first marriage. Marriage number one had taken place long ago when he was still a young man. When he and his first wife divorced, it took him only a year to meet and wed Phyllis Miller. The two daughters who blessed their union were a gift from God.

Members of the church shook their collective heads. The reverend wasn't taking his loss well. Of course, they had no way of knowing the Lord had provided Clark with the foresight to insure Phyllis's life for a cool $50,000 just two months before she departed this cruel world.

To ease his great pain, the reverend purchased a couple of new cars, which more than replaced the rickety old rattletrap he had been forced to drive before the tragic loss of his wife. Clark just loved to roar down the country roads in his new Camaro. He changed in other ways, too. When Phyllis was hale and hearty, he attended to his church duties punctually and with great diligence. Now he neglected the church and his devoted flock.

The elders of the church, while sympathetic toward their minister, felt that enough was enough. About a year after Phyllis's departure, they advised Clark that his services were no longer required. They gave him a month's notice, requesting he move out of the church's property by March 31, 1983. Then the date was extended to April 27. A lot happened in that one month.

Let's start off with Ronaele "Candy" Rotz. On April 7, Candy's nude body was found in the bathtub of her home in Chambersburg. An electric space heater was in the tub with the attractive 40-year-old divorcee. She also had a severe gash on the back of her head. It could have been one of those weird accidents that happen from time to time. Candy could have stumbled, hit her head, and knocked the heater into the tub as she fell in. Then again, she could have been murdered.

And how did the unfortunate death of Candy Rotz

involve the good and holy Rev. Clark? Well, I'll tell you. Investigators learned that Candy had been an extremely religious woman, who had belonged to every religious organization in the area. Somewhere along the way, she had met Clark, while he was mourning the departure of dear Phyllis. On January 20, 1983, the reverend and Candy had married secretly, but did not live together. No one else knew about their wedding.

After detectives learned the details of the reverend's third marriage, they uncovered other sensitive information. Clark had never told Candy he was a minister. He posed as a police officer to his bride and to the officiating minister. He claimed to be an undercover narcotics agent, explaining to Candy that until his current assignment was concluded, they would have to live separately for her safety.

Clark was in hot water. And speaking of hot water, an autopsy was performed on Candy's body. It was discovered that she had been struck on the head with a sharp instrument and placed in the tub with the space heater in a crude attempt to make her death appear accidental.

Detectives looking into the reverend's activities were now hot to trot. They delved deeper into the devious life of the preacher man. Eight days after his marriage to Candy, he had insured her life for $50,000. Not satisfied with this amount of protection, he waited only a week longer before increasing his bride's insurance to $200,000 should she expire due to an accident.

On April 13, authorities paid a visit to Rev. Donald Lewis Clark. When they received no response to their knocking on his door, they forced their way into his home. There was the minister's body lying nude on the bathroom floor. An autopsy and toxicology tests indicated that he had taken small amounts of arsenic for several days as the circle of evidence drew him into the police investigation. Two days before his body was found, he gave himself a massive dose, which killed him. The reverend left suicide notes that have never been made public.

Police backtracked. They looked into the untimely demise of wife number two. After conducting an extensive investigation, they concluded that Phyllis had been systematically poisoned with arsenic. Weak and racked with stomach cramps, she had either fallen or been pushed down the stairs and had died within a few days.

Despite Clark's elaborate plans, Candy's murder was botched. The blow to her head had killed her. She was already dead when she was placed in the tub with the heater.

The motive for the murders was the insurance money, but there was another reason for the reverend's strange behaviour. Investigators discovered he had had a teenage lover all the while he was burying and marrying his wives. No doubt Phyllis was murdered so he could gain his freedom, as well as a tidy sum, to carry on with his mistress. He gave himself a false occupation and lived separately from his third wife to avoid her finding out about his lover. Many believe the minister killed Candy for the insurance money to finance a $90,000 home he had purchased in Shippensburg, where he planned to install his teenage paramour.

It matters little. A private funeral service was held for Rev. Donald Lewis Clark, after which he was buried in nearby Burns Hill Cemetery.

The Macedonia United Brethren Church hired a new minister.

Eric Cooke

(Australia)

THE CITY of Perth, Australia, was in a state of crisis. A serial killer was at large and the police appeared powerless to apprehend the murderer.

The first killing took place on February 2, 1959, a sultry summer night down under. Pnena Berkman, a beautiful 33-year-old divorcee, had just returned from an upscale party. Her escort kissed her goodnight at the door of her luxurious apartment. Pnena undressed and retired for the night. Next morning, a neighbour and close friend, who had a key to the apartment, received no response to her ring. She entered and made her way to the bedroom. There lay Pnena amidst blood-soaked bedclothes. She had been stabbed many times all over her body. The neighbour rushed back to her apartment and called police.

It took only a few minutes for homicide detectives to arrive. Their preliminary investigation indicated there was no forced entry, which didn't mean much in Perth. Many residents left doors unlocked due to the low incidence of crime in the city. Pnena's date was questioned and exonerated of any complicity in the crime. Robbery was dismissed as a motive since Pnena's open purse was in plain sight and no money had been removed. There was no indication of a sexual attack of any kind. This was verified by autopsy results.

Because there was no sign of a struggle, police theorized that Pnena might have known her killer and might have welcomed him into her bedroom. Acquaintances of the dead woman came under investigation, but all were able to prove their innocence. The murder, considered an isolated incident, went unsolved.

Ten months later, on December 19, Jillian McPherson Brewster, a 22-year-old heiress, was dropped off at her apartment around midnight by her fiancé. The happy couple had a golfing date for the following morning. At 9 a.m. Jillian's fiancé let himself into the apartment with his key. He found Jillian dead on her bed. She had been stabbed many times.

Detectives noted the similarities between the two murders, one of which was that both women had been stabbed to death while sleeping in their own apartments. Like Pnena's date, Jillian's fiancé was immediately cleared of any guilty knowledge of the crime.

Murder took a sabbatical until January 27, 1963. In the middle of that night, the Walmsley family was awakened by the persistent ringing of their doorbell. George Walmsley, a retired grocer, woke up, threw on his bathrobe and answered the door. He was immediately shot in the head by an intruder who ran away. George's daughter was the first family member to reach the grievously wounded man. No amount of assistance helped. George died moments after arriving at Royal Perth Hospital.

A few blocks away from the Walmsley residence, a 19-year-old student, John Sturkey, was taking advantage of the warm weather. He was fast asleep on his front veranda when someone approached him and shot him in the head. His landlady found him unconscious and bleeding profusely. John was rushed to Royal Perth Hospital, where he died only a few hours after George Walmsley.

Both Walmsley and Sturkey had been murdered with a .22-calibre weapon and both had been shot in the head. Police were reluctant to couple the murders with the earlier Berkman and Brewster killings because the weapons were different. Yet there were similarities. All four murders had taken place between midnight and dawn. There was some evidence the killer had spied on all four victims before killing them.

Six months passed. On August 10, 1963, a cold, windy day, Shirley McLeod, a 19-year-old babysitter, was taking care of a baby on Walell Road. At 2 a.m. the baby's parents returned home. Shirley didn't respond to their greeting. When they heard their infant daughter crying, they knew something was wrong. Shirley would never let the baby cry unattended. In the living room they found Shirley sitting grotesquely in a chair. She had been shot in the head.

Police ascertained that she had been killed by a .22-calibre bullet. Detectives discovered that the killer could have entered the premises through an unlocked garage that had a door leading to the living quarters. Nothing had been taken from the residence. Neighbours had not heard or seen anything unusual.

Another unsolved murder gave the good citizens of Perth something to think about. It seemed that no one was safe. The string of victims came from all walks of life. None were engaged in criminal activity, nor were they connected in any way with each other.

The first real break in the case came August 17, 1963, when an elderly man gathering wildflowers came across a .22-calibre rifle under some brush. Because of the wide publicity given the murders, the man didn't touch the weapon, but went directly to police. Ballistics experts proved that the striations on test bullets fired from the weapon matched those on the bullet taken from Shirley McLeod's head.

Detectives wondered why a killer would toss a murder weapon under brush rather than throw it in the nearby Canning River. They concluded that the murderer was hiding the rifle to retrieve it later rather than attempting to get rid of it. Investigators substituted a similar weapon and placed it under the brush exactly where the killer had hidden it. The area was staked out in the hope that the murderer would show up to collect the rifle.

It took two weeks. On September 1, a car stopped near the planted weapon. A short, slim man walked directly to the rifle and was picking it up when two burly officers took him into custody.

The suspect was Eric Edgar Cooke, a five-foot four-inch, 32-year-old truck driver. Eric was married and the father of seven children. He led detectives to the Swan River, where divers retrieved another .22-calibre rifle. This weapon proved to be the one which had taken the lives of John Sturkey and George Walmsley.

On November 25, 1963, Eric stood trial for three murders. At his trial, his rather difficult childhood was reviewed by defence counsel. Evidently, Eric, who had a harelip and cleft palate, had been cruelly taunted by school chums. He had been abused by his parents and had later suffered several industrial accidents, incurring trauma to his head.

The prosecution hammered away at the cold-blooded acts that had taken three lives. In the case of John Sturkey, Cooke said, "He was on his back sleeping and I walked up to about four feet from him. I pointed the rifle at him and I shot him. I do not know why. I did not have the slightest reason for harming him. He was a complete stranger to me." Eric went on to say that he had tremendous urges to kill. All his victims were strangers. "The power was so great that I could not stop myself. It was not until afterward, when I read the details in the papers, that I fully realized the dreadful things I had done."

Although Eric was strongly suspected in the Berkman and Brewster murders, he never confessed to them and was never charged with these crimes.

Eric Edgar Cooke was found guilty of murder and sentenced to death. On October 24, 1964, he was hanged.

Margaret Crump
(England)

MARGARET CRUMP felt life was passing her by. There she was, decidedly plump, with ever so tiny crow's feet making their unattractive appearance beside her eyes, which in recent months had developed an involuntary squint.

Margaret, who had seen four decades come and go, looked across the breakfast table at her husband of 14 years. Wasn't he a prize? she thought. David spent most of his time collecting money for worthy causes in and around Folkestone, England. When he wasn't complaining about the state of the Commonwealth, he was moaning about his ulcerated leg. Among David's more disagreeable traits, Margaret felt his bouts of depression ranked right up there as the most annoying. Sometimes David was so low he threatened to commit suicide. No one, least of all Margaret, took his threats seriously. The Crumps' marriage had produced no children.

Year after dreary year, David collected funds for charity, while Margaret pursued her hobby of citizens' band radio. Each evening, after David had taken his sleeping pills and she could hear him snoring, she would plug in her equipment. Her CB handle was Maggie Boo. Her hobby was her one escape from her boring, loveless marriage.

One fog-enshrouded night in 1986, Maggie Boo received a response from Hawaiian Cruiser. It was like no other response she had ever received. Hawaiian Cruiser had a melodious, sexy voice. He flattered Maggie Boo. What's more, he was suggestive. Maggie Boo said nothing to discourage the naughty boy. Each day she would wait to hear David snoring so she could exchange sweet sly insinuations with her Hawaiian Cruiser.

It was agreed. The pair had to meet. Margaret hid those crow's feet as best she could and plucked out the few invading gray hairs. She and Hawaiian Cruiser met in a restaurant. The sexy voice belonged to 20-year-old David Belsham, a skinny young man with a severe case of acne. If you can imagine a young Ichabod Crane, you pretty well have the picture.

Despite the physical deficiencies and the discrepancy in their ages, Maggie Boo and Hawaiian Cruiser got along famously. They met often and soon became lovers. Juices dormant those many years once again flowed freely within Margaret Crump. Life was worth living after all. Belsham was attentive, polite and, above all, terrific in bed.

In time, Margaret introduced Belsham to her husband. David never suspected for a moment that this young lad was anything more than a fellow citizens' band enthusiast. Eventually Margaret met two of Belsham's friends, Stephen Farthing and teenager Paul Thompson. When Belsham requested that the two men, who had recently been asked to leave their rooming house, move in with the Crumps, Margaret agreed it would be a good idea. Even David liked the arrangement. Their boarders could do odd jobs around the place, allowing him more time for his charity work.

For a while, all went well. Farthing and Thompson had a roof over their heads, David had two live-in handymen, Belsham had done a favour for two friends and, of course, we all know what Margaret was receiving in quantities she had once only fantasized about.

In the deception business, one must realize that things can't go on forever. In 1987, David's ulcerated leg bothered him so much that he had to be hospitalized. By this time, the relationship between Margaret and Belsham was such that he moved into the Crump house to keep Margaret company.

Playing house appealed to Belsham. There is good evidence he had fallen in love with Margaret and dreaded the fast-approaching day when her husband would be released from hospital. He and Margaret discussed their predicament. They would do the honourable thing. They would tell David of their love for each other. No doubt, he would be civilized and drop out of the picture. After the divorce, they would marry and live happily ever after.

Well, folks, David did come home from the hospital. Margaret and Belsham told him of their intentions. Rather than take the news calmly, David said he would rather die than grant his wife a divorce. In addition, loud and clear, he ordered Belsham and his two buddies out of the house.

No one left the Crump residence. In the next few days, you could cut the tension with a knife. Each evening, David went to his room, took his sleeping pills and went to sleep alone. Downstairs, Belsham, Margaret, Farthing and Thompson plotted his death. They would make the murder appear to be a suicide. After all, David had suffered from depression for years and had often mentioned suicide to anyone who would listen.

On July 16, 1987, David went to his room. He extracted several sleeping pills from a bottle on his night table and took them with a glass of water, as was his custom. Margaret, realizing that he would take his usual large quantity of sleeping pills as he read his Bible in bed, brought him up a cup of coffee. She had solicitously dissolved several sleeping pills in the coffee before taking it upstairs. David grumbled a thanks and drank his coffee.

Next morning, Stephen Farthing found David dead in bed. He called an ambulance. The ambulance attendants noted the empty medicine bottle, observed the room was otherwise neat and tidy and concluded that David had committed suicide by means of an overdose.

Nothing would have been done about the open-and-shut case had a relative of David's not called the Folkestone Police Station the day following his death with the information that David had written her two weeks before, informing her that he believed the four conspirators living in his house planned to kill him. He also told her of his wife's ongoing affair with Belsham. Evidently, David had sneaked downstairs one night and had overheard the entire plot. Although he was alarmed, he couldn't bring himself to believe that his wife and her friends would actually kill him. David was wrong.

An autopsy was performed. The results indicated that David had taken a large quantity of barbiturates, about 12 pills, several of which had not been absorbed into the bloodstream by the time death occurred. The attending pathologist also discovered cotton fibres in David's nose, mouth and lungs, indicating that the victim could have been suffocated with a pillow.

The investigation might have bogged down at this point had David Belsham kept his mouth shut. However, like so many killers before him, he had an irresistible urge to tell someone that he had committed the perfect murder. Belsham chose a buddy in a pub. He related in detail how Margaret had laced the coffee with sleeping pills. They had waited awhile before climbing the stairs and finishing the job with a pillow. Belsham's drinking buddy scampered down to the Folkestone Police Station and told what he had heard.

All four conspirators were arrested, tried and found guilty of David Crump's murder. Because of his youth, Paul Thompson received an indefinite prison term, while Stephen Farthing, Maggie Boo and Hawaiian Cruiser were sentenced to life imprisonment.

John David
(England)

DISPOSING OF embarrassing bodies has always been the bane of those ladies and gentlemen who choose to kill. Over the years we have heard about many varied and novel methods of disposal—from a killer who dropped body parts from an airplane over the English Channel, to a demented man who kept his wife's frozen body in a freezer for several months.

This grisly tale breaks new ground!

Beautiful, 25-year-old Miriam Jones lived in the English town of Reading. She ran with the motorcycle crowd and loved life in the fast lane. She loved bikers too. Despite her mother's warnings that no good would come of her association with such unsavoury companions, Miriam ended up marrying one of her biker boyfriends. As her mother had predicted, the marriage wasn't a happy one. For one thing, her hubby was a wild and crazy guy who just wouldn't settle down.

Miriam, who wasn't a saint herself, also had difficulty lavishing her affection on only one man. The newlyweds argued incessantly, but finally came up with a solution to their problems. A baby was exactly what the marriage required. Nine months after that decision was made, Miriam became a mother. The addition to the family didn't help one iota. In due course the couple separated, which left Miriam with a new set of problems, not the least of which was making a living for herself and her baby.

Miriam obtained a position as barmaid at the Cider House Pub in the village of Winkfield. The pub was not exactly a high-class establishment. Not by a long shot. The fact is, the Cider House was a hangout frequented by members of the Hell's Angels. Miriam hung around with the bikers.

One day, charming John David walked into the pub for a refreshing Guiness Stout. John was a handsome 25-year-old hunk who had a way with words. Miriam took one look and thought to herself, "That's for me." It wasn't long before the young people became lovers. Once again, Miriam's mother wasn't thrilled with her daughter's choice of men. Still, the woman thought, it was nice that she had a man to care for her and her child. It wasn't easy for Miriam to keep up her tiny apartment on her income from the Cider House.

John's job wasn't what you would call a top-flight position. He worked part-time as a labourer taking care of hogs at a nearby large hog farm. Be that as it may, during the winter of 1987, John and Miriam were seeing each other on a steady basis. He often stayed all night at her apartment. Many thought they would marry.

Just when events were proceeding smoothly, who should return to the scene but Miriam's estranged husband. He, too, often downed a few at the Cider House. Isn't love grand? Miriam discovered that those feelings she once felt for hubby were now revived. There was one iceberg in the tranquil sea of love and his name was John David. Miriam could see no way out. She would simply have to tell the hog tender that he was out and hubby was in. That's exactly what she did. John David was devastated. He beseeched Miriam to reconsider, but nothing he did or said had any effect. Miriam was adamant that she would return to her husband's bed and board and that was that.

John David didn't take rejection well. He had been abandoned by his mother shortly after his birth. Eventually he was adopted, but always resented that his biological mother had set him adrift. Because of his good looks and charming demeanor, John had no difficulty attracting girlfriends. However, they all broke off with him when he grew serious.

In 1984, 22-year-old Jacqueline Cheer had gone steady with John for some time. At one point, she decided that John was not for her. On December 23, 1984, in nearby Maidenhead, Jacqueline was found dead on her bed. An autopsy indicated that she had engaged in sexual intercourse immediately before her death and that she had been manually strangled. Although John was suspected, he was never charged, due to lack of evidence.

Now, in 1987, it was happening all over again. John was being rejected, but no one knew of his previous brush with the law. On April 9, John called on Miriam's mother with the upsetting news that she was missing. He had been babysitting for her the night before, but she had not returned to the apartment. Miriam's mother reported her daughter missing to the police.

A preliminary investigation revealed that Miriam and her husband were about to be reunited. In fact, Miriam, her husband and baby were scheduled to leave for a vacation in Spain the day after she went missing. Police conducted a massive search of the area. Her husband and John David searched side-by-side for the missing woman. She wasn't found.

John David was routinely questioned. He swore that he had no idea of Miriam's destination on the night she disappeared, nor did he know whom she was meeting. During the course of the interrogation, a detective noticed a small cut on John's cheek. John claimed he had received the cut while shaving, although it was obviously above his beard line. John was asked to remove his shirt. There for all the world to see were a number of scratches on his chest and back. He explained that he had scratched himself while working with wire down at the hog farm. No one was buying his story.

John was lodged in a cell overnight. Apparently the long dark night had its effect. Next morning at dawn, he requested to see his interrogators. He told them that he had been rejected all his life and that Miriam had cooled toward him. On the night of April 8, he decided to make one last attempt to win her affection. In no uncertain terms, Miriam told him thanks, but no thanks. Their affair was over. She was returning to her husband.

John attempted to make love to his former girlfriend, but Miriam pushed him aside. The rejection was complete. He clasped Miriam's throat in his strong labourer's hands until she was dead. At this point, John paused in telling his story, then ceased talking altogether. Detectives urged him on. "What did you do with her body?" they wanted to know. It was as if John wanted to get the actual killing off his chest, but was reluctant to go further.

Finally, he confessed that he had wrapped the body in a bedsheet and carried it down to a car he had borrowed for the evening. He drove to the farm where he worked looking after a hundred fully grown hogs. John managed to lift

Miriam's body over a fence and into the hog enclosure. John David wept hysterically as he concluded his terrible recitation.

Police descended on the hog farm. Their disgusting task was to recover what might be left of Miriam's body. At the conclusion of their three-day hunt, they had recovered a small piece of her dress and four bone fragments.

While John awaited trial, additional evidence was provided against him regarding the 1984 murder of Jacqueline Cheer, but it was decided that nothing was to be gained by trying this case.

On December 6, 1988, John David was found guilty of the murder of Miriam Jones. He was sentenced to life imprisonment.

John Du Pont

(United States)

DAVID SCHULTZ didn't pursue his dream of another gold medal at the Atlanta Olympics. A madman shot him dead.

It is difficult to pinpoint just when John Eleuthere Du Pont went around the bend. He was always a bit strange, which is referred to as eccentric if you happen to be very rich. Financially speaking, John was loaded. We are talking here about a family tree dating back to 18th century France. One of John's ancestors had a monopoly on gunpowder. Du Pont's business conglomerates have given us nylon, rayon, lucite, lycra, mylar and teflon. The empire had, and still has, its tentacles in so many enterprises that it would be difficult for you or me to go through a single day without using a Du Pont product.

John was born a multimillionaire. He lived with his divorced mother at Foxcatcher Farm, an 800-acre spread in Newtown Square, Pennsylvania. Naturally enough, as a young man he attended private schools. After graduating from high school in 1957, he enrolled at the University of Pennsylvania, but higher education was not for Du Pont. John knew that with his vast wealth he could do or have anything he wanted. With this in mind, he embarked on various projects that interested him. When he tired of his most recent fad, he moved on to another.

In the early sixties, John devoted himself to birds and seashells, spending most of his time collecting in the South

Pacific. After gathering hundreds of thousands of specimens, he quit to take up competitive swimming. His aim was to win a gold medal in the 1964 Olympics, to be held in Tokyo. John enrolled in Villanova University and later switched to the University of Miami, where he earned a place on the varsity swim team in 1962 and 1963. With a singleness of purpose, he joined the Santa Clara Swim Club, then the most prominent club in the United States. Competing with the top swimmers in the world, John was to learn that while he was an excellent swimmer, he would never be world-class.

Undeterred, John switched interests, as he would do all his life. He decided to win a gold medal in the pentathlon, a five-discipline event consisting of swimming, pistol shooting, horseback riding, running and fencing. Unfortunately he sprained his ankle at the Olympic trials and had to withdraw.

John did manage to compete in his specialty all over the world, becoming good enough in 1965 to win the Australian championship. He was enthused about his win, so much so that he invited the National Pentathlon Association to hold its 1967 championship competition at Foxcatcher Farm. The association was thrilled to accept. After all, what organization wouldn't desire to have a wealthy competitor and possible patron interested in its sport? John didn't disappoint. He built an Olympic-size pool and an indoor shooting range on the estate. Other amenities were added, until Foxcatcher Farm was a state-of-the-art facility where John practised and where the championship competition could be held.

In August 1967, John finished fourteenth in the compe

tition. At age 29, in a subsequent competition, he finished twenty-third and dead last. In 1976, he made it to the Montreal Olympics as manager of the U.S. pentathlon team.

For a while, John tried to form an unbeatable swim team. He hired the best coaches, but after sinking a cool half-million dollars into the project he abruptly closed the club. He married an occupational therapist, Gail Wenk, in September 1983. The union lasted until March 1984, exactly six months. The divorce made headlines. Financial arrangements were settled out of court for megabucks.

John needed a diversion. He found it in amateur wrestling. It was John's idea to gather the best coaches, provide the ultimate facilities and attract the most outstanding amateur wrestlers in the country to Foxcatcher Farm. His aim was to have the United States dominate amateur wrestling, in particular to win world championships and gold medals at the Olympics for years to come.

As one of Villanova's prime benefactors, John had no trouble associating himself with the university after promising to finance its entire wrestling program. Of course, John Du Pont took the title of head coach. He gathered the top wrestling coaches in the country. Amateur wrestlers who in the past had to take jobs to finance their low-profile sport were now offered deluxe facilities, a regular salary and a home for themselves, their wives and children, all on the Foxcatcher estate. Many were suspicious, thinking this was too good to be true. But John kept his word. The eccentric Du Pont built the facilities, hired the coaching staff and started a wrestling program. It mattered little to the wrestlers that their sponsor liked to drive round the estate in an armored personnel carrier when he wasn't hopping about in his helicopter.

By 1986, Team Foxcatcher was a major force in U.S. amateur wrestling. World-class athletes were attracted to the club. Everything was provided. David Schultz, a 1984 Olympic gold-medal winner, was the shining star of the Du Pont stable of athletes. He lived on the estate with his wife and children.

David had devoted most of his life to his sport. He had won athletic scholarships to universities and had reached the pinnacle of his career when he won an Olympic gold medal to go with his world championship victory at Kiev, Russia, in 1983. Amateur wrestling is not a financially rewarding sport. While baseball, football, basketball and hockey pay huge salaries, there is no such reward at the end of the rainbow for amateur wrestlers. David considered himself fortunate to have a rent-free home, a regular salary and, above all, another chance at Olympic gold.

The first few years at Foxcatcher went well for David, although it was difficult for him not to notice that John Du Pont's behaviour was becoming more and more erratic. John drank heavily and suffered from severe mood changes. David seemed to be the one person at Foxcatcher who could calm him down. It wasn't easy to stay friends with a sponsor who, from time to time, referred to himself as the Dalai Lama. No question about it, John was operating a couple of bricks short of a full load. David assured his wrestling buddies that John was harmless. He was wrong.

On January 26, 1996, John placed a .38-calibre pistol in his belt, jumped into his Lincoln Town Car and drove to Dave Schultz's house. For reasons known only to himself, John believed David was his enemy. He aimed the .38 a

David, who was sitting in his Toyota Tercel. The rear window shattered. David screamed as he got out of the Toyota and walked toward the Lincoln. John took careful aim. From a sitting position in his car, he extended his arm and fired. David fell onto the snow-covered ground.

Inside the house, David's wife, Nancy, and their two children, Alexander, 9, and Danielle, 6, heard the shots. Nancy opened the front door and gasped in horror. There lay David, face down in the snow. As she stared at the unbelievable scene, John aimed his pistol at her. Nancy retreated into the house. John again focused on the still form in the snow as if transfixed. He aimed twice more at David and fired. The shots went into the fallen man's back. Nancy again opened the door and again was forced back inside when John pointed his pistol at her. Finally, John stepped on the gas and drove to his 18-room mansion on the estate.

Nancy dialed 911 and observed John leaving the scene. She ran to her husband's side and cradled his head in her lap as a red puddle of blood spread around his body. David was still breathing but died as Nancy comforted him.

Police rushed to the estate. It was evident from the outset that John had no intention of surrendering. Police decided against forced entry. They would wait outside the eccentric millionaire's home, all the while attempting to communicate with him. The house was surrounded by police and lit with floodlights. Expert hostage negotiators managed to speak to John by phone. He pleaded with them to turn off the lights so he could sleep. The police complied.

Saturday came and went with no new developments in the standoff. Authorities turned off the heat in the house.

By Sunday John complained of the cold. When told that they would turn the heat back on, John, as the experts had anticipated, became angry. Who did these people think they were, telling a Du Pont that they would turn on his heat? He knew how to do it and would turn on the heat himself. The ploy worked. John left the house and started to walk towards a boiler room that supplied heat to the mansion. A SWAT team converged on him and took him into custody. The siege was over.

John Eleuthere Du Pont, one of the richest men ever charged with murder in the United States, was found guilty of murder in the third degree. He was sentenced to 13 to 30 years' imprisonment.

Christopher Enderly
(New Zealand)

WHEN HER husband was lost at sea in 1977, Sarah Enderly, at the mature age of 45, made up her mind that she was far too young to take her place on the proverbial shelf. Sarah not only scorned the shelf, she made a concerted effort to sample every available male in Christchurch, New Zealand. It was an open secret that Sarah was a woman of, how shall we put it, loose moral standards.

Sarah lived with her 19-year-old son, Christopher, at 7 Oakdene Road, just outside the city in a rather pleasant, rambling old villa. She worked part-time at a university restaurant. Usually there was a man waiting for her to get off duty at eleven each night.

I would be leading you astray if I have given the impression that our Sarah was a raving beauty. Nothing could be further from the truth. She was decidedly overweight, had pronounced bags under her eyes and wore far too much makeup. To compensate for her unattractive appearance, Sarah often trolled for male companions. She wasn't above picking up sex partners in the various parks around Christchurch. It was these gents who would come a calling at the restaurant at closing time.

For six years, Sarah had one of the busiest sex lives in all of Christchurch. I mean four or five times a week, usually with different partners.

On January 25, 1983, her son showed up at police headquarters and reported his mother missing. She had not returned home after work the previous evening. Christopher provided the police with a photograph of his 51-year-old mother. Two days later, when Sarah still hadn't shown up, police commenced to interview neighbours and acquaintances. It was then that they learned of Sarah's over-active sex life. This knowledge opened up a myriad of suspects. Had one of her lovers done her in for any number of reasons that lovers do away with partners?

Detectives also learned that Chris was as straight as an arrow and had no idea that his mother was so sexually active. It appeared that as far as he was concerned, she worked in the house all day, went to work in the restaurant each evening and returned home.

Colleagues at the university restaurant stated that, uncharacteristically, no boyfriend had shown up for Sarah on January 24, the night she went missing. Since Sarah always travelled by bus, police interviewed bus driver Ralph Daniels, who knew Sarah well. He told investigators that on the night in question, Sarah had been the last person to get off his bus.

What in the world had happened to Sarah? Police speculated that the missing woman might have run off with one of her male friends. However, they felt she would not have left a son she loved, nor would she have left without taking any of her belongings. It just didn't make sense.

Police concentrated their efforts on the area between the bus stop and 7 Oakdene Road. Residents of the neighbourhood were again questioned. All knew Sarah by reputation, but none knew her well. Some expressed sympathy for Chris, whom they felt was not aware of his mother's nocturnal dalliances.

In a weed-infested yard behind a vacant house, police found the body of Sarah Enderly. She had been struck on the head seven times. Four of the blows had been delivered elsewhere and the last three had been inflicted after she lay dead in the field. Sarah might have been attacked as she walked from the bus stop to her home, authorities speculated, after which she had been dragged into the vacant lot, where the killer had struck the last three blows to make sure she was dead.

No money or jewellery had been stripped from the dead woman, nor had Sarah been sexually interfered with in any way. That left investigators with the idea that the culprit was a jealous or vengeful lover. Police undertook the tedious task of seeking out the scores of men in Sarah's life. This process had barely begun when Roger Ackworth walked into police headquarters with a most unusual story.

Straitlaced, artistocratic Ackworth explained that his 23-year-old daughter, Melanie had been engaged to Christopher Enderly. He and his wife had met Chris over the Christmas holidays and found him to be a charming young man. They totally approved of their daughter's choice of a husband. However, since the Ackworths were bluebloods, it was most natural for them to delve into their future son-in-law's family. Their investigation revealed that Chris's mother was nothing more than a tramp. To the Ackworths' way of thinking, although Chris was not responsible for his mother's behaviour, he was not a suitable husband for their daughter.

On January 18, Melanie returned Chris's engagement ing. She told her parents that he was extremely bitter when she advised him of the reason for the termination of their engagement.

Police interviewed Chris. He explained that for the past two years he had been aware of his mother's sex life. He had found out by accident. One night, he was studying late for an exam and left his room to fetch a glass of water. He was walking by his mother's room at the other side of the house when he heard loud moans. Thinking that his mother might be ill, he opened her door. Sarah was too busy to notice her son. She was engaged in frenzied activity in her bed with a member of the opposite sex.

Chris was devastated. Since that incident, a service club had refused him admittance, citing his mother's reputation as their reason. On another occasion he was asked to leave a private club because of Sarah's well-known activities. He grew to hate his mother. For two years, the thought of killing her never left his mind. The broken engagement had been the last straw.

Chris had concealed himself near the bus stop each night, waiting for his mother to come home alone. When she got off the bus on the night of the twenty-fourth, he sneaked up behind her and struck her over the head with a hammer. He then dragged his mother's body into the vacant lot and proceeded to strike her three more times to ensure she was dead.

Christopher Enderly was tried and found guilty of murdering his mother. He was sentenced to life imprisonment.

George Farmakopoulis
(England)

GEORGE FARMAKOPOULIS met his girlfriend Maureen in a rather unique way. He was serving time in an English prison for a minor con job, and his cellmate was none other than Maureen's husband. When George was released from the slammer, he visited Maureen, whose husband was still in prison.

George was a tall, handsome rascal who could charm the birds out of the willows. His guile worked on Maureen. Before you could say "why not," she and George were living and loving under the same roof. Soon their union was blessed with a baby.

What more can I tell you about George? He was one of those fellows who insisted on living well without an adequate income. When pressed for cash, he delved into crime. Just as many Canadian criminals seem to enjoy preying on convenience stores, British rounders thrive on sub-post offices, where many English people deposit their savings. George picked out a likely target in the village of Thriplow, Cambridgeshire.

On an overcast day in the fall of 1984, George and Maureen dropped off their baby and Maureen's other child by her still-incarcerated husband with friends who would babysit the children for the day. After a pleasant lunch, they proceeded to Thriplow. George had been talking about robbing a sub-post office for weeks. It was his way of getting out of debt in one fell swoop. Initially, Maureen was against the idea, but gradually George wore her down. Now it was too late.

George and Maureen walked into the shop of 53-year-old Doreen Smith. Doreen had lost her husband years earlier. She was alone in the sub-post office. Maureen was shocked when George produced a gun and pointed it at the postmistress. She would later state that she had no idea a weapon was to be used in the robbery. George handed Mrs. Smith a bag with the terse order to fill it with money. As Maureen stepped around a partition, she heard the terrified Mrs. Smith shout, "No, don't!" George responded, "Get in here." Then Maureen heard the sound of a door closing.

As Mrs. Smith cowered in the cupboard where George had placed her, she recoiled in horror as George pointed his gun at her head and fired four times. Three slugs entered Doreen's head. The fourth bullet missed its mark. George and Maureen left the sub-post office, jumped into their van and drove away. George bragged about the shooting to Maureen. They drove to Grantchester, where they had a spot of tea before picking up the kiddies and making their way to the home of Maureen's mother. Once there, they counted their loot. It came to £415.

Back in Thriplow, Doreen Smith, although horribly wounded, was still alive with three slugs in her head. She crawled out of the cupboard, across the floor of the post office and out into the street. Neighbours immediately rushed her to Addenbrooke's Hospital in Cambridge. Throughout her ordeal, Doreen remained conscious and was able to relate her terrifying experience to police. Unfortunately, this courageous woman died from her wounds after lingering in hospital for 18 days.

The day after the robbery, George and Maureen travelled to Amsterdam. A few weeks later, they read about Doreen Smith's death in the newspaper. Maureen was devastated. What had started out as a grab-and-run theft had turned into the brutal murder of an innocent woman. She implored George to go back to England and face the music. He wouldn't hear of it. George confiscated Maureen's passport, making flight impossible. To complicate matters, Maureen informed George that she was pregnant.

Undeterred, George talked Maureen into moving to Athens. Once in Greece, he kept a tight rein on her, occasionally locking her in their home. As luck would have it, Maureen found her passport. Without hesitation, she flew to England and gave herself up to police. That June, she gave birth to a daughter in prison.

In order to apprehend George, authorities approached Maureen with a deal. She went along with the arrangement. George had no idea she was in custody. In fact, he had often called Maureen's mother's home to speak to her. Maureen was delivered by police to her mother's house to receive his calls from Athens, which were always prearranged. George coaxed Maureen to meet him on the continent. Police urged her to arrange to meet him in Amsterdam.

George travelled to Amsterdam and rang Maureen's hotel before showing up. The hotel staff had been briefed. They told him she was breast-feeding her baby and would call him back shortly. Maureen returned his call. Little did

George know that she was still in England. However, he was a cautious man and, at the last moment, changed the site of the reunion to Antwerp, Belgium. He was arrested as he stepped off the aircraft in Belgium.

George was returned to England to stand trial. He swore that he was innocent, insisting that he had been shopping in Cambridge at the time of the crime. His protestations were in vain. Maureen's evidence relating every detail of the cold-blooded crime sealed George's fate. He was found guilty of murder and sentenced to life imprisonment with no possibility of parole for 20 years. When the sentence was read in court, George attacked the officers guarding him. It took a half-dozen police to subdue him.

The same jury found Maureen not guilty of murder, as it was felt she was an unwilling dupe in the hands of her manipulative lover. She was complimented on the assistance she had given authorities in apprehending George Farmakopoulos as well as in giving evidence against him. However, Maureen didn't get off scot-free. She was found guilty of robbery and sentenced to five years' imprisonment.

Ken Fromant & Elizabeth Thompson

(England)

OCCASIONALLY MURDER cases reveal titillating sexual details that dwarf the crime itself. One such murder occurred on November 5, 1971, along a lovers' lane known as Purbrook Heath Road outside Portsmouth, England. A police officer discovered the body of 35-year-old Peter Stanswood in his car, which was parked on the road. He had been stabbed to death with a Japanese paper knife, which was protruding from his chest. The handle was covered with blood.

It was ascertained that Pete and his partner, Ken Thompson, were owners of a boating business on the Isle of Wight. Pete lived in Portsmouth with his wife, Heather, and their two children, Tina and Charles.

An officer had the disagreeable task of informing Mrs. Stanswood of her husband's murder. To say that he was shocked at her reaction would be an understatement. Heather told the investigator that her husband had several mistresses. She provided him with a list of 25 ladies whom she knew had been intimate with her Pete. She added that two of the women had presented Pete with illegitimate children and a third was currently pregnant. Heather thought that her husband had spent the previous evening, the night of the murder, with Wendy Charlton, who was heavy-laden with Pete's child. Detectives scrambled over to

Wendy's digs. She confirmed that she had spent the previous evening with Pete. During the course of the evening he had phoned Linda Reading, one of the two women who had borne his offspring. It was Wendy's opinion that he had intended to visit Linda after leaving her flat.

Police scratched their noggins. This guy Pete Stanswood had been one busy boy. It was apparent that he had been carrying on adulterous affairs with more Portsmouth ladies than a porcupine had quills. And there was more. It was learned that Heather Stanswood had none of those attributes that would make her a candidate for sainthood. Heather confessed that she too played the field and had had scores of affairs, some of which were known to her husband. Her current beau was Ken Fromant, a native of Berkshire, who was also married with two children. When questioned, Ken swore that he had been in Berkshire on the evening of the murder. Furthermore, he had broken up with Heather two months before the murder. He had no reason to kill Pete Stanswood, a man he had never met.

Meanwhile, minor mysteries cropped up. Blood found on the handle of the murder weapon and the steering wheel of the car did not match the murder victim's blood type. There were no fingerprints on the Japanese paper knife and it was never traced. Above all, it appeared that all those involved in the case were promiscuous and took their adulterous affairs very lightly.

Nine months passed. While detectives were turning up more dirt than a landfill site, they were having great difficulty coming up with a clue to the killer's identity. Their luck changed while interviewing one Portsmouth woman who mentioned that she had been visited by her lover, Ian

Dance, the night Pete was killed. Since police had already interviewed Dance, who had sworn he hadn't been in Portsmouth on the evening in question, they now had someone who had given them a conflicting statement.

Dance was questioned again. When told of his girlfriend's faux pas, he admitted that he had been in Portsmouth with an acquaintance, Ken Fromant. Well, son of a gun, Ken was the lover of Heather Stanswood, the murdered man's wife. Dance was able to prove that Ken had dropped him off late in the afternoon and that he had had absolutely nothing to do with Pete Stanswood's murder.

Matters became complicated. Upon being reinterviewed, Ken Fromant was confronted with Dance's statement. He now admitted he had lied when first questioned. His reason for being in Portsmouth was simple enough. He had spent the night in bed with Elizabeth Thompson, the wife of Pete Stanswood's partner. When Elizabeth was interrogated, she broke down and admitted she had spent the night with Fromant. She too swore that neither she nor Fromant had had anything to do with Pete's murder. They were guilty of adultery and lying, but nothing more.

Police weren't so sure. They located the vehicle that Ian Dance and Ken Fromant had driven to Portsmouth on the night of the murder. By sheer good fortune, it had broken down the day after the murder and been left undriven in a garage parking lot ever since. Samples of earth were taken from the vehicle's tires. This earth proved to be identical to earth taken from the site of the murder. In addition, Fromant's blood type matched the blood found on the murder weapon and on the steering wheel of Pete's car.

Although their case was far from airtight, the police took Ken Fromant and Heather Stanswood into custody and charged them with Pete's murder. After being charged, Heather informed police that Elizabeth Thompson had told her that she and Fromant had murdered Pete. She revealed all the details of the crime. According to Heather, her husband had received a telephone call from Elizabeth to meet her at the Purbrook Heath Road car park with sexual intercourse in mind.

When Pete drove up, he found Elizabeth and Fromant waiting in Elizabeth's car. The two joined Pete in his vehicle. The men argued. Fromant took out his Japanese paper knife, but momentarily Pete got the upper hand and managed to cut Fromant's arm, accounting for the presence of his blood on the knife and the steering wheel. When Ken gained control, he stabbed Pete seven times, causing his death. Elizabeth and Fromant drove to her house, where they changed clothing and patched up Ken's arm.

Heather's startling revelations were extensively investigated. As a result, the charges against her were dropped. In her place, Elizabeth Thompson was charged with Pete's murder.

On October 21, 1975, the 17-day murder trial commenced. It caused a sensation throughout England, mainly because of the sexual dalliances of the participants. It was proven that Elizabeth was in the midst of an affair with Pete Stanswood. Although both were married, she felt that if she couldn't have him exclusively, no one could. Fromant, who was infatuated with Elizabeth, murdered a man he had never met. Both defendants admitted that they had been at the scene of the crime at the time of the murder.

Each accused the other of committing the actual stabbing. It mattered little.

Ken Fromant and Elizabeth Thompson were found guilty of murder. Both were sentenced to life imprisonment.

Dennis Golding
(Canada)

IN THE FALL of 1974 everyone was wondering what had happened to Lisa Golding. Her husband, Dennis, told friends that he had driven her from their Clonsilla Avenue apartment in Peterborough, Ontario, to Highway 401 so that she could hitchhike to Georgia. According to Dennis, he and Lisa had had a bit of a squabble and Lisa had wanted a little time to herself. He would join her to begin a new life in a couple of weeks when she phoned him to let him know her location.

Acquaintances couldn't quite swallow Dennis's story. Dennis, 24, had a real estate business in Peterborough. It didn't seem likely that he would give up his career to resettle in Georgia without any prospects in that American state.

One of the missing woman's friends called Lisa's mother and stepfather in Halifax and was told that they, too, were concerned. They had not heard from Lisa in several weeks, which was very unusual. The friend's phone call so upset Lisa's parents that they informed Halifax police of their daughter's strange disappearance.

Halifax police listened in when Lisa's stepfather called Dennis in Peterborough. Dennis now told a somewhat different story. He said he had no idea where Lisa had gone. He had driven her to the highway 19 days earlier. At that time she told him that their marriage was finished and that she was never coming back. Dennis claimed he was embarrassed to relate the tale to friends, but felt that Lisa's parents deserved to hear the truth.

Lisa's family conferred with police. They felt that she might very well have walked out on her husband, but they could not believe that she would not have contacted them in almost three weeks.

Within days of these suspicious developments, a male friend of Lisa's visited Peterborough police. Upon hearing that Dennis had officially reported his wife missing, he revealed the saga of his involvement with the missing woman. As a result, police delved into the life and loves of Lisa Golding.

Lisa had met 19-year-old Dennis Golding in Halifax when she was 17 and he was serving in the Canadian navy. He was her brother's closest friend. Dennis spent all his shore leave with Lisa. Soon the young people were deeply in love. Everything was coming up roses. Lisa and Dennis were married in All Saints Cathedral and set up housekeeping in Dartmouth, Nova Scotia. As is the case of thousands of newlyweds, the future appeared bright and full of promise. But with the glamour of the uniform removed and the practical problems of earning a living closing in on the Goldings, their relationship deteriorated.

Dennis received his discharge from the navy and decided that Ontario held far more promise than Nova Scotia for a young fellow who wanted to get ahead. He accepted his stepfather's offer of a place to live in Peterborough until he got on his feet. In the meantime, he would take a real estate course with the idea of joining his stepfather's real estate firm.

Lisa was furious. This wasn't in her plans at all. A gift of a motorcycle pacified her enough to facilitate the move, but Lisa was an unhappy camper. She demanded to hit the open road in an attempt to get a proper perspective on the direction her life was taking. Despite the built-in risks in her plan, Dennis reluctantly acquiesced to his wife taking off with a few friends on their motorcycles headed for Halifax. They would check in with Lisa's parents upon their arrival in the Nova Scotia capital. All seems to have gone well with the Halifax visit. Three weeks later, Lisa arrived back in Peterborough.

Shortly after Lisa's return, Dennis had had enough. He ordered his wife out of the apartment, suggesting she go find the life she sought with her biker friends. Lisa took up the challenge and conferred with a particular friend in Sudbury. Together the couple headed for western Canada. Within a month they reversed their direction and crossed the country to Halifax. When Lisa ran out of money, she called Dennis for airfare back to Toronto. She had a buddy in nearby Ajax and would stay there for a while.

Dennis came through as he always did. He figured his wife was finished with her wild lifestyle and was susceptible to returning to him. He was wrong. Lisa once again flew to Halifax, but was immediately disillusioned.

Dennis was beside himself with his wife's machinations. She was charming one minute, but the next minute treated him like dirt. It was lonesome living alone in the Peterborough apartment, so he took in a border, David Sing-Woon Chan, who occupied the spare bedroom.

For the umpteenth time, Lisa made another move. She returned to Peterborough. The troubled couple seemed to be on the verge of a shaky reconciliation. On October 20,

1974, Dennis took his wife out for dinner. That night they made love, not a frequent activity in the Golding residence. They agreed to start over. Dennis's real estate career was taking off. In the years that lay ahead, they would carve out an idyllic life together. Arm in arm, they arranged a $15,000 loan to see them through the next year. At last their hectic relationship was on an even keel.

That's when Lisa Golding disappeared.

The Ontario Provincial Police (OPP) questioned Dennis. He told them that he had left his wife hitchhiking on the highway. Next day, Dennis's stepfather called police. Dennis hadn't shown up for work and couldn't be reached by phone. For three days authorities had the disconcerting task of attempting to find out what had happened to both Dennis and Lisa.

The mystery of Dennis's absence was soon solved. He had been found unconscious in a hotel room in Toledo, Ohio. Apparently he had taken an overdose of barbiturates and was recovering in hospital. OPP detectives were dispatched to Toledo to accompany Dennis back to Ontario. Initially he stuck to his story of dropping off his wife at the edge of the highway, but changed his tune on his lawyer's advice.

Dennis told detectives that after obtaining the $15,000 loan, he and Lisa had argued over the disposition of the money. He thought a large portion of the loan should go toward a down payment on a house, while Lisa believed that she should receive more than the $500 Dennis had given her. The argument continued in the bedroom. Even after they were in bed, Lisa wouldn't stop. Finally, she blurted out that Dennis wasn't adequate in the lovemaking department. To add insult to injury, she told her husband that her biker friend was a far better sex partner than Dennis would ever be. She went on to tell him that even when he was in the navy she had seen other men and used to joke about how stupid he was not to catch on.

Dennis broke. He bent over his beautiful wife, clasped his hands around her neck and strangled her. He told police that he dressed himself and Lisa, all the while making sure he didn't wake up his roomer, David Sing-Woon Chan, who'd slept through the entire incident. He then had the difficult task of carrying the body out of the apartment and down six flights of stairs. Dennis placed his wife's body in his car and drove around for three hours before deciding to bury Lisa near Chandos Lake.

Throughout his gruesome dissertation, Dennis swore that he had loved his wife and had made every allowance for her erratic behaviour, until he finally had seen red and couldn't control himself. Police located Lisa's body, which was buried in soft earth exactly where Dennis had indicated.

Dennis was charged with murdering his wife. Later the Crown accepted his plea of guilty of the lesser charge of manslaughter. On February 17, 1975, he was sentenced to 10 years' imprisonment, the initial portion of his sentence to be served at the Penetanguishene Hospital for the Criminally Insane. When deemed fit to be released from the hospital, he was to be transferred to prison.

Dennis Golding has long since been paroled.

Steve Gray
(United States)

STEVE GRAY knew Dolores's family didn't like him. He attributed their obvious displeasure to the fact that he was black and Dolores was of Hispanic stock. That's not the way Dolores's family saw it at all. They couldn't put a finger on the reason they disliked Steve. It was just one of those things. They simply couldn't stand Steve Gray.

It didn't matter who disapproved of the match. The young couple, in their mid-twenties, appeared to be madly in love. They dated for only a few months before marrying on August 29, 1987. Dolores knew she was marrying a navy man. She realized right from the beginning that she could never get accustomed to being separated from her husband.

A month after their marriage, Steve was assigned to sea duty on the *USS Enterprise*. After a couple of weeks ashore, he was again at sea on the *Enterprise* for more than a month. Dolores, who worked for the U.S. government in Fresno, California, was elated when Steve informed her that he had been granted a 17-day leave. At last they would have a real honeymoon. They would take off in Dolores's 1982 Camaro and drive away with no destination in mind, no schedule, just each other and the good times to cherish and enjoy.

On Saturday December 5, they decided to visit Yosemite National Park at Curry Village. The young couple purchased food and a bottle of champagne. They ate the food before driving up to Discovery View to take in the outstanding view of the valley and consume the champagne. Dolores didn't care for any champagne, so Steve drank it as they listened to the car radio in the parking lot. He became drowsy. As he dozed off, Dolores said she was going to take a walk and enjoy the scenery. It was around 5 p.m., just about the time the setting sun cast brilliant red and orange shadows against the geological outcroppings that dominate the surrounding hills.

Steve remembered Dolores leaving the Camaro. He fell asleep. When he awoke, it was pitch-black and Dolores was nowhere to be seen. The next thing anyone was to hear of the fate of Dolores Gray was when Steve dialled 911 from the Curry Village ice-skating rink and told the dispatcher his wife was missing. He had searched for her, but simply couldn't locate her in the dark. The dispatcher told Steve not to worry, many people get lost in that area. A U.S. park ranger would be sent to meet him at the rink immediately.

The ranger met with Steve, who repeated the details of his wife's disappearance. Together, they drove to the Discovery View parking lot. The ranger turned on his loudspeaker, broadcasting Dolores's description and requesting a response from her in case she was injured or immobilized for any reason. When he received no response, he phoned his command post for additional assistance. He couldn't help but wonder why Steve had not used either of the two pay phones he had passed between Discovery View and the Curry Village rink.

When reinforcements arrived, one of the Rangers asked Steve if he and Dolores were happily married. Steve assured him that his three-month marriage was extremely happy. About the only negative he could think of was his wife's family's racial attitudes. As Steve was being questioned, several rangers noted he referred to Dolores in the past tense.

As the night wore on, Steve indicated that he had promised to return to Fresno that evening to stand guard for a buddy. It seemed strange that a man whose wife was missing would want to leave the scene to do a favour for a friend. The rangers had to coerce Steve into staying the night at a nearby motel.

Next morning, the search for Dolores in the treacherous terrain intensified. Around noon, a mountain climber came across her battered body at the base of a cliff. She had apparently stumbled over the cliff in the dark. An autopsy indicated the death was accidental. Because of Steve's rather weird behaviour, the rangers decided to discuss the case with the FBI, who agreed a full-scale investigation was warranted.

Friends of the newlyweds were questioned. It was learned that on his wedding night Steve had gone out, found a willing female companion and hadn't returned to his bride's side until 4 a.m. You wouldn't call that getting off on the right foot. They also found out the he'd had several one-night stands with a variety of women since his marriage.

Steve had inquired about insurance on Dolores's life 10 days before she plunged to her death. He said it was the normal inquiry of a man who was newly married. When asked to take a polygraph test, Steve agreed. The test indicated he was giving deceptive answers concerning the events leading up to calling 911. Faced with the lie detector results, Steve weakened and changed his story. He now told detectives that after arriving at the Discovery View parking lot, he and Dolores stood beside the Camaro listening to the car radio and drinking champagne. Dolores left to look for a washroom along one of the trails.

Steve said he heard a blood-curdling scream moments later. He panicked, took a quick, unsuccessful look for Dolores in the dark before jumping in the car and driving to the Curry Village rink. Steve said he had lied for two reasons: he hadn't acted very heroically, and he knew Dolores's family would never accept his story. The investigating officers didn't believe his story either, but they realized they didn't have enough evidence to convict the man they were now convinced had killed his wife.

Although Steve denied having any life insurance outside his normal naval protection, detectives discovered he had three policies on Dolores's life that would pay him more than half a million dollars in case of his wife's accidental death. Despite the undeniable proof that the policies existed, Steve insisted that he had no knowledge of them. Detectives were able to dig into the insurance company's files and find Steve's fingerprints on an application he had signed to take out one of the policies.

A short time after Dolores's death, Steve set himself up with another woman. He didn't treat his live-in girlfriend much better than Dolores. One night, police were called to his apartment. Steve had beaten the girl and had threatened to throw her out a second-storey window. For this adventure, he was charged with assault, found guilty and sentenced to 60 days in jail. He was charged with Dolores' murder while still serving this sentence.

In June 1989, Steve stood trial for his wife's murder. The prosecution proved beyond a reasonable doubt that Steve had lied to Dolores about himself from their very first date. He had falsely glamorized his rank in the navy, had constantly seen other women and had contrived to insure Dolores' life for sums far exceeding his ability to pay for such insurance. There was little doubt he had contrived to kill Dolores, collect the insurance money, leave the navy and live a life of leisure. Had he not passed those pay phones or had he shown more concern for his missing wife before she was found, he might very well have gotten away with murder.

It took the California jury only five hours to find Steve Gray guilty of murder in the first degree. He was sentenced to life imprisonment with no possibility of parole.

George Green
(Canada)

MURDER AT any time is a repugnant act. When committed by an adult, we look for deep-rooted motives. What drove the murderer doing the deed? Was it greed? Was it anger or passion? But when murder is committed by a child, we look elsewhere. What emotion or drive could compel a child to take another's life?

In 1849, in the township of Emily, near Peterborough, Ontario, a murder took place that shocked the community and the nation. Eliza and Thomas Rowan were God-fearing, honest folk, who laboured long and hard on their farm. When they heard that the widow O'Connor was having a difficult time making ends meet since the recent loss of her husband, Eliza and Thomas agreed to take in tiny, five-year-old Margaret O'Connor.

Soon the little girl was an integral member of the Rowan family. She loved to play with and feed the animals on the farm, and seemed to be always laughing and smiling. The Rowans loved the little girl as if she were their own. Previous to Margaret's joining the family, the Rowans had adopted another youngster. For two years, young George Green had been living with the family.

As an infant, George had been placed with Rev. Mr. Dick, a Presbyterian minister. Then in 1847, the Rowans had taken George to their farm. When the boy reached the age of nine, the Rowans realized he needed some formal education, but the district school was too far away for him to attend regularly. Every so often they would sit George down at the kitchen table and go over some reading and sums.

The boy seemed to take to his farm chores with vigour and good humour. He fed the chickens, milked the cows, and was a pretty helpful hand around the farm. When Margaret joined the Rowans, George and the little girl often performed chores together.

In the autumn of 1849, George was 11, Margaret was 5. Events were about to unfold that would affect both their lives forever.

Samuel Hannah lived about a mile down the road from the Rowans. One fine day Thomas hitched up his team. He was going to a ploughing bee at Samuel's place. Eliza was planning on spending some time with a neighbour while Thomas was ploughing. Her husband would drop her off on his way to the bee.

Before the Rowans left their farm for the day, Thomas instructed George to "raise ten or twelve rows of potatoes." This sort of casual instruction was over and above the normal chores the young lad was expected to do around the farm. Thomas shouted to George as the team galloped out of the yard, "When Margaret goes out to you, you may have her help you to pick the potatoes, and place them in the wheelbarrow."

George nodded and waved to the Rowans as they drove out of sight. The next time Thomas Rowan was to see George, the boy was running toward him on Samuel Hannah's farm shouting, "Margaret has been eaten by a bear!"

For some reason that he had difficulty explaining later, Thomas Rowan instinctively felt George was lying. He angrily turned upon the young lad, "You have killed the little girl. You have murdered Margaret." The words came fast and furious. They were unnatural words, directed against a protesting, sobbing 11-year-old child. The youngster swore he was telling the truth.

All the men rushed to the Rowan farm to hunt for some trace of the missing girl. George pointed out where the bear had come upon little Margaret. He illustrated how the unsuspecting child had held out her hand to the bear, an act she had performed many times when she gave young calves their milk bottles. The boy pointed to the place in the fence where the bear had jumped, carrying Margaret with him.

The men searched until darkness made it impossible to continue. They could find no evidence that a bear had dragged a child in the soft earth. They found no bear tracks or torn clothing. In fact, they could find no evidence that a bear had been anywhere near the Rowan farm.

With the search at a standstill, the men turned their attention back to George Green. They grilled him until finally he fell asleep, still insisting that a bear had carried away the unfortunate Margaret.

All the farmers in the area, as well as young George, were up bright and early the next morning to continue the search. Around noon they found the pathetic body of tiny Margaret O'Connor. She had been bludgeoned to death with a hoe, which lay beside her body. Her attacker had struck her repeatedly in the head and all over her body until she was dead. Adhered to the blade of the hoe that George had been using to "raise the potatoes" were blood and strands of the dead girl's hair.

The men fixed their stares upon 11-year-old George Green. The savageness of the attack upon the helpless child was beyond comprehension. Adamantly proclaiming his innocence, George was taken into custody and lodged in the Peterborough jail. On May 3, 1850, to my knowledge the youngest defendant ever to stand trial for murder in Canada, faced his accusers.

The scene was strange. Solemn, educated men were to argue the merits of his case. A black-robed, learned judge was to direct the proceedings and, in the end, a jury was to pass judgement on George's innocence or guilt. The object of all this attention was a small, trembling child.

Thomas Rowan explained the circumstances leading up to the discovery of Margaret's body. Eliza Rowan then took up the story. She told the court that George confessed to the murder after he had been placed in jail. Margaret had come out to the field where George was digging the potatoes. George had never thought of killing Margaret before. It was only when she was with him in the field that he had "taken the notion of killing her." All of a sudden he struck her with the hoe again and again until she lay still.

The crowd in the courtroom looked down at the young lad in the prisoner's box. They stared in disbelief. The defence called no witnesses.

George was found guilty of murder and sentenced to hang on June 26, 1850. On June 4, his sentence was commuted to life imprisonment in Kingston Penitentiary.

After a few weeks of confinement, George became pale and weak. Several months later, two prisoners were relieved of their usual work detail. They slowly carried a tiny pine box, which they placed in an unmarked grave. The little boy who had hacked Margaret O'Connor to death had arrived at his final resting place.

Simon Gun-a-noot
(Canada)

IF SIMON Gun-a-noot had lived, loved and roamed the wilds of the United States, his saga would be as well-known to us as that of Sitting Bull, Geronimo or Cochise. But Canadians appear to be inherently reluctant to glamorize their heroes or, for that matter, their villains. I'll leave it up to you into which category you wish to place Simon Gun- a-noot.

Come along with me now to a different time and place, where men worked hard and played hard. It is June 18, 1906, and the place is Two Mile Creek, British Columbia. The closest real town is Hazelton, home to some 200 hardy souls.

Simon Gun-a-noot was a Kispiox native who trapped and hunted year round in the wilderness between the Skeena and Stikine Rivers. He often sold the products of his labours in far-off Vancouver, purchasing supplies that he lugged back north to sell in the small shop he owned near Kispiox village. Simon, a handsome, well-built man, lived in harmony with his wife, Sarah, and one child on a small ranch where, in addition to his other activities, he raised cows and horses.

On the fateful night in question, Simon dropped into James Cameron's licensed watering hole for a few drinks. Among the patrons was one Alex McIntosh, a heavy-drinking prospector who would rather fight than eat. That's exactly what happened. No one could remember how the fight started, but before you could say mink pelt, Alex and Simon were going at it hammer and tongs. After each had taken severe punishment, the combatants were parted. Simon said that, given the chance, he would fix McIntosh good. McIntosh had his own problems. During the fight he had badly injured a finger, which required medical attention. He took off on horseback for the hospital in Hazelton. Alex didn't make it. Next morning his body was found face up on the trail about a mile outside town.

The coroner stated that Alex had been shot. The bullet had travelled diagonally upward, exiting through the man's collarbone. Its trajectory was compatible with someone firing from a horizontal position on the ground. While police were surveying the scene of the crime, they were informed that another body, that of Max Leclair, had been found on the trail leading to Kispiox village on the other side of Hazelton. Like McIntosh, he had been shot while travelling on horseback.

Provincial Constable James Kirby, in charge of the investigation, soon learned of the bad blood between Simon and Alex. Although Leclair had not attended the drinking bout the night before, it was felt that Simon might very well have met him on his way home.

An inquest into the deaths of Alex McIntosh and Max Leclair was speedily conducted. The jurors concluded that Simon had murdered McIntosh. They also strongly suspected that Simon and his brother-in-law, Peter Hi-madan, were responsible for Leclair's death. Evidently Peter had been seen travelling with Simon after the scuffle at Cameron's drinking establishment.

Kirby, with five other constables, travelled to Kispiox village to pick up the wanted men, and so began the Gun-a-noot saga. Simon was not at home, and his wife had no idea where he might be hiding. Later it was learned that he had correctly surmised that the law would widen the search, so he stayed close to home. When the heat died down somewhat, Simon gathered up his wife and child, together with Peter and his wife, and headed north into the wilderness he knew so well. His father, Nah-gun, joined the well-equipped and experienced band of travellers.

All that summer the hunt for the wanted men continued. North West Mounted Police lent their assistance. A $1,000 reward, a small fortune in 1906, was posted for the capture of the two men. Despite the mammoth effort, authorities had difficulty penetrating the rugged mountainous terrain. Summer gave way to one of the coldest winters on record. On occasion, the hunted band was sighted, but not once did they come close to being apprehended. When the weather became intolerable, the hunt was intermittently suspended.

With the coming of summer, the search for Gun-a-noot once again intensified. Expert guides and prospectors were hired to help police, but all were unable to locate or keep up with the fugitives. It was learned that Gun-a-noot and his band occasionally joined other groups of natives for short periods of time, but they were always able to anticipate the authorities and move on.

Years passed. Gun-a-noot was unlike many other wanted natives in several ways. He had no urge to return to his village to visit his wife and child for the simple reason that he had taken them with him. Most important of all, he was intimately acquainted with the uninhabited territory he traversed. He often found himself in remote areas into which no white man had ever ventured. Natives, who usually resented anyone trespassing on their hunting and fishing grounds, became Gun-a-noot's allies and assisted him in any way they could.

Natives and whites alike came to admire Gun-a-noot's endurance and courage. To those who crossed his path in the first decade of his freedom, he swore he had murdered no one but was certain he would not be believed. Years later, Gun-a-noot was at least partially vindicated when his sister-in-law, Peter Hi-ma-dan's wife, confessed on her deathbed that she had killed Max Leclair after he had made sexual advances toward her. According to her story, Gun-a-noot came along the trail moments after the incident and then and there decided to take the blame for Leclair's murder.

By 1919, the now-legendary Gun-a-noot had been at large for 13 years. During his sojourn in the wilderness, he had lost three children to natural causes and longed for a better life for his two remaining offspring. Both his parents had died and his wife was in the midst of a prolonged illness. In essence, Gun-a-noot was tired of running. Word spread throughout the territory that the most notorious fugitive of the era was negotiating a surrender. Friends put him in contact with Stewart Henderson, a graduate of the University of Toronto who had originally headed west to seek gold in the Yukon. In 1919, he was a successful criminal lawyer practising in Victoria.

Henderson met Gun-a-noot in the forest outside Hazelton. To Henderson's surprise, Gun-a-noot had saved up the proceeds of years of trapping while a fugitive. He could easily afford to pay Henderson for his services.

On June 24, 1919, Gun-a-noot, accompanied by his lawyer, gave himself up to authorities at the Hazelton jail. In October of that same year, he stood trial for the murder of Alex McIntosh. After 13 years, Crown witnesses were vague in their recollections. Stewart Henderson tore their testimony to shreds. He relentlessly pointed out that there was no concrete evidence linking his client to the murder, other than a fistfight, which was more the norm than the exception when rugged, tired men have one too many. It took the B.C. jury only fifteen minutes to bring in a verdict of not guilty.

A few months later, no doubt influenced by Gun-a-noot's success, his brother-in-law, Hi-ma-dan, turned himself in. With lawyer Henderson at his side, he was freed following a preliminary hearing.

Gun-a-noot lived on until October 1933, when he collapsed and died while tending his traplines.

Debra Hartmann

(United States)

TO SAY WERNER HARTMANN was not a devoted family man would be to understate the case. He lived under the same roof with both his current wife and his ex-wife. Folks, that takes guts.

Werner made his bundle in the car-stereo game. It was a prosperous business, but simply didn't pull in enough loot to keep him in the lifestyle to which he had become accustomed. Let's see now, Werner and the ladies lived in Northbrook, a classy suburb of Chicago. They had three vehicles, a Mercedes, a Rolls-Royce and a Lincoln Con-tinental at their disposal. You get the idea. Business was good, but not that good.

On June 8, 1982, Werner was alone in his palatial home. It was a pleasant, warm evening. With nothing else to do, he decided to take a shower. Upon leaving the shower, he wrapped a towel around his body and placed one foot outside the shower stall. Someone poured several shots directly into Werner's chest. The seriously wounded man turned as if to stagger out through the bathroom door. His assailant fired more bullets into his back. Werner Hartmann, 38, lay lifeless on the bathroom floor with a total of 12 bullet holes in his upper torso.

In the wee hours of the morning, Werner's current wife, Debra, returned home after a tour of nightclubs with her 14-year-old stepdaughter. When she went upstairs and found her husband's body in the bathroom, she and her stepdaughter ran out of the house and drove to the nearest police station.

Detectives accompanied Debra to her home. They immediately ruled out robbery as a motive for the murder. Absolutely nothing was missing from the house, and besides, robbers don't usually overkill to such an extent. To the veteran police officers it appeared that someone hated Werner enough to shoot him 12 times. When it was established that a .38-calibre pistol had been the murder weapon, police knew that the killer, in the midst of his murderous spree, would have had to reload in order to keep on shooting.

As the investigation proceeded, detectives learned of Werner's rather weird domestic setup. About a month before the murder, he had contacted his first wife, who lived in Florida with their two daughters. Werner had been married to the woman for 13 years, having tied the knot when he was 20 and the blushing bride a mere 15 years of age. In 1977, they divorced, but before that, wife number one had been bookkeeper for the family business. Now, a month before his demise, Werner had asked his ex-wife to return to Chicago to help him in the business. Debra, his current wife of four years, also worked in the family business. The two women got along so well that Debra invited her husband's former wife and children to move into the large home in Northbrook. All were out of the house on the night of the murder.

An additional complication came to light when a police pathologist informed investigators that several of the fatal bullets had been fired hours before the balance of the bullets had been discharged. All the slugs had been fired from the same .38-calibre weapon.

During the course of the investigation, detectives learned that Debra was having an affair with a tennis pro, one John Korabik. When Debra was faced with the investigators' knowledge, she readily admitted her involvement. In fact, since her husband's death, she had moved in with Korabik. Demure Debra stood to gain approximately a million dollars in insurance from her husband's estate. Surely she had a double-barrelled motive for murder most foul.

Still, there was no proof that Debra had committed the murder. Shortly after the body was found, paraffin tests were conducted on her hands in an effort to trace gunpowder. None was found. Inexpli-cably, small traces of gunpowder were detected on the hands of Debra's 14-year-old stepdaughter. Months drifted into years. Wife number one returned to Florida with her children.

In 1987, some five years after the murder, out of the blue, convict Ken Kaenel told prison officials that back in 1982 he had been approached by tennis pro John Korabik to murder Werner Hartmann for a fee of $50,000. Korabik had given Ken a .38-calibre pistol to do the job with, but when Ken fired off some rounds in his basement, he found that the pistol misfired. He lost faith in the scheme and returned the weapon. Ken was now coming forward in an attempt to get his own sentence reduced. Such admissions are viewed with a degree of suspicion by police. In order to verify his story, detectives went to Ken's former home and dug the old slugs out of the basement wall. The slugs were compared to those removed from Werner's body. Wouldn't you just know it, they matched perfectly.

Ken agreed to work with police to get the goods

on Korabik. Debra and the tennis pro had long since parted company. About a year after Werner's demise, Korabik had been shot in the leg, ostensibly by a prowler. Shortly after the incident, the firm of Debra and Korabik was dissolved.

Detectives outfitted Ken with a wire. He visited with Debra. During the course of their conversation, he told her that he had almost become the killer of her husband, but had turned down Korabik's offer. Debra rose to the bait. She volunteered that she had promised Korabik $200,000 to kill her husband. After the murder, they were planning to go into business together, but her ex-boyfriend had become too greedy and had wanted everything for himself. Their relationship understandably had deteriorated after she shot him in the leg.

In January 1989, Debra Hartmann, John Korabik and Ken Kaenel were arrested and charged with conspiracy to commit murder. Although it was never proved, it is believed that when Debra and her 14-year-old stepdaughter returned home on the morning of the murder, they were met by Korabik, who had killed Werner hours earlier. Realizing that Debra's stepdaughter knew too much, the two schemers had her fire several shots into her father's already-dead body. She was told she was equally guilty of the foul deed and was frightened into silence.

The charges of conspiracy to commit murder were never pursued. Instead, the state felt it could more easily obtain convictions on lesser charges, which carried equally harsh sentences. All three had at various times used the mails to implement their murderous schemes. They were each found guilty of mail fraud. Eight years after the murder, Debra Hartmann was sentenced to 22 years' imprisonment; John Korabik received 20 years; and Ken Kaenel, who was looking to have his sentence reduced, was instead sentenced to 20 years' imprisonment.

Debra Hartmann's stepdaughter who, at the time of the sentencing was 22 years old, was not charged with any crime.

Walter Herbert

(Canada)

A FEW MILES north of London, Ontario, lies the tiny, peaceful hamlet of Arva. Paved roads have replaced the old dusty thoroughfares, but once you venture off the main road, the area is much the same as it was a hundred years ago when intrigue and bloody murder paid a visit to the Ontario countryside.

Joe Sifton had gone through two wives and was 55 years old if he was a day. You had to hand it to Joe, he looked ten years younger.

Joe lived on his son Gerald's farm, but the two men never got along. It didn't matter what the topic—if Joe said black, Gerald said white. In order to keep peace in the family, Joe moved away to his own farm nearby. Truth is, Joe owned several choice acres in the area. The Sifton clan was never considered poor.

Mary MacFarlane was a fresh, 20-year-old dairy maid who worked for Gerald on his farm. The decaying trial transcript of the case reveals the facts, but only the imagination can do justice to Mary. One can picture the rosy-cheeked lass working away at the butter churn or scurrying around the farm doing her chores. Mary was engaged to Martin Morden, a fine broth of a lad who had formerly worked on Gerald's farm. The young people were to marry the following spring.

Who knows how it started. Maybe it was those rosy cheeks. Maybe Joe was one of those men who require a woman's company. Whatever the reason, 55-year-old Joe took a shine to 20-year-old Mary. Actually, he took more than a shine. He took Mary.

Now don't go blaming Joe. It takes two to tango and the evidence indicates that Mary simply loved to dance. Well, folks, Joe and Mary danced to such an extent that lo and behold, Mary noted the distinct absence of the regular monthly biological occurrence that had never deserted her in the past. Yes, of course, she was pregnant.

Mary approached Joe on Thursday, June 27, 1900, with the disconcerting news. Joe took it well. They would get married. Indeed, there were certain complications. There was the little matter of Mary's engagement to Martin Morden. Mary assured Joe that it was nothing more than a childish infatuation to be ignored. Number two wasn't as easy to dismiss. Gerald would be furious. He stood to inherit his father's substantial estate. The marriage would change all that. Joe assured Mary that Gerald would just have to grin and bear it.

The die was cast. Joe would make arrangements with the Rev. Cooper. The date and time were set. The wedding would take place at 5 p.m. on the following Sunday.

Weddings were never meant to be secret. Mary revealed her marriage plans and delicate condition to Gerald. He reacted as expected and flew into a rage.

That very evening, Joe called on Mary. He was discreet enough not to knock on the farmhouse door, but parked his buggy in the yard. Mary ran out and the pair drove away. That night they told Mary's mother of the impending nuptials. Mrs. MacFarlane was none too happy with the match, but in the end reluctantly gave her blessing.

At 11 p.m., Joe parked his buggy in his son's yard. Before Mary could depart, farmer Edgar Morden suddenly appeared on the scene. Edgar had startling news. In a whisper, he told Joe, "You better get away—out of the country, your life is in danger." Edgar, good friend that he was, insisted that Mary and Joe stay over at his house for their own safety.

The couple took Edgar's advice. They were served supper by Edgar's wife, after which they sat around the stove before going to bed.

On Sunday, Mary awoke brimming with joyful anticipation. This was to be her wedding day. Joe told her the plans. They would drive over to his place, where he would change into his best clothing. From there they would make their way to the church. Despite Edgar's warning, Joe couldn't believe he was in any real danger. After all, Gerald was his own flesh and blood.

Joe had just put on his Sunday best when Gerald showed up with hired hand Walter Herbert, ostensibly to return some equipment. They would place it in the barn. Joe said he would give them a hand when he finished dressing. Mary implored Joe not to go, but he insisted.

Shortly thereafter, Walter Herbert ran to the house and excitedly blurted out, "Oh, Mary, Mr. Sifton has fallen out of the barn and killed himself!" He then called across the road to neighbour John Sinker, "Mr. Sifton fell out of the barn and killed himself!"

Sinker asked, "How did he fall out of the barn?"

"He was knocking boards out of the haymow and fell out of the barn."

Sinker ran to assist his fallen neighbour. He noted an

axe and some bricks not far from Joe's head. The badly injured man was carried indoors.

Gerald and Walter rushed the short distance to Dr. David McNeil's home. Gerald told the doctor, "Father is terribly hurt. He fell out of the barn and may not be alive when you get there." Rev. Cooper, a neighbour of Dr. McNeil's, overheard the conversation and he too showed up at Joe's side a few minutes after the doctor. That afternoon, Joe Sifton died.

Initially, Joe's death was considered an accident. Then rumours began to spread throughout the area. Rev. Cooper remembered seeing two pools of blood beside Joe's fallen form, rather unusual for a fall. There were also the axe and bricks close to Joe's head. Dr. McNeil, who was the coroner, also became suspicious.

Twenty-five days after the tragedy, Joe's body was exhumed. There were two distinct and terrible wounds to the man's scalp. Police were called in. They learned that Gerald had offered Martin Morden and his brother, James, $1,000 each if they would help him kill his father. Gerald had suggested a fake suicide. Both men, who had been approached separately, refused the offer. Later, when the investigation into Joe's death intensified, Gerald offered the brothers $1,000 not to tell the authorities about his proposition.

The police, led by famed Detective Inspector John Wilson Murray, picked up Gerald Sifton and Walter Herbert. Both men were charged with murder.

A short time after being taken into custody, Walter confessed. He told authorities that the night before the tragedy, Gerald had offered him $1,000 to be a witness "in case anything should occur to make people suspicious about the job." Walter said that he would go with his boss but would have nothing to do with putting old Joe out of the way.

After breakfast on the day of the murder, they left Gerald's house in a horse-drawn cart. When they arrived at Joe's, Gerald fetched an axe and entered the barn. He then took a large hammer and proceeded to knock boards off the top of the barn up in the haymow. Gerald told Walter, "If my father comes up in the mow, hit him in the head with the axe."

A short while later, Joe came into the barn and climbed up the ladder into the haymow. Walter crouched low. "When his father came up, I struck him with the axe. Gerald came over and struck him three or four blows on the top of the head with the hammer. His father's legs seemed to cave in and he fell through the trapdoor. His legs went through the rungs of the ladder and he hung there. Gerald told me to get down and shove him up. I did so and Gerald pulled him out of the hole and hit him two or three more blows.

"Then we picked him up into the mow and placed him on his back. Gerald picked up the axe and hit him again a couple of times. Gerald took hold of his shoulders and I took his feet and we carried him over and threw him out the end of the barn."

Gerald then told Walter to fetch some bricks and put blood on them. Gerald threw the axe out of the barn and instructed Walter to run to the house and tell Mary of the horrible accident.

A year later, Gerald Sifton was brought to trial. Rarely has a more graphic tale of murder been related in a

Canadian court. Defence counsel produced doctors who felt that had Joe received the terrible punishment outlined by Walter Herbert, his injuries would have been more severe. After deliberating for six hours, the jury reported that they could not reach a verdict.

Another long year went by before the entire process was repeated. Once more the crowded courtroom was transfixed by Walter Herbert's account of the murder. After almost five hours of deliberation, the jury returned a verdict most startlingly at odds with the evidence—not guilty. Gerald Sifton was a free man.

Walter Herbert, who had confessed to murder, which the court had ruled was not murder at all, was allowed to change his plea from guilty to not guilty. He, too, was set free.

The notoriety of the murders and the two trials forced the two main participants in the drama to leave the area forever.

Wanda Holloway
(United States)

WHEN THE story broke in 1991, it was beyond comprehension. A woman down Texas way had planned a murder so that her teenage daughter would be assured a place on a seventh-grade cheerleading team. Impossible? Yet it did happen.

Channelview, Texas, is located a few miles outside Houston. It's an industrial blue-collar town, distinct from its sprawling neighbour. Religion is big in Channelview. Most of the hard-working inhabitants belong to one fundamentalist group or another.

Ranking right behind religion for the people of Channelview is football. It is not unusual for 25,000 fans to show up for a high school football game on a Saturday afternoon. Parents groom their sons to excel at the game, knowing full well that only a minuscule few will go on to play college or pro ball. In many cases the athlete's high school football career is the highlight of his entire life.

Just as boys aspire to make their high school football team, ambitious girls attempt to become high school cheerleaders. Positions on the squad are few, and require good looks, athletic skill and a certain charisma. Usually the entire student body votes for candidates to the team. In Texas they take their cheerleading seriously.

Verna Heath and Wanda Ann Holloway were good friends. Both were attractive women in their late thirties. Verna had three children: Sean, age 10, and Aaron and

Amber, 14-year old twins. Her husband, Jack, was the manager of a grocery store. Verna was active in church affairs and saw to it that she and her family regularly attended the Truth Tabernacle Pentecostal Church.

Verna had been steeped in the art and lore of cheerleading from childhood. Her mother ran a school solely to train potential cheerleaders. Verna taught at her mother's school. It was only natural that Verna's daughter, Amber, displayed the ability and determination to make her mark in the cheerleading game. At age 14, Amber was one of the finalists trying out for a spot on the Grade 7 cheerleading team.

Wanda Holloway had been married three times. Each time she sashayed down the aisle, she bettered her social and financial position. She had one daughter, Shanna, 14, the product of her ill-fated first marriage to a local man, Tony Harper, whom she had married directly out of high school. But all that was behind her now.

Wanda's third husband, 20 years her senior, was prosperous businessman C.D. Holloway. Wanda had all the creature comforts—fine home, expensive jewellery (some pieces were valued in excess of $100,000) and a Jeep Grand Wagoneer in which to cruise around the countryside. Wanda wanted for very little, but she had a burr under her saddle. There was one thing that eluded her. She longed for her daughter to be a high school cheerleader.

Amber Heath and Shanna Holloway were also good friends. When the two youngsters were in Grade 5, they were deeply involved in training to become future cheerleaders. Their parents encouraged them. Wanda in particular pressed her daughter to excel. She went so far as to build a stage in her garage, complete with lights and mirrors so that Shanna could observe herself going through her routines.

When Shanna finished the fifth grade, Wanda had her transferred to Cobb Elementary Public School. There was a method to her madness. Grade 6 youngsters at Cobb were able to try out to be cheerleaders at Alice Johnson Junior High the following year. Only two girls from the entire student body at Cobb would be chosen.

In the spring of 1989, Shanna tried out for one of the two spots available at the junior high. Wanda kept her daughter on a strict regimen of practice and more practice. She felt Shanna couldn't miss. After all, one of the best cheerleading aspirants, Amber Heath, had chosen to stay at her old school, Channelview Christian, for the sixth grade and so would not be eligible to compete.

Unknown to Wanda, halfway through the school year, Verna Heath went to the junior high school and asked officials to let Amber try out for the school cheerleading team since she was planning to attend the following year. Officials saw no harm in the request and advised Verna that her daughter could try out with the Cobb Elementary applicants.

Here's what happened. Another girl, Summer Rutledge, won the competition. Amber came second. Both girls made the team. Shanna came in third and lost out. Wanda raised Cain with school officials. In her mind, the rules had been changed to include Amber in the competition and eliminate her daughter. Wanda's blind ambition for Shanna became an obsession. She grew to hate Verna and Amber. Next year would be different. Her Shanna would win.

In 1990, Shanna was again a finalist for the team, as was current team member Amber Holloway. Strange as it may seem to us, these youngsters conducted campaigns to garner votes from the student body. The committee governing such events prohibited the use of giveaway gifts by the competing girls. Wanda gave out rulers inscribed with her daughter's name during the campaign. Officials deemed this to be in direct defiance of the rules and disqualified Shanna from competition.

Wanda was fit to be tied. She didn't blame the officials. She blamed Verna Heath and Amber, telling everyone in town in no uncertain terms that Shanna had been cheated out of her rightful place in the sun. When the football season started, Wanda couldn't stand the sight of Amber Heath out there strutting her stuff.

During the 1990 football season, Wanda decided that something drastic had to be done to put those Heaths in their place. She looked up her first husband's brother, Terry Harper. Now, Terry was not what you would call a sterling individual. Over the years he had been arrested for drunk driving, causing a disturbance, and on several drug charges. In recent months, he had been going through one of his crime-free intervals. Terry was also quite the marrying man; he was currently living with his seventh wife.

Wanda approached Terry and didn't mince words, "I hate this girl. I want to get rid of her. I hate her mother. I want to get rid of her." Despite his checkered past, Terry listened in surprise as Wanda asked him if he knew anyone who would do away with Verna Heath and her daughter. Terry related the incident to his brother Tony, who insisted that he contact police. Terry took his brother's advice.

Detectives listened to the unbelievable tale. It was difficult to fathom that this churchgoing wife of a pillar of the community was soliciting the murder of a woman and her teenage daughter all because of a position on a high school cheerleading team.

Police asked Terry if he would wear a wire for his meetings with Wanda. He agreed. A series of encounters took place. The substance of these meetings constituted a verbal contract. Terry would acquire a hit man to kill Verna for $5,000, and Amber for an additional $2,500. Wanda agreed to hand over $2,500 in jewellery as a down payment for Verna's murder, with the balance to be paid in one month. On January 28, 1991, a tape recorder on Terry's body recorded the entire transaction. Wanda handed over the jewellery in a plastic bag. Two days later, she was taken into custody and charged with "solicitation of capital murder," an offence that carries a sentence of five years' to life imprisonment.

Wanda, christened "Pom Pom Mom" by the press, was found guilty. She received a 15-year prison sentence and a $10,000 fine. Two days later, she walked out of court free on $10,000 bail pending appeal. Since 1991, the strange case of Wanda Holloway has not disappeared from public view. In 1994, her defence team was successful in having a new trial ordered on a technicality.

In a civil action, the Heath family sued Wanda and was successful in obtaining a settlement of $150,000 from Wanda's insurance company. Lawyers' fees ate up $50,000 of the settlement.

Meanwhile, life goes on in Channelview. The Holloway family and the Heath family still live only a few blocks from each other. Occasionally, Wanda and Verna bump into each other, but do not exchange pleasantries.

Juliet Hulme & Pauline Parker

(New Zealand)

IN 1953, AT the age of 16, Pauline Parker was an overweight, awkward teenager. She walked with a slight limp, the result of contracting osteomyelitis as a child. Because of her limp, she didn't take part in sports at Christchurch High School in her native New Zealand, but she did own a pony and was an avid member of the Horse and Pony Club.

Pauline's father, Herbert Rieper, was an inoffensive little man who owned a relatively successful wholesale fish business. Herb never did get around to officially marrying Honoura Parker, but their common-law marriage had survived 23 not-always-tranquil years. The Rieper-Parker union produced four children. The eldest, Wendy, 18, was a normal, affectionate daughter who had never caused her parents one moment's anxiety. A younger brother was born mentally ill and was confined to an institution, while a fourth child died at birth.

Dark, brooding Pauline, as we shall soon see, marched to her own drummer. We will never know how Pauline would have turned out had not the fates decreed that her life become entwined with that of 15-year-old Juliet Hulme.

Juliet's father, Dr. Henry Rainesford Hulme, was tall, stooped and cultured. During the Second World War, at age 46, he was one of England's leading mathematical scientists. He was considered a fine acquisition when he became rector of Canterbury University College in Christchurch. With the position came membership in the senate of New Zealand University.

No question about it, Hulme was a heavyweight. But it was not academic recognition that enticed him to leave England for New Zealand. It was his daughter, Juliet. Doctors told him that her tubercular condition would improve in the fresh, clean air of New Zealand. In 1948, Hulme, his aristocratic wife, Hilda, daughter Juliet and his youngest son, Jonathan, arrived in Christchurch.

As part of his compensation, Dr. Hulme was given the use of a 16-room mansion in which to live and entertain. Certainly the brilliant doctor, who held one of the most prestigious positions in Christchurch, could look forward to a bright and promising future.

Things didn't work out as Dr. Hulme planned. After a few years of apparent tranquillity, 15-year-old Juliet met Pauline Parker. Adolescent girls often develop close attachments, but this was different. The two girls were inseparable. The bond between them bothered both families. To Pauline's parents, it appeared the Hulme girl was the cause of all their daughter's problems. Conversely, the Hulmes felt Pauline was an extremely bad influence on Juliet.

But the gods in the heavens decided they had more in store for the two families. Walter Andrew Bowman Perry arrived in Christchurch from England on a prolonged business trip. He became acquainted with the Hulmes, who invited him to be their houseguest in a self-contained flat that was part of their large home. Walt was delighted to partake of Henry's hospitality. Unfortunately, he partook of Henry's wife as well.

One fine afternoon, when everyone was supposed to be out, Juliet strolled into her mother's bedroom. Who should she find there in bed with Mummy but Walter Andrew Bowman Perry? Things were never quite the same between Mummy and Juliet after that.

Dr. Hulme picked this inopportune time to resign his position at the university. He told his family he had decided to return to England with son Jonathan. Dr. Hulme suspected his wife of adultery and his daughter of having a lesbian affair with Pauline Parker. He discussed the situation with Pauline's father, but nothing seemed to do any good. Dr. Hulme decided he would take Juliet as far as South Africa. He would continue on his way to England and she would return to Christchurch.

When Juliet heard of this scheme, she was furious. She wouldn't budge a step unless Pauline went with her. The girls asked Pauline's mother for permission to have Pauline go on the trip. They were bluntly refused.

The human mind is a complicated mechanism. The more the two girls thought about it, the more it seemed to them that Honoura Parker was the one who stood in the way of their happiness. They decided to kill her.

On June 22, 1954, an overcast winter's day in Christchurch, Honoura, Pauline and Juliet walked together along a path. The murder scenario was already in motion. That morning, Juliet had brought half a brick to her friend's house. Now that very brick was in Pauline's pocket inside the foot of an old stocking. Pauline pointed to some pretty pink stones on the path. As her mother stooped to examine the pebbles, Pauline extracted her homemade murder weapon and set it crashing over and over again on her mother's head. She passed the bloody stocking to Juliet, who proceeded to hit Honoura repeatedly. Together, the two girls beat Honoura Parker to death.

Pauline ran to a nearby kiosk, shouting, "It's Mummy. I think she's dead. We tried to carry her. She was too heavy."

Hysterically, Juliet added, "Yes, it's her mother. She's covered with blood."

Pauline interrupted, "We were coming back along the track. Mummy tripped on a plank and hit her head when she landed. She kept falling and her head kept banging and bumping as she fell." The girls washed their hands. Later, witnesses said the pair could be heard laughing uncontrollably as they washed away the blood.

Police examined the 45 wounds that had been inflicted to Honoura Parker's head and detained the girls for questioning. Three weeks later, they were charged with murder. Both girls confessed, making the salient point of New Zealand's most infamous crime not who committed the murder but whether the perpetrators were sane or insane.

The star of the proceedings was not a witness, but Pauline's diary. It remains one of the most diabolical pieces of evidence ever read in a courtroom. Here are a few excerpts:

> February 13, 1954. *Why could not Mother die? Dozens, thousands of people are dying. Why not Mother?*

> April 28, 1954. *Anger against Mother boiling inside me as she is the main obstacle in my path. Suddenly, means*

of ridding myself of the obstacle occur to me. If only she were to die.

June 21, 1954. *We have decided to use a brick in a stocking rather than a sandbag. Mother has fallen in with our plan beautifully.*

June 22, 1954. *I felt very excited last night and sort of night-before-Christmas.*

On the top of the page dated June 22, Pauline printed: THE DAY OF THE HAPPY EVENT.

As the trial progressed, it was revealed that the two girls spent much of their time writing stories, which they believed were potential best-sellers if they could ever make their way to America and have them published. Honoura Parker had crystallized in their minds as the main obstacle standing between them and their goal. As a result, she had to die. The thought of being apprehended and punished had never entered their minds.

After retiring for 2 hours and 13 minutes, the New Zealand jury found both girls guilty of murder. They were sentenced to prison "during Her Majesty's pleasure," which is usually around 25 years. Pauline Parker and Juliet Hulme spent only four years in prison before they were released.

Author's Note: The movie *Heavenly Creatures* is based on this old New Zealand murder. New Zealand journalists have traced Juliet Hulme to a small village in Scotland, where she now lives. The literary world was shocked to learn that Juliet Hulme is internationally renowned mystery writer Anne Perry, who has written more than twenty murder mystery novels.

Dailrene Ingram & Matthew Peiris
(Sri Lanka)

FROM TIME to time the faith-healing business has had the misfortune to fall into disrepute. Remember Mr. Swaggart who, between leading assorted heathens to the light, took great joy in bedding down with prostitutes. Then there was Jim Bakker, who was more concerned with renting the rooms of his luxury hotel than with saving souls.

Now let me introduce you to Father Matthew Peiris, who was somewhat of a heavyweight in his chosen field of healing the afflicted. The good father, a native of Sri Lanka, received his religious education at Lincoln Theological College in England. He held down several ecclesiastical positions there before returning to his native land.

While in England, Father Matthew had met and married Eunice Lois, herself the daughter of a preacher man who claimed to have a direct line to the Archangel Michael. At the time our story unfolds, the couple had three adult children: a son, Munilal; and two daughters, Mihiri and Mairani. Obviously, Father Matthew was partial to the letter M.

For years Father Matthew went about praying, healing and curing with a degree of success. At age 60, something happened to the man of the cloth that cannot be laid at the feet of his profession. It seems that Father Matthew had earthly concerns known to lure less religious men off the straight and narrow. Shall we get right to it?

In 1976, Eunice returned to England for a visit. During her absence, Father Matthew acquired a secretary. He was writing a book and planning to take a future book tour with his wife. The secretary could take care of the vicarage while they were gone.

Dailrene Ingram was a beautiful, ripe 27-year-old when she applied for the position. She had been married for eight years, had three young children and an unemployed husband named Russel. Never mind, Father Matthew would take care of all the problems. To alleviate Mrs. Ingram's pressing financial situation, he moved her entire family into the vicarage. He was successful in finding a job for Russel as an advertising salesman for a local newspaper. Everyone was happy as a bed of clams. Especially Father Matthew. Before you could say Casanova, he was bedding down with Dailrene right there in the vicarage. For shame.

Well, now, Mrs. Peiris returned from her trip abroad, which was most inconvenient for the lovers. Still, they made do with lovemaking on the sly, so to speak. Dailrene in particular was in a tight pickle. With three children and a husband underfoot, it was difficult to find the time and the energy to make love to Father Matthew. It was most annoying on Sundays to have to drag hubby and the kids to church in order to hear her lover's sermon, complete with occasional healing sessions.

Something had to give. Russel was the first to take ill. One fine morning, this healthy athletic specimen could hardly get out of bed. In fact, he remained in bed for five weeks. Rather than call in curious doctors, Father Matthew attempted to cure Russel by his own devices. When incanting a few choice phrases over Russel's stomach failed to bring the desired results, Russel was rushed to hospital. He was hooked up to a saline and dextrose drip, which improved his condition markedly. A few weeks later, he was sufficiently well to be sent home to the vicarage and into the care of Father Matthew and his own ever-loving wife, Dailrene.

When Dailrene was asked why Father Matthew was giving her husband so many pills, she became indignant. "Father knows what he is doing," she replied. The good Father's eldest son, Munilal, also inquired why his father was purchasing so many tablets. He never received a satisfactory explanation. Father Matthew had been buying as many as a hundred tablets of the drug Euglucon at a time.

Father Matthew tried to think of everything. He felt he should have independent witnesses in the vicarage and decided to invite another preacher, Russell Jackson, and his wife, Bridget, ostensibly to observe Russel Ingram's agony. Four days after the patient returned from the hospital, he died. Later, Jackson testified that the sleeping arrangements at the vicarage were somewhat unorthodox. Father Matthew was sleeping with Dailrene, while poor Russel was locked in a room all by his lonesome. Bridget had a most unusual and incriminating story to tell. She revealed that she had overheard a conversation between Father Matthew and Dailrene after Russel's death. He said, "Don't worry, Dailrene, soon I will be in the same condition as you, bereft of a partner."

Russel's death was attributed to hypoglycemia, which had caused irreversible brain damage. Hypoglycemia is due to an extremely low level of sugar in the blood. Diabetes, which is caused by too much sugar in the blood, is sometimes treated with Euglucon. Small amounts of Euglucon, such as a single 2.5 mg tablet, are prescribed to bring down blood sugar. Father Matthew had given Russel, who had suffered from no illness whatsoever, as many as seven tablets at one time, telling Russel that a doctor had prescribed the tablets. He had lied.

A few months after Russel's untimely demise, it was Eunice's turn. She lapsed into unconsciousness and was diagnosed with hypoglycemia. As he had done during Russel's illness, Father Matthew led doctors astray with false information.

He did everything in his power to make an accurate diagnosis an impossibility. Eunice remained unconscious for 47 days before dying. Doctors were extremely suspicious of the death. It could have been suicide or homicide. Several put their feelings on record

In May, 1979, Father Matthew and Dailrene were taken into custody and charged with the murders of Russel Ingram and Eunice Peiris. The case, built solely on circumstantial and medical evidence, was a complicated one. It took four years for the unholy duo to be placed on trial. The trial lasted 163 days.

Defence lawyers contended that death had been due to natural causes, which accounted for the low levels of sugar in the blood of the victims. Similar to the more recent O.J. Simpson defence, the pair's lawyers claimed that samples of blood had been contaminated during the testing process.

The prosecution came up with a witness who had overheard Father Matthew tell his wife that that Christmas would be her last on earth. Other witnesses revealed the strange sleeping arrangements they had observed on visits to the vicarage.

In the end, Father Matthew and Dailrene were done in by the medical evidence, which proved that Russel and Eunice had died from hypoglycemia. The condition was induced by medication, namely the drug Euglucon, which had been purchased by none other than Father Matthew. Witnesses testified that Dailrene knew what was going on all the time. In Dailrene's closet, police found a book on the topic of sugar in the blood. She had been reading up on the subject.

Father Matthew Peiris and Dailrene Ingram were found guilty of conspiracy to commit murder and murder in both cases. They were sentenced to death, but their sentences were later commuted to life imprisonment.

Zein Isa

(United States)

TO THEIR customers at the Alliance Market, the Isa family appeared to be a happy, industrious one, busy carving out a new life for themselves in America. Their small Shaw Boulevard grocery store in St. Louis was light-years removed from the life they had led in Palestine.

Maria and Zein Isa had four daughters. The three eldest girls worked diligently in the store and strictly adhered to their father's stern Muslim code. Although Zein had become a naturalized American citizen, he felt compelled to maintain his Midddle Eastern ways, as his father had before him. To Zein, modern American customs and loose moral standards were for heathens, certainly not for his family.

The three older daughters never questioned their father's wishes. Their lives were directed by the head of the family which, to Zein's thinking, was as it should be. Not so to the youngest daughter, Tina. In 1989, 16-year-old Tina was a beautiful youngster, full of the joy of life. She was a popular, straight-A student at Roosevelt High School. A natural athlete, Tina was on the school's soccer, tennis and hockey teams. She was also a member of the school band.

Zein hated the idea of his daughter taking part in any activities outside the home and the store. He berated Tina on a daily basis. Tina's three oldest sisters, who had been brought up so strictly themselves, sided with their father.

his religious values had been good enough for them, surely Tina should follow his wishes. On occasion, when Zein's wife, Maria, took Tina's part, the wrath of the entire family fell on her shoulders. Soon she was pleading with Tina to change her ways.

But Tina believed America was a land where one should be able to express one's free will. She was doing nothing wrong, simply living the life of an American girl. When her father talked in Arabic to his Mideastern friends, Tina couldn't understand why he didn't speak English. On one occasion, American officials had questioned her father about his association with the Palestine Liberation Organization (PLO). Tina didn't want to know about her father's political leanings. She merely wanted to be herself. It wasn't easy.

There were continual embarrassing incidents. Once Zein, accompanied by his eldest daughters, practically broke up the junior prom dance Tina was attending by dragging her off the gymnasium floor. In her senior year, Tina was forbidden to accompany her class on a trip to the nation's capital. That summer, she begged her parents to allow her to attend a six-week summer course at the University of Missouri. They wouldn't consider such an idea.

In 1989, Tina made the acquaintance of Cliff Walker, a tall, good-looking 18-year-old who often shopped at the Alliance Market. When Zein learned that Tina and Cliff were dating, he was furious. Cliff was black and Zein didn't approve. Despite her father's constant tirades on the subject, Tina continued to see Cliff.

Zein fervently objected to his daughter's lifestyle. He

believed there was no hope for his youngest child and convinced his wife that Tina could only be saved by having her leave this world for a far better one beyond. He felt the family's honour was at stake. He believed that Tina was a disgrace to herself, her family and her heritage. In time, Maria came around to his way of thinking.

In November 1989, Tina told her family she was taking a nighttime job at a nearby Wendy's. Zein forbade it. His own store had been good enough for her sisters and it should be good enough for Tina, he told her. Over her father's objections, after finishing her school work, Tina went to work at the fast-food outlet for the first time. She proved to be an excellent employee and a joy to have in the establishment. At the conclusion of her shift, Cliff walked her back to her Delor Street apartment.

One evening, Zein and Maria were waiting for Tina when she got home. They were beside themselves with anger. Their daughter had disobeyed them once too often. Furious Maria yelled at Tina as soon as the apartment door opened. Zein appeared from the kitchen, his right hand concealed behind his back. He accused his daughter of being a prostitute and told her she was a disgrace to the family. Mother and father shouted that they would throw Tina out of the apartment and out of their lives. Tears streaming down her cheeks, Tina volunteered to leave. Her father screamed, "You she-devil, don't you know this is your last day? You are going to die tonight."

From behind his back, Zein extracted a vicious-looking, long boning knife. Maria, who weighed 200 pounds, clutched her daughter's hair from behind and threw her to the floor. Zein bent over Tina and thrust the knife into her chest six times. He shouted at the top of his voice, "Die, die, my daughter."

Then Zein picked up the phone and called each of his daughters, informing them of Tina's death. He called police and told them that Tina had attacked him, but with the aid of his wife he was able to thwart the attack. Unfortunately, in the act of self-defence, he had killed his daughter.

Detectives were dispatched to the Isa apartment. They were amazed at Maria and Zein's calm demeanor as they related how their insane daughter had arrived home demanding money from them. When they refused, she had lunged at them with a knife. Zein had managed to direct the knife away from himself, as his wife had attempted to pull Tina away.

It didn't take long for detectives to learn of the animosity between the entire family and the attractive teenager. An autopsy proved Zein's story didn't wash. The six stab wounds were very close together, which is not compatible with a wild struggle. In addition, the angle of the wounds indicated the victim was lying on her back when the knife entered her chest.

Maria and Zein were charged with the murder of their daughter. Before the trial, the FBI contacted St. Louis police. Because of Zein's involvement with the PLO, the Isa apartment had been bugged for over a year. Every argument and threat directed toward Tina had been recorded. The buildup of hate was there for all to hear. Most relevant of all was the recording of the actual murder. Tina was heard to frantically plead, "Mother, please help!" To this plea, her mother responded, "Shut up."

Maria and Zein claimed self-defence, but the Missouri

jury found both defendants guilty of murder. Both were sentenced to death. In 1993, the Missouri Supreme Court overturned Maria's death sentence because of the jury had been given flawed instructions. However, her conviction was upheld and she is currently serving a life sentence in prison with no possibility of parole. Zein Isa awaits his fate on death row in Missouri State Prison.

In April 1993, the Isa murder case took a strange turn, when the FBI revealed there might have been an additional motive for the murder of Tina Isa. A federal indictment stated that Zein and three other men in St. Louis were associated with the terrorist arm of the PLO known as Abu Nidal. The indictment accused the four defendants of conspiring to kill Tina, allegedly because she might reveal the Abu Nidal's St. Louis connections. The indictment also accuses the four men of terrorism and of planning to blow up the Israeli embassy in Washington.

Jack Kirschke
(United States)

IF EVER A married couple had a unique marital arrangement, it was the one that existed between Elaine Terry Kirschke and her husband, Jack. They agreed in writing that for a full year ending on May 1, 1967, they would not have sex with each other, nor with anyone else. They also agreed that after that date they would continue to live together, but would go their separate ways sexually, if you get my so obvious drift.

Now, folks, these were no lightweights, not by a long shot. Until she sold her lucrative business, Elaine Terry was one of California's leading fashion designers. Jack was considered one of the most accomplished criminal prosecutors in the United States. He held down the position of deputy district attorney and appeared to be a shoo-in for a judgeship. At 45 years of age, handsome Jack had the world by the tail. Elaine, 43, was an attractive redhead who looked 10 years younger. The pair had been married for 24 years and had two adult children.

On April 8, 1967, Frank Cornell, who lived in the same apartment building as the Kirschkes at 185 Rivo Alto Canal in Naples, California, thought he heard a loud noise emanating from the Kirschkes' home at 2:30 a.m. Later that morning, when things were abnormally quiet in the Kirschke apartment, he sent a relative, James Miller, downstairs to take a look.

James couldn't get a response to his loud knocking. He

peered through a window and saw two blood-spattered bodies in the bedroom. James called police.

The bodies were quickly identified as Elaine Kirschke and Bill Drankhan. Bill was a well-known local businessman. Among his many accomplishments were his ability to fly a plane and his acrobatics in bed with other men's wives.

Under the circumstances, it was most natural that hubby Jack was strongly suspected of drilling his wife and her lover. Jack was detained as he sped through the Mojave Desert towards Los Angeles.

When he was informed that his wife and Bill were dead, Jack suggested that they must have been shot by a robber, which was rather revealing since no one had mentioned where they had been killed or that they had been shot to death. Jack refused to take a lie detector test and was immediately charged with two counts of murder.

Detectives soon learned of the strange marital arrangement between Jack and Elaine. They also learned that Bill had been bedding down with Elaine for months and that all their acquaintances knew it. No doubt Jack had found out.

Indignant, Jack swore he was innocent of any involvement in the murders. He told his interrogators that he had prosecuted many men, any of whom might have sought revenge. One of them had obviously mistaken Bill for him.

Jack's theory made a lot of sense, particularly when doctors estimated that the time of death was between midnight and 4 a.m. Jack claimed that on the night before the morning of the double murder, he had driven in his daughter's 1963 beat-up Volkswagen to the Los Angeles

International Airport to catch a plane to Las Vegas. He had a speaking engagement the following morning at a Rotary Club convention.

However, at the airport, he learned that three consecutive flights at 8:30 p.m., 9:30 p.m. and 11:30 p.m. were totally booked. At 11 p.m. he gave up and decided to drive to Las Vegas. He drove through San Barnardino to Yermo, where he purchased gas between three-thirty and four in the morning.

At around sunup he arrived in Las Vegas and spent a few hours gambling in order to pass the time until he was scheduled to speak to the Rotary Club. Jack gave his speech and was in the Volkswagen on his way back to Los Angeles when he was stopped and informed of his wife's death.

Jack's attempt to get on three successive flights at the airport was confirmed. Two Yermo gas station attendants, Dennis Baily and Gene Ledet, were located. Both swore they had served gas to Kirschke around three-thirty on the morning in question.

Frank Cornell told police that he had heard a noise, which could have been gunshots, around 2:30 a.m. Another neighbour stated that at 4 a.m. he got up to use the bathroom, looked out the window and saw the light go out in the Kirschke bedroom.

There seemed to be no way that Jack Kirschke could be the killer. If the murders had taken place at 2:30 a.m., it would have been impossible for Jack to have driven the 155 miles to Yermo and have been there between 3:30 and 4 a.m. He would have to have averaged 103 miles an hour in the 1963 Volkswagen which, upon testing, wouldn't go over miles per hour. Of course, if the killer had remained in the Kirschke residence until 4 a.m. when the light was turned off, it was out of the question for Jack to have been the guilty party.

Police went to work in an attempt to dismantle Jack's seemingly airtight alibi. They learned that shortly after the crime, a private detective had accompanied Jack to the garage where Baily and Ledet were employed. At that time, Baily didn't recognize Kirschke. Ledet only said that Kirschke looked vaguely familiar. They also vacillated about the exact time that Kirschke might have stopped for gasoline. Detectives felt that these two men had not lied about the time that Kirschke had been in the garage, but were simply confused.

When the gas station attendants faltered in their evidence, the possible scenario changed abruptly. The murder could have taken place at 2:30 a.m. when Cornell heard what he thought could have been shots. Kirschke would have had plenty of time to drive to Las Vegas and give his speech to the Rotarians at 9 a.m.

Homicide detectives still had to cope with the neighbour's evidence that the bedroom light had gone out at 4 a.m. Once more, they examined the murder scene. This time an investigator had the presence of mind to try to switch on the light. It didn't work. Upon examination, it was discovered that the lightbulb had burned out. The neighbour who had seen the light go out hadn't been privy to the killer turning out the light. He had merely seen darkness envelop the room because the bulb burned out.

Bullets removed from the victims' bodies had been fired from a .38-calibre revolver. The slugs were in such go shape that experts were able to ascertain that they had been fired from a rather rare revolver, a Harrington and Richards Defender. Jack admitted that he had once owned such a weapon. It had been given to him as a souvenir of a case he had prosecuted years before, but he hadn't seen the weapon for months.

The hunt was on for Jack's .38-calibre Defender. Fields and ditches near the murder scene were searched without success. The serial number, 22068, was known to authorities. They traced the weapon to the manufacturer. They learned that it had initially been sold to a sporting goods store in Long Beach, which had been burglarized. One of the weapons stolen had been a Harrington and Richards Defender, serial number 22068. Later the criminals were apprehended and the weapon returned to the sporting goods store. It was verified that while these criminals were in possession of the revolver, it had been used to shoot a woman, one Toni White, in the hip.

After an exhaustive search, detectives found the evidence box pertaining to the Toni White shooting. Inside a dusty file cabinet, in a sealed envelope, were bullets taken from Ms. White's rump. A ballistics expert compared the bullets with those taken from the bodies of Elaine Kirschke and Bill Drankhan. They matched. In this way police were able to prove that the gun given to Kirschke as a souvenir had been used to shoot his wife and her lover.

The Kirschke trial took 121 days to complete. A California jury took another six days to reach a verdict. They found Jack guilty of murder in the first degree and the famous prosecutor was sentenced to life imprisonment.

Jack Kirschke spent eleven and a half years in prison before being paroled in February, 1977. He has since remarried and today lives with his wife, Sara, on an island off the coast of Washington State.

Ralph Leahy
(Canada)

"THERE WAS no direct evidence that murder had been committed, not even a body, yet I knew that Viola had been murdered, and I had a pretty good idea who killed her. The case was bizarre in many ways," said Inspector Bill Perrin of the Ontario Provincial Police. Sitting in his office at police headquarters talking about the apprehension of murderers, I got the distinct impression that once Bill Perrin becomes convinced of something, he doesn't let go until he either proves or disproves his beliefs.

Inspector Perrin now operates out of the Anti-Rackets Branch, but for years was attached to the Criminal Investigation Branch, where he was in charge of many of Ontario's strange murder cases. None was stranger than that of Viola Leahy.

The Leahy farm is situated along Rural Route 4, outside Lakefield, Ontario, and has been in the Leahy family for as long as anyone can remember, certainly four or five generations. Jim Leahy worked hard on the farm, and supplemented his income by operating heavy excavation equipment. Everyone agrees that Jim was one of the best operators in the Peterborough area. Viola, his wife of over 25 years, also had interests that drew her away from the farm. Before her marriage, she received formal training as registered nursing aide, a vocation she continued to fol- after she became Mrs. Leahy. Both Jim and Viola had independent natures, and this independent bent, combined with their physical absence from each other, drove a wedge into an otherwise normal relationship.

Viola in particular craved some sort of social life. She enjoyed taking in the local dances, and sometimes visited a tavern with a woman friend, Emgard Woodzack, although Viola never drank anything stronger than a soft drink.

The long-standing marriage deteriorated until, finally, in 1972, Jim and Viola had an argument that turned into a fight. Viola charged her husband with assault. He was forced to appear in family court in Peterborough, where the charge was dropped. Viola then separated from Jim for a while and took legal action to obtain a half share of the family farm. For some reason known only to herself, she changed her mind and returned to live with Jim. Things were never the same after that. The Leahys settled down to a strange and unusual lifestyle. Viola supported herself. Jim did likewise. They conversed only when necessary. Viola continued to cook Jim's food and wash his clothing. They slept in separate rooms.

Every Friday, Viola would leave the farm and visit with Emgard. She always returned on Monday. And so, month after month, year after year, the strained lives of Viola and Jim Leahy continued.

Jim's brother Emmett worked a farm directly south of the Leahy farm. Actually, Jim had sold the house to Emmett some years before. Besides farming, Emmett had been steadily employed at the Westclox plant in Peterborough for the past 25 years. Emmett was raising four sons; the oldest, Ralph, was nineteen.

Although all was not well with the Leahy marriage, there was really nothing to distinguish them from hundreds of other farmers throughout the country: two brothers with adjoining farms, supplementing their incomes by working away from the soil—hardly the scene for a bizarre and unusual murder.

In 1975, Jim suffered a fractured skull in a farm accident. From that time on, Emmett and his sons gave Jim a helping hand with the chores. Viola, too, was not well. She suffered from arteriosclerosis, hardening of the arteries, which resulted in serious memory losses.

Because of the coolness between husband and wife, Viola came to depend a great deal on her brother and sister-in-law, Jack and Zetta Leeson. She phoned them every day. If she wanted to go anywhere, it was the Leesons who picked her up and brought her back to the farm.

On Friday, September 17, 1976, Viola was picked up by Jack Leeson and taken to Peterborough, where she stayed with her friend Emgard. Two days later, on Sunday, Jim was admitted to Sunnybrook Hospital in Toronto to have bone chips removed from his skull. This confinement was the result of the fracture he had suffered two years previously. Thus Jim was away from the farm from September 19 until his return from Sunnybrook on October 3. He was never to see his wife again.

Meanwhile, Viola's movements are well documented. On Monday, September 20th, she paid a visit to her doctor in Peterborough. Jack and Zetta Leeson picked her up at Emgard's and gave her a lift to Dr. Flak's office. He prescribed pills and rest. The Leesons then drove Viola back to the farm. They helped the 65-year-old woman into the house with her luggage. They left the farm at about 7 p.m. It was the last time they ever saw Viola.

A half-hour later Emgard received a phone call from her friend. The conversation was normal in every way. Viola gave no indication of unusual stress or anxiety. Emgard assumed that everything was fine.

Next day, Zetta Leeson tried to reach Viola on the phone all day, with no success. On Wednesday, Zetta and Jack drove to the farm. They found Viola's luggage exactly where they had placed it the previous Monday. There were several cigarette butts in an ashtray, which bothered the Leesons, because they knew that neither Viola nor Jim smoked.

On Thursday, they notified Emmett Leahy that Viola could not be located. Together with Emmett, they searched the farmhouse but found nothing that could lead them to the missing woman. On Saturday, five days after she made the phone call to Emgard, Viola was reported missing by Jack and Zetta Leeson. The report was turned in to E.D. Martin of the Peterborough detachment of the OPP.

During the preliminary investigation into the missing-person's case, the OPP turned up three pieces of information that would be of the utmost significance. David Ramsay had cleaned the furnace of the Leahy home on September 22. The only person he had come in contact with on the property was young Ralph Leahy. Ramsay stated that the boy seemed to be lurking near an open barn door when he spotted him. Ramsay was interested in getting someone to sign his bill that the work on the furnace had been completed. He thought it odd that when he approached Ramsay with the bill, the boy said, "I'm not supposed to be here." But Ralph signed the bill.

Another bit of information that gave the investigators food for thought was Emmett Leahy's statement that although he was taking care of his missing sister-in-law's mail, it had disappeared from his house. Jack, Zetta and Emmett remembered that when they searched the house on September 23, Ralph had mentioned that he'd seen Viola at about 8 a.m. on September 21. He thought she was heading for the bus.

The investigation continued. Jim Leahy came home on October 3, into the midst of an investigation into his wife's disappearance. All of Viola's personal effects were found in the house. Increasingly, it became apparent that she had met with foul play.

Two weeks went by. The Lakefield postmaster received an unusual piece of mail. It was a change-of-address notice apparently signed by Viola Leahy, directing her mail to the Sudbury post office, general delivery. The card was turned over to the OPP. They quickly established that the signature on the card was a forgery.

In the meantime, Ralph left his father's farm to seek employment in Edmonton, Alberta. The police checked his handwriting against the signature on the change-of-address card and established that the signature had been forged by Ralph.

Detective Inspector A.D.R. Smith and Constable G. Katz thought that Viola Leahy had been murdered. Despite snide insinuations that she had taken off with a man, neither policeman believed it was true. They flew to Edmon-on to interrogate Ralph. At first he denied rging the signature. Then he admitted to having done so, ing that a friend of Viola's had given him $50 to do it.

Ralph was returned to Peterborough, and charged with uttering a forged document. On June 9, 1977, he received three months' imprisonment, to be followed by a two years' probation.

On June 13, Detective Inspector Bill Perrin was assigned to the case. "I believed that Viola Leahy was dead," the inspector says, "and that the case could only be solved through her nephew, Ralph Leahy." Perrin made the decision to place Constable Bill Campbell, of the Intelligence Branch of the OPP, into jail with the suspect. Within a day, Campbell was playing cards with Ralph in the Quinte Regional Detention Centre in Napanee. Other prisoners were preparing for a transfer to Kingston Penitentiary. Ralph told his new friend that he too would probably be transferred before he finished his current sentence. He bragged that he and a friend had killed someone during the course of a robbery. Campbell didn't press the matter, but made a date to get in touch with Ralph when both men were released.

On August 9, Ralph Leahy was released. Unknown to him, he was under constant surveillance by the OPP. The following night Campbell met with Ralph at the Jolly Roger Lounge of the Holiday Inn in Peterborough. During their conversation, Ralph boasted to the undercover agent that he had killed his aunt the evening after his Uncle Jim had gone to hospital in Toronto. Once Ralph began talking, he wouldn't stop. He confessed to 17 or 18 robberies, and bragged about serving two years in jail. Ralph thought he was impressing Campbell, who had posed as a member of an auto-theft gang working between Montreal and Ontario. Ralph wanted a job with the gang.

Campbell didn't believe any of Ralph's bragging, with one exception. He firmly believed that he had a murderer on the line. They made a date to meet again on August 13. This time Campbell brought along Constable Terry Hall, posing as his brother and fellow member of the auto-theft gang. Ralph was duly impressed, talked incessantly of having killed his aunt. Late into the night the three men talked. In the end, Ralph promised to show them where he had hidden Viola's body.

The following Friday, the two officers and Ralph left the Holiday Inn at 1:30 a.m. for the Leahy farm. In deep bush beside a swamp, the three man dug for a body. Later, the officers were to relate that while Ralph dug, he made derogatory remarks about his aunt. "You old bitch, where are you? You've given me enough trouble."

Throughout the early morning, the men dug by flashlight, but Ralph couldn't find his victim's body. He promised his two friends that if they returned with him at some future date, he would produce the missing woman.

On August 25, at 11:05 p.m., Inspector Perrin decided to pull the plug on the investigation. He arrested Ralph and, at the same time, picked up Ralph's girlfriend, Barbara Hartwick, for questioning. At the time, Ralph remarked, "You'll never find her in a million years." When questioned, Barbara revealed that Ralph had admitted to her, back in November 1976, that he had killed his aunt. He said he had shot her three times.

Perrin interrogated the suspect. Ralph claimed he had nothing to say. Then he informed Perrin, "You made a mis-ke picking me up today—you should have waited a day d you would have had the body."

In the wee hours of Friday, August 26, Ralph indicated that he wanted to see Perrin. Perrin questioned and informed the suspect of his rights: "Are you prepared to show us where Viola is buried? You know you don't have to show us or do anything that may be used as evidence, Ralph."

At the ungodly hour of 3:30 a.m., Ralph Leahy led the officers to the area beside the swamp where he and the two undercover agents had dug previously. He stated that he had marched his aunt down to the edge of the swamp, and had shot her three times with her husband's .22-calibre rifle. The murder weapon was turned over to Perrin.

Digging began later the same day, but try as they might, they couldn't find the body. Finally Perrin brought in some heavy earth-moving equipment, and on Tuesday, August 30, the shovel uncovered the body of Viola Leahy. She had been shot three times in the area of the chest and abdomen. Ballistics tests confirmed that two of the bullets had been fired from the Leahys' .22 rifle.

Later, Ralph told doctors that he hated his aunt. The killing had not been a spur-of-the-moment sort of thing. He had mulled over the possibility of killing her for several weeks. After murdering his aunt at the edge of the swamp, he left her where she fell, but returned the next day with a shovel and buried her. He told the doctors that his aunt was not worth the time he was going to spend in prison. He had no remorse for what he had done and was only sorry that he would have to go to jail.

The rather smallish five-foot-six-inch farm boy had killed his aunt because he didn't like her. All indications a that she was kind and considerate to her nephew.

Viola Leahy had spent 11 months and 10 days buried on her farm. On February 4, 1977, her nephew, Ralph Leahy, was sentenced to life imprisonment.

George Lemay
(Canada)

GEORGE LEMAY is unique. Strongly suspected of one murder, acquitted of another, he was also the brains behind one of Canada's most dramatic robberies. Toss in recent capers such as assorted burglaries and trafficking in drugs and you begin to get the idea.

George was born into a well-to-do Montreal family. His early years gave no hint of what was to follow. His mother employed George in her successful real estate business.

In 1950, George met beautiful 19-year-old Huguette Daoust, a Montreal bank secretary. Huguette was petite, weighing no more than 105 pounds, with dark hair that accentuated her large, bright eyes. George fell hard. He pursued Huguette with a passion, until the lovely girl from the respected family consented to marry him.

On May 19, 1951, over the objections of her family, Huguette and George were wed. They honeymooned in Florida, familiar territory to George, who had often been on fishing expeditions to the Sunshine State.

When the newlyweds returned to Montreal, it was evident that they were having difficulty adjusting to married life. For one thing, George didn't seem to be very interested in working for a living. For another, he displayed a nasty temper.

Seven months passed, strained months for the good-looking young couple. When George suggested a second honeymoon in Florida, Huguette thought it was a gre idea. On December 27, the Lemays drove to Miami in George's red Studebaker convertible. They rented a room and fished every day.

On Friday, January 4, 1952, they went fishing along the Florida Keys, stopping at Tom's Harbor Bridge #4. According to George, they were fishing off the bridge at around 8 p.m. Huguette, clad only in a halter and shorts, complained of the cold. She told George that she was going back to the Studebaker to change into something warmer.

Fifteen minutes passed. When George's fishing line broke, he walked the hundred feet to the car to get a new line. It was only then that he missed his wife. George shouted. He peered into the car. His wife's shorts and halter were on the seat. A sweater and a pair of jeans were missing. No doubt Huguette had wandered off, but as time passed, George became frantic. He raced to a toll gate and, crying hysterically, told attendant Les Baker, "My wife has been kidnapped! Stop all cars! Have them searched!" Baker called the Florida Highway patrol.

Despite an extensive investigation, and despite the suspicion that George may have been involved in his wife's disappearance, no trace of Huguette Lemay has ever been uncovered since that day 47 years ago when she went fishing with her husband.

For the next ten years, George, who maintained a chalet near St. Jerome in the Laurentians, continued to get into minor scrapes with the law. On the Dominion Day weekend of 1961, he graduated to the big time. That's the weekend he directed the novel and daring break-in of the Ste-Catherine St. branch of the Bank of Nova Scotia in Montreal.

Lemay had rented a building across the street from the bank. Using walkie-talkies, he directed his confederates as they worked all weekend digging a tunnel into the bank's safety deposit box vault. Three hundred and seventy-seven safety deposit boxes were looted. The official loss reported was well over $600,000, but it's believed that many victims were reluctant to disclose the amounts removed from their safety deposit boxes. Some feel that George relieved the bank's clients of over $4 million that weekend.

Within two weeks, the gang was rounded up. Andrew Lemieux, age 27, his brother Yvon, 19, their sister, Lise, Jacques Lajoie, 37, and Roland Primeau, 35, were taken into custody. The four men were convicted and given lengthy prison sentences. Lise pleaded guilty to being an accessory and was sentenced to time already served. Later, she would become George Lemay's second wife.

But where was our George? The answer to that question was partially revealed two weeks later, when George's 42-foot cruiser was found docked near Miami. George had piloted the cruiser almost 2,500 miles from Montreal to Florida. The police had the cruiser, but its owner was long gone.

Meanwhile, a raid on George's St. Jerome chalet uncovered a small portion of the loot taken from the bank's safety deposit boxes. Police found a few thousand dollars secreted in a false panel in George's bedroom.

Two years later, the RCMP, the FBI and Scotland Yard cooperated in using an Early Bird satellite for the first time to send pictures of internationally wanted fugitives across the United States. In this manner, Lemay's picture showed up on TV screens in Florida. Sure enough, a boatyard worker in

Fort Lauderdale recognized the wanted Lemay as Rene Roy, the owner of the 43-foot sloop *Tirana*. Within the hour, Roy was fingerprinted. He was indeed the internationally-sought bank robber from Canada, George Lemay.

Lodged in Dade County jail while deportation proceedings were being instituted, George seemed to take a great interest in strengthening his somewhat flabby, squat physique. He also found time to marry Lise Lemieux. Active George was successful in turning on the charm and bribing the guard with a whopping $35,000 to aid him in his escape. It was a daring venture in the Lemay style.

George was allowed to slip out of his first-floor cell and take the elevator to the seventh floor, where he entered a room with an unbarred window. He fastened a rope to a radiator and made his way seven floors down the rope to freedom. Now everyone knew why George had been devoting so much time to building up his strength. He had, as usual, planned every facet of his escape.

The FBI, RCMP and Interpol searched for George throughout the world. It took them almost a year. On August 19, 1966, the FBI received a phone tip. They picked up Robert Palmer in the Golden Nugget Casino in Las Vegas. Fingerprints proved that Palmer was really our George. To change his appearance, George had shaved off the remaining hair from his almost bald head.

It took four months to get George back to Canada to face the music. On November 16, 1966, he was charged with the old Dominion Day break-in of the Bank of Nova Scotia. His confederates described in detail how he had masterminded the entire operation. They related that, when their hard tunnelling had been completed, George had, like a conquering general, insisted on being the first to enter the vault.

In January 1969, after one of the longest criminal trials in Montreal history, George was found guilty and sentenced to eight years' imprisonment.

After serving his sentence, George was out of jail only a short time before being picked up on a drug trafficking charge. While back in jail awaiting trial, George and three confederates are believed to have orchestrated the killing of one Pierre Quintal to prevent him from testifying against them. Despite Quintal's death, they were convicted on the drug charge.

In 1984, George stood trial for Quintal's murder. He was acquitted, but still had to serve the remainder of his drug-related sentence. Once again, George completed his term in prison and was released.

Where is George now? Your guess is as good as mine. Quebec prison officials assure me that George is now "on the streets." They nonchalantly add that they expect him back any time. George is like that.

Darren Huenemann, Derik Lord & David Muir
(Canada)

DORIS LEATHERBARROW worked hard all her life, and her efforts bore fruit. By 1990, at age 69, she was the sole owner of four prosperous ladies' dress stores in the Vancouver area. Her personal wealth was estimated at between four and five million dollars

Doris had one daughter, Sharon, who had gone through two husbands by the time she met and married Ralph Huenemann in 1976. Eventually Ralph obtained a doctorate and became a respected professor at the University of Victoria. Sharon brought Darren, her four-year-old son by a previous marriage, to the union.

The Huenemanns maintained a rather palatial home in the Saanich area, just north of Victoria on Vancouver Island, while Doris lived alone at Tsawwassen, near Delta, on the mainland. Despite her age, Doris exercised a hands-on policy regarding her chain of stores. She had the reputation of being a hard-nosed businesswoman, but was also known to be generous to her daughter and grandson.

Sharon raised Darren to be obedient, punctual and polite. Friends of the family felt that the lad was almost too perfect. He was immaculately dressed, never took part in athletics and was overly respectful of his superiors.

Although many believed Darren was the ideal son, others felt that his behaviour was unnatural for a teenager.

Doris doted on the boy. On his sixteenth birthday, she presented him with a shiny black Honda Accord. She also saw to it that he had a bulging bank account, amounting to several thousands of dollars. Money played a large part in the lives of Doris and Sharon. Both had known hard times and both appreciated the security and power that money brought to the family. Darren couldn't help but be influenced by the constant references to monetary subjects by his mother and grandmother.

In the spring of 1989, mother and daughter made wills. Doris's will was simple enough. Half of her fortune would go to her daughter, and the other half would be left to her grandson. Sharon left the money inherited from her mother to her son, Darren. Both women told Darren the terms of their wills. In so doing, they signed their death certificates. You see, Darren Huenemann, the perfect teenager, who had never received as much as a traffic ticket in his life, had made up his mind to murder his mother and grandmother.

A short time after learning the terms of the wills, Darren began talking openly to school chums about killing his mother and grandmother. They didn't take him seriously. A devotee of the game Dungeons and Dragons, at first he may have been merely voicing fantasies. At some point, however, the fantasies became a diabolical reality.

Darren went about formulating a plan to commit double murder. He picked his co-conspirators carefully. Fellow high school student, 15-year-old David Muir was a straight-A student. The only son of highly educated parents, Dav had never been in any trouble in his life. Derik Lord, 16, was also the product of a fine family. Like Darren and Dave, he had never been in any difficulty with police. The three boys lived within a half-hour's drive of each other.

Unbelievably, Darren's suggestion that his two friends carry out the killings was not greeted with revulsion by the boys. Darren made it all sound so convincing, so very easy. He offered them money, cars and property when the deed was done. Cold-bloodedly the boys discussed the method by which they would snuff out the lives of the two innocent women. With Darren acting as leader, it was decided they would wait until Doris and Sharon were together. The boys would club them unconscious then slit their throats.

Darren was ecstatic that his plan was taking shape. He took great pride in confiding the plot to his girlfriend, Amanda Cousins. At first, 16-year-old Amanda didn't believe that clean-cut, polite Darren was serious, but as time went by she realized she was privy to dangerous information. When she asked what would happen if she told police of the plot, Darren vacillated between telling her that no one would believe her and threatening to kill her. Amanda didn't mention a word to anyone about the murderous scheme that was taking shape on a daily basis.

All was set. Darren bought two crowbars at the Capitol Iron Store in Victoria, and outfitted David and Derik with them. They would use knives from Doris's kitchen to slit the women's throats.

On September 21, David and Derik took the ferry cross the Strait of Georgia to Tsawwassen, but couldn't nd Doris's house from the information supplied by

Darren. Although Darren was furious at the failure, he wasn't discouraged. They would try again.

On October 5, all was in readiness for a second attempt. Sharon was visiting her mother in Tsawwassen. The two boys, equipped with crowbars in a knapsack, took the ferry across the strait. This time they had no trouble locating the correct address. Doris and Sharon had just started dinner when the doorbell rang. The boys said they were in the area and had stopped by to say hello.

Sharon greeted her son's friends warmly and asked them to stay for dinner. She quickly put two additional plates on the table. When the women's backs were turned, the boys struck. In minutes, Doris and Sharon lay unconscious on the floor. David and Derik picked up two knives from the kitchen, just as Darren had instructed. They slit their victims' throats. The boys then scurried about the house, opening drawers and scattering their contents. Darren had wanted the scene to look like a robbery. They removed a total of $1,580 from the women's purses.

When the killers returned to Saanich, Darren, accompanied by Amanda, was pleased with a job well done. He reviewed their alibis. If they were ever questioned, Amanda was to say she was with the two boys all afternoon and had dinner with them later in the evening. Darren could easily establish an alibi because he was nowhere near the crime scene at the time of the murders.

That night, Dr. Ralph Huenemann was concerned when his wife failed to return home from a visit with her mother. He couldn't reach either woman on the telephone. Finally he called Delta police, who promised to look in at Doris' address. It was they who found the bodies.

Detectives felt something was wrong with the crime scene right from the outset. Valuable jewellery and electronic equipment had not been touched, yet the contents of drawers were strewn about the premises. It looked as if someone had amateurishly attempted to simulate a robbery. Two plates on the table were partially filled with food, while two were untouched. It appeared that the victims had invited their killers to dinner.

Doris and Sharon had been clubbed before they were stabbed. Although the knives used to slay the women had been left behind, the instruments used to club the victims were nowhere to be found. The murders had all the aspects of a premeditated assassination.

When Darren was told of the murders, he became hysterical. Relatives and neighbours were sympathetic. After the initial shock wore off, Darren's behaviour abruptly changed. He seemed obsessed with his grandmother's wealth, taking time to inquire how much her car was worth and the value of her jewellery. He told friends jubilantly that he stood to inherit everything.

When police questioned Amanda Cousins, she told a straightforward story of spending the afternoon and evening with Derik and David. The two boys corroborated the details of her story. Darren offered $12,500 reward for the apprehension of the killers. The offer was duplicated by his stepfather.

Darren's other school chums were questioned. They told police that he had often talked about killing his grandmother. Authorities located a taxi driver who had driven the boys to the ferry on the date of the murders. He picked David's and Derik's pictures out of a police photo line-up.

So did a youngster who had seen them near Doris's home on the date of the murder.

David was the first to break under questioning. He confessed in detail to the premeditated murders. When offered the opportunity to testify for the Crown instead of standing accused of being an accessory, Amanda Cousins confessed to her involvement as well. All three boys were arrested and charged with murder in adult court.

David Muir and Derik Lord were found guilty and sentenced to life imprisonment with no possibility of parole for 10 years. Darren Huenemann also received a life sentence, but with no possibility of parole for 25 years.

The perfect son who orchestrated the murders of his mother and grandmother didn't collect a cent of his family's money. Doris Leatherbarrow's brothers and sisters inherited the bulk of her estate.

Frank & Fred MacTemple
(Canada)

ST. THOMAS, Ontario, is a peaceful community located south of London, just up the road from Lake Erie. But one day in the spring of 1934, guns blazed and bodies fell like something out of a Wild West shootout.

It all started innocently enough. Fred MacTemple, 21, was wanted for stealing a bicycle. Constable Colin McGregor and Sergeant Sam McKeown were dispatched to bring in the local youth for questioning. By chance, Detective Bert McCully of the Michigan police happened to be in the St. Thomas police station. He volunteered to give the officers a lift to 13 Queen Street, where the MacTemples lived. The street was in the rougher part of town, and the MacTemples were known as tough customers.

The officers decided to take the necessary precautions. They asked McCully to cover the back door as they approached the rundown house. They knocked on the front door. A young boy answered. When the officers asked to speak to Fred MacTemple, the lad was so frightened he could only point to the rear of the house.

The two officers entered. A door opened, and there stood Fred MacTemple, brandishing a wicked-looking blue-black U.S.-army-issue .45-calibre automatic. "Stick 'em up!" he shouted.

Neither officer was expecting such a move. They had felt, at worst, that their young suspect might try to run out of the house. Now they stared at a nervous young man waving around a dangerous weapon. McKeown tried talking his way out of a tough jam. "Just a minute," he said, "We've got a warrant against Fred MacTemple for stealing a bicycle. Why all the gunplay?"

The tall young man rasped, "No cops is going to take me!"

McKeown continued, "It's not that serious."

He was interrupted. "Shut that talk!" Fred shouted.

From a door leading off the kitchen, 55-year-old Frank MacTemple emerged, waving a revolver in each hand. One was an ugly-looking German Luger, the other a white .38 Ivor-Johnson. He took command of the situation and shouted orders. "Shut that talk and both of you put your guns on the table! No tricks!"

McKeown couldn't believe he was facing a total of three handguns, all over a stolen bicycle. Once again he attempted to talk his way out of this unlikely predicament. "You're Frank MacTemple, I take it. Your son is wanted for bicycle stealing. It isn't a serious charge."

MacTemple would have none of it. He pushed a gun into McKeown's ribs and commanded, "Shut the talk and put your gun on the table! We're not going to be taken by any damn cop." Fred MacTemple grabbed Constable McGregor's gun. McKeown didn't respond to the elder MacTemple's orders.

McGregor warned, "Be careful, Sam, the hammer of that Luger is up."

For the third time, Frank cursed, "Put your gun on th

table or I'll let you have it!" At that precise moment, McKeown jumped Fred MacTemple. Frank started cursing and shooting.

Constable Colin McGregor took a slug directly in the stomach and fell to the floor. McKeown, in a desperate struggle with Fred, was shot in the wrist. He grimaced in pain as his hand went numb. Frank was still shooting. A bullet entered Fred's neck, spinning him to the floor. MacTemple had missed McKeown and shot his own son.

Frank MacTemple, guns blazing, backed out a side door and escaped. Detective McCully raced into the house but was too late to apprehend the crazed man. McKeown managed to get off one shot, which missed.

From upstairs, Mrs. MacTemple and her young son heard the shooting. When it stopped, she ventured downstairs and saw her son, Fred, lying on the kitchen floor with a bullet through his neck.

The two wounded officers and Fred MacTemple were rushed by ambulance to hospital. The day after the shooting, Constable Colin McGregor died of his wounds. Fred MacTemple lingered between life and death for some hours, but gradually recovered. McKeown's hand was bandaged and he was released from hospital.

As soon as Fred was able to talk, police questioned him. They wanted to know what had motivated the shooting. Fred explained that it was a grudge shooting, not particularly against McGregor, but against the police in general. Evidently, the threat of going to reform school for the theft of the bicycle and of the older MacTemple going to jail for other minor thefts had caused father and son to flee the area. Only after they had purchased guns in Erie,

Pennsylvania, did they return, swearing that the police would never take them.

Fred explained, "Police had broken up our home, separated our family and made it impossible for Dad and me to come home."

After they procured the weapons, the MacTemples decided to chance returning to St. Thomas.

Now the hunt was on for Frank MacTemple. One of the largest manhunts ever conducted in that section of Ontario was quickly organized. Frank was spotted in several places, but the quarry always managed to elude the hunters.

On May 9, two days after the shooting, a 16-year-old farmhand, Clifford Anderson, was pitching hay from the haymow to the barn floor below. There was a scream and out popped a dirty man in ragged clothing. The old man implored Clifford not to tell his boss, Malcolm McNeil, that he was hiding in the haymow. Clifford, who suspected he was talking to the most wanted man in the province, was frightened out of his wits. He was relieved when MacTemple allowed him to leave the barn to go to his supper. Two hours later, Clifford told the McNeil family about the stranger in the barn. McNeil immediately called police.

MacTemple left the barn and stayed in nearby woods until dark. He then made his way to West Lorne, where he had a friend, Dick Carnegie, 58, who operated an antique store. Police felt the wanted man might seek refuge in his friend's spartan two-room shack. They decided to encircle Carnegie's home, but to remain hidden. Carnegie was told to expect MacTemple. He agreed to co-operate with police and do anything in his power to apprehend the suspected killer.

About 11:30 that same night, MacTemple showed up at Carn-egie's door. He claimed he had been hunting squirrels and had accidentally shot himself in the hand. He showed Carnegie his slightly wounded hand, which he had acquired in the melee two days earlier. Carnegie washed and bandaged the wound.

About an hour after he entered the house, MacTemple jumped up. He thought he had heard a noise outside the shack. Before he could respond further, Carnegie exclaimed, "It can't be anything. I'll go out and see, though." With that, he dashed out the door. He was met by police officers, who were in position around the house.

Carnegie confirmed, "I got him inside. What am I going to do with him? If anyone but me goes in that door, he'll shoot. He's got a gun and he's ready to use it." The courageous man continued, "I guess I'll hafta hold him so he can't use his gun while you boys come in."

Carnegie returned indoors and offered his guest a cigarette. After the man accepted the cigarette, Carnegie threw himself upon the startled MacTemple. He yelled for help and, within seconds, it was over. Carnegie was so exhausted and excited, he fell to the floor in a faint.

On March 26, 1935, Frank and Fred MacTemple were tried for the murder of Constable McGregor. Both were found guilty and sentenced to death. There was a great hue and cry to save Fred's life as he hadn't actually fired the murder weapon. However, all appeals failed. On June 27, 1935, father and son were hanged in the St. Thomas jailyard.

Chris Magee
(Canada)

THERE ARE monsters among us. Psychiatrists describe them as pathological personalities of the antisocial type. This is the story of one such deranged individual.

On the night of March 1, 1974, Judy Barksey, 19, purchased a pizza and two bottles of pop to take with her. She already had a chocolate bar. Judy was making her way home that night in Strathroy, Ontario, when she was attacked.

Later, her assailant was to describe the incident in his own words: "It was late at night. I was at home watching a hockey game and I decided to go uptown to get some raffle tickets on the game at the News Depot. After getting the tickets, I started for home. I noticed a girl walking on the street in front of me. I started fantasizing sex with her and I was trying to build up nerve to approach her. As we walked along, I finally built up enough courage, or else my sickness was coming to a head, then I grabbed her after we crossed over the tracks. I told her what I wanted. She struggled and refused. I grabbed her by the throat. She goes down, then I panicked, took my jackknife out and stabbed her in the throat. I got scared and I went into her purse and took some money."

Judy Barksey's monster cleaned off his bloody jackknife in a mud puddle and went home to his wife.

The morning after the attack, Dallas Allan, 66, left his

home at 11:45 to mail a letter. As he walked by a fertilizer shed, he looked to his left and spotted the body of a young girl lying on the ground. A pizza, two bottles of pop and a chocolate bar were strewn around her. Moments later police were viewing the body of Judy Barksey.

Despite an extensive investigation, detectives were unsuccessful in tracing the killer.

A year and three months later, the man with the uncontrollable desires was absently looking out the window of his home as Rosalie Winters, 18, wandered into Alexandra Park. A short while later, she felt strong hands clamped around her neck. Schoolbooks flew into the air. Rosalie lost consciousness. She was raped and left in the park. She was unable to give a good description of her attacker.

On October 20, 1975, exactly four months after the attack on Rosalie Winters, the unknown assailant struck again. Twenty-four-year-old Denys Jenner arrived home from work and entered his Strathroy home by the back door. His wife, Louise, was lying dead on the kitchen floor. Someone had slashed her throat and tightly tied a black bootlace around her neck.

Realizing his wife was dead, and fearing for his baby's life, Denys walked over his wife's body to his daughter Rachel's room. He found Rachel unharmed in her crib.

Ontario Provincial Police detectives theorized at the time that Louise's killer was known to her. Photographs were found on a chesterfield as if an acquaintance had been scanning them. Possibly, Mrs. Jenner had excused herself to change her baby's diapers upstairs, giving the killer time and opportunity to undo his bootlace. When Mrs. Jenner came back downstairs, the killer struck. Mrs. Jenner had been sexually attacked but then had been given the opportunity to dress before she was killed.

A 74-year-old neighbour of the Jenners reported seeing a late-model cream-coloured or yellow vehicle, possibly an Oldsmobile, enter the Jenner driveway on the day of the murder. She said the occupant of the vehicle, a white male with dark, collar-length hair, had stood at the Jenner door for three or four minutes before entering the house.

Police conducted thousands of interviews in the Jenner investigation. One man, Chris Magee, loosely fitted the description given by the Jenners' neighbour. He knew Mrs. Jenner, as well as Judy Barksey. His father owned a light-colored Oldsmobile.

Magee remained a suspect, but there was nothing of a definite nature to label him a killer. When interviewed he vehemently denied having any knowledge of the murders.

Sylvia Holly Jennings, 19, was hitchhiking to London. She accepted a lift. She was driven well past her destination to an abandoned sideroad near Mount Brydges, Ontario, where she was raped, beaten over the head with a pop bottle, and left for dead. Mira-culously, she survived the attack.

James Frayne, 16, of Forest, Ontario, drove a farm tractor and hayrake to a farm his family owned about four and half miles from his home. When he arrived at the abandoned farm site he spotted a leg and knee in the grass.

Initially, James thought someone was sunbathing. He blew the tractor horn and went about changing the hayrake for a mowing machine. James commenced to cut hay, but the sight he had seen upon entering the property bothered him. He returned to the spot and took a much closer look. What he thought was a sunbather was, in reality, the body of 15-year-old Susan Lynne Scholes. Susan had been raped and stabbed in the throat. The Scholes family resided in London but was spending the summer at their cottage in nearby Hillsboro Beach.

At 1:00 p.m. Susan had left the cottage with her brother, Geoffrey, to go into Forest to buy batteries for her portable radio. Geoffrey dropped Susan off in town. She purchased the batteries and was seen walking out of town towards County Road 12.

McFarlane's Tile Yard is situated on that road. Mrs. McFarlane heard of the murder on the radio and immediately went to the police. She reported seeing the murdered girl walking in front of the tile yard at 1:30 p.m. Susan was wearing a distinctive green sweater with the word "Hillsboro" printed in white letters across the front.

Mrs. McFarlane's son had been using a forklift to transfer tile to the yard when he saw Susan, who he knew through his association with her brother, Geoffrey. As he watched, a truck stopped and gave Susan a lift. He recognized the truck as the one used in the area to pick up and dispose of dead animals.

OPP inquiries soon uncovered that the suspect truck, a 1975 Ford, was owned by Mr. John Grinsven, a Strathroy-based dealer in dead stock. On the day of Susan's murder, the truck was operated by none other than Chris Magee, the suspect in the Barksey and Jenner murders.

Taken to the OPP detachment in Forest, Magee admitted picking up Susan but claimed that he dropped her off and continued on his way. He told investigating officers that he was married and his child-ren were presently living with his father in Strathroy. Magee had no police record but had been dismissed from various jobs because of petty theft.

Authorities found out that Magee's truck was usually outfitted with a filleting knife, used in his work with dead animals. When the truck was searched, the knife was missing. It was later found on Grinsven's property, sharpened and cleaned. It was obvious that all traces of blood had been thoroughly cleaned away by Magee.

On October 21, 1977, Chris Magee was arrested and stood trial for the murder of Susan Scholes. At no time did he confess to the crime. He was found not guilty by reason of insanity and sent to the Mental Health Centre at Penetanguishene.

Magee, always suspected of committing the other crimes in the area, was reinterviewed on May 11, 1979, by OPP Constables P. De Vlugt and B. Linker. They learned nothing new from their two-hour session with Magee, but a half-hour after they left the institution they received a radio message that Magee wanted to see them again.

When they returned, Magee blurted out a confession to the two officers: "I'm guilty of everything you suspect me of." He went on to give detailed statements concerning the murders of Barksey, Jenner and Scholes, and the rapes of Winters and Jennings.

On January 18, 1980, Chris Magee stood trial for the murders of Barksey and Jenner. Once again he was found not guilty by reason of insanity and once again confined to the Mental Health Centre at Penetanguishene.

Lindley Charles McArthur

(Canada)

IN 1972, when Lee Marie Conway graduated as a registered nurse from St. Joseph's Hospital in Toronto, the future looked bright. She was now qualified to pursue a satisfying and honourable profession. Besides, she had met someone she really cared for—Joe Di Palma. Affection turned to love, and on October 20, 1973, Lee and Joe became husband and wife.

Eventually, the couple moved to Angus, Ontario. In April 1979, a son, Anthony, was born. Joe had a good sales position with Rothmans of Pall Mall Ltd. The pieces were falling into place for the Di Palma family. Sure, there were a few rough spots. Joe had the exasperating habit of putting off fixing things around the house. When Anthony hit the terrible twos, he proved to be a hyper youngster. Lee also felt a bit confined in her rural home and often expressed a desire to move closer to Toronto. But these small differences or complaints were superficial. The Di Palmas had a very successful marriage.

All this was to change on Tuesday, September 21, 1982. On that day, quite by chance, Lee was to cross paths with an amoral monster.

On that fateful morning, Joe got up as usual and left at 7:30 a.m. for his job in Toronto. Lee's parents, Kevin and Audrey Conway, who had spent the previous night with the Di Palmas, rose and had breakfast with their daughter. They left the house at 10:30 a.m. to visit their son in Levack, Ontario.

Lee Marie cleaned up the dishes and tidied the house. She then dressed Anthony for the short ride into Barrie in her black-and-silver 1972 Buick. At twelve o'clock, Lee pulled into Don and Ron's Sunoco Service Station in Angus to purchase gas. Anthony was enrolled at a Stay-and-Play program at the Y. Each Tuesday and Thursday, Lee would drop him off at 1:15 and pick him up at 3:15 p.m. Promptly at 1:15 p.m. she dropped little Anthony off at the Barrie YMCA. The hour between 12:15 and 1:15 is unaccounted for. Quite possibly, Lee went window-shopping and had lunch. There is also the possibility that she was being stalked by a madman.

The previous day Lee had made a hairdressing appointment for that Tuesday at 1:30 p.m. at the House of Bellini's, located in the Bayfield Mall. She never kept the appointment. Later that afternoon, at 3:15 p.m., when she failed to arrive at the Y to pick up Anthony, social program director Heather Fraser grew apprehensive. She called the Di Palma residence and the Royal Victoria Hospital, where Lee worked as a part-time nurse. When she could find no trace of Lee Di Palma, she called police.

At 8:44 that evening, Lee's Buick was found parked in the Bayfield Mall opposite the Pit Stop Gas Bar. The car was unlocked, the window open and an interior garbage container was overturned, all conditions that were foreign to Mrs. Di Palma.

At the request of Barrie police, the Ontario Provincial Police were brought into the case. Inspector Norton

Rhiness headed the investigative team. Rhiness had precious little to work with. Mrs. Di Palma had disappeared as if swallowed up by the earth.

Lee Marie Di Palma's past was scrupulously investigated. There were no hidden boyfriends, no affairs, no logical reason why this housewife, nurse and mother would meet with foul play. The disappearance was given wide publicity. A dramatization of the mystery appeared on television. Police were deluged with tips from well-meaning citizens. All had to be checked out. One tip was thought to hold real significance. A citizen came forward stating that she and her daughter had been on a bus on October 22, 1982, a month after Mrs. Di Palma's disappearance. She claimed that she chatted with Lee.

The woman, who was travelling to Sudbury, overheard Lee saying that she was going to Calgary. She said a friend had a large dog. She talked about places she had visited in Calgary and people she had met there two years earlier. She complained that her husband was negligent in fixing things around the house. The woman said she had often been to Bayfield Mall in Barrie. She talked about her sister, Nancy, and said she had a small son. The blond woman with the shoulder bag even stated that her husband once drove a van for Rothmans. Unbelievably, each one of these statements was dead on. They all applied to Mrs. Di Palma. However, the woman on the bus was not Lee Marie Di Palma.

Other sightings occurred in Calgary, Blind River and Vancouver. On December 20, about three months after Di Palma's disappearance, an alcoholic confided to a friend that he had murdered a woman near Barrie. He then committed suicide. For a while, he too was considered a prime suspect.

On May 15, 1983, eight months after Lee Marie failed to pick up her son, her body was found. Malcolm Urquhart and his wife, Pauline, were out picking mushrooms on Laurence Henderson's property in nearby Mulmur Township. Urquhart notice a white object on the ground. At first he thought it was a puffball. It turned out to be the skull of Lee Marie Di Palma. Police were soon at the scene. Nearby, they found evidence that before death, Lee had been tied up with shoelaces and the straps from her shoulder bag.

Five months after Lee Di Palma's disappearance and before her body was found, Lindley Charles McArthur first came to the attention of police. McArthur was accused of kidnapping a 13-year-old girl and driving her to a secluded area, approximately three-quarters of a mile from where Mrs. Di Palma's body was eventually found. The youngster was sexually attacked. McArthur was arrested at that time and lodged in the Barrie Jail.

Once in jail, McArthur had an overwhelming urge to talk about the Di Palma murder. He told several inmates details of the murder. Some thought he was lying; others didn't care one way or the other; many grew tired of listening to him.

During the spring of 1983, McArthur was transferred to the Mental Health Centre at Penetanguishene for assessment. That May, Mrs. Di Palma's body was found. McArthur told a psychiatrist that he thought fingerprints would connect him to the Di Palma killing. After the assessment was completed, McArthur was sentenced to two years less a day for the assault on the 13-year-old girl.

He was returned to the Barrie Jail to serve his time.

Inspector Rhiness, aware of McArthur's loose tongue, decided to place an undercover agent in McArthur's cell. Fabricating a story that he had been picked up on Highway 400 and was being held until he could be returned to Calgary to face a rape charge, the undercover agent ingratiated himself with his cell mate. Soon McArthur was confiding in his new friend. "Yeah, I expect to be charged with murder in the first degree." When the undercover policeman feigned ignorance, McArthur went on, "So you never heard about Di Palma The broad was taken from her car and strangled."

Two days later, McArthur was charged with murder. He told the undercover policeman, "I'm charged with murder. As far as I know, they have three things on me. I hung around there. I was in town that day and I know the area where the body was found. Man, after a year, I thought it was over." Then McArthur, cool as a cucumber, took in a movie on television. He really enjoyed the horror movie, *The Changeling*

During his stay in jail, McArthur revealed details only the killer would know. He told one inmate that he jumped out of his truck, ran to the driver's side of Mrs. Di Palma's car, stuck his head through the open window and caught her by the throat. She said, "Please don't hurt me." He dragged her from her car to his truck.

Who was Lindley Charles McArthur?

McArthur was born in Collingwood, Ontario on September 21, 1962. He successfully completed Grade 12 at Collingwood High School. He was married on February 28, 1982, but at the time of his confinement, he was already separated from his wife. Factors leading to the breakdown of his marriage were his long stretches of unemployment and his desire for nonstop sex. His wife told police that McArthur demanded sex sessions that sometimes lasted for 12 hours. He was also rough and abusive during sex games. On some occasions, he insisted on performing the sex act as many as 15 times a day.

McArthur's wife revealed that the day after the sex attack on the 13-year-old girl, her husband shaved his beard. He did the same thing the day after Lee Di Palma was reported missing. Mrs. McArthur also told police she noticed that her husband had inexplicably lost the laces to his blue Adidas right after the woman's abduction. She had purchased a new pair.

What had triggered the abduction, rape and murder of a defenceless woman? As McArthur told one of his fellow prisoners, "I done it for kicks." The day he murdered Lee Di Palma was his twentieth birthday.

In June 1984, Lindley Charles McArthur was found guilty of first-degree murder. He was sentenced to life imprisonment with no possibility of parole for 25 years.

Herbert McAuliffe
(Canada)

NOT MANY men attempt to get rich by counterfeiting 50-cent Canadian coins. Herbert McAuliffe not only attempted the trick but did a fairly good job. Unfortunately, Herbie's rather comical criminal endeavours ended in tragedy when his bungling efforts turned to murder.

Born in North Bay, Ontario, Herbie was an above-average student during his formative years. He showed a natural mechanical bent and attended a technical school before leaving North Bay for the tobacco belt around Simcoe.

In 1939, along with thousands of other young Canadians, Herbie joined the army. While in the service, he used his mechanical ability to good advantage and quickly rose to the rank of staff sergeant. However, there must have been a little larceny in his heart even then. In 1944, he was dishonourably discharged for stealing money from his comrades.

Herbie gravitated to Windsor, Ontario, taking with him one of the army's .45-calibre Thompson submachine guns and eight automatic pistols. We have no reason to believe that he intended to use the army weapons. No, Herbie had other devious plans. He had decided to counterfeit 50-cent Canadian pieces, something never accomplished in Canada before.

To facilitate his operation, Herbie rented a double garage from Germain Noel on London Sreet, using the alias Frank West. Noel listened as Herbie explained that his work was rather noisy and was a top-secret government project concerning the invention of a revolutionary new weapon.

Now that his cover was established, Herbie wrote away for books and manuals on coin minting. For weeks he pored over the technical articles. There was one immediate problem—the lack of funds. In order to implement his scheme, he required money to purchase machinery. He overcame this minor difficulty with ease: Herbie became extremely adept at holding up service stations and grocery stores.

Coincidental with his successful robberies, a steady stream of rather sophisticated machinery arrived at the garage on London Street. A turret lathe, dies and punch presses worth more than $15,000 were delivered to Herbie's factory. A $10,000 hydraulic press for stamping out the coins was installed in the garage. Herbie didn't do things half way.

It was hard work. Herbie carried out his experiments from scratch. He had no assistants and no technical advisors. His painstaking experiments continued for four years, interrupted and financed by his periodic stick-ups.

At last he'd perfected his technique. He had invented his own alloy and was actually able to stamp out coins from cheap metal and coat them with silver in an electroplating bath. The end result looked perfect. Just for fun, Herbie produced a bucketful.

That same night, Herbie tested his newly minted 50-cent pieces at a gambling joint in Detroit. He knew betting quantities of 50-cent Canadian coins would be unusual and focus attention to him, but he wanted the coins to be examined. If they were accepted in a gambling den, he decided they would be accepted everywhere. Herbie and his phony fifties passed with flying colours. His coins were identical to the real thing.

Next day, back at the garage, Herbie decided to figure out just how much he would net from his operation. He added up his expenses and was dumbfounded to find out that it cost him 48 cents for every 50-cent coin he produced. If he threw in his own labour he was losing money!

There was a solution. If he had the capital to modernize his plant with new equipment, he could lower costs. Herbie decided that the quickest way to raise capital would be to rob a bank.

In his usual methodical manner, he drove throughout the countryside looking for a suitable bank. He found it in the Imperial Bank of Canada at Langton, Ontario. Now, Langton was not a hustling, bustling metropolis. Located about 20 miles from Simcoe, it was not likely that the 250 souls who called Langton home would interfere with Herbie's nefarious scheme.

In preparation for the heist, Herbie stole a car in Windsor. Into it he threw his .45-calibre Thompson sub-machine gun, a Luger and a .45 revolver. He tossed in a brown paper shopping bag to hold his anticipated loot.

Herbie walked up to bank accountant Henry Thompson and announced, "This is a stick-up. Listen, chum, if you don't open up the combination on that vault, I'll be back tonight to drill you dead." Thompson filled Herbie's paper shopping bag with $22,577 in bills and coins. Herbie waved his gun menacingly and herded 11 customers into the bank vault. He then took off for his waiting car, but in his haste our boy neglected to lock the vault door.

Inside the vault, Arthur Lierman, a 31-year-old tobacco-farm owner, pushed the door open. He shouted to William Goddyn, 24, "Come on, Bill, I've got a .22-calibre rifle in my Buick. Let's get him."

Herbie knew he was being followed. A few miles down the road near Frogmore he stopped, took out his submachine gun and fired a burst at the pursuing car. Lierman and Goddyn died in a hail of 30 bullets.

Herbie abandoned the shopping bag full of money on the front seat of his stolen car and took off into the bush. Word of the dramatic daylight bank robbery and the murders of two popular citizens of the area spread like wildfire.

The hunt was on. Herbie was headline news across the nation. The largest manhunt in Canadian history up to that time was organized. For three days Herbie hid out in barns, stole food from farmers and swatted mosquitoes, until Graham Haggerty, a 20-year-old farmhand out deer hunting, discovered Herbie in an old shack near Straffordville.

Initially, Herbie was identified as Frank West or George Walker, the two aliases he had used during his years developing fake 50-cent pieces. Eventually his true identity and his counterfeiting career were uncovered and revealed to the public.

Herbie was tried in Simcoe, found guilty of murder and sentenced to death. On December 19, 1950, he was given the last rites of the Catholic Church and walked briskly to his death on the scaffold at the Simcoe Jail.

So ended the career of Herbert McAuliffe, who will go down in Canadian history as the only man to successfully produce counterfeit 50-cent pieces.

Dana McIntosh

(United States)

YOU CAN NEVER be sure what goes on behind the closed doors of someone else's home, can you? Let's take a peek behind the portals of the McIntosh family of Dallas, Texas.

Susan and Dana McIntosh had been high school sweethearts in Tyler, where both were born. On August 8, 1970, the attractive young couple were married. Those who knew them believed they were made for each other.

As the years drifted by, nothing happened to change anyone's mind. They were as much in love as they had been when Dana carried Susan's books home from school back in Tyler. When Susan's dad died seven years after her marriage, he left her a sizable sum, estimated to be several hundred thousand dollars. That didn't hurt a bit.

By 1990, the McIntoshes had two lovely daughters, aged 8 and 12. Dana was the president of his own computer software company. They all lived in a luxurious home on Sunny Land Lane in the Lakewood section of Dallas. Dana and Susan attended church regularly and were extremely active in church affairs, as well as charitable causes. The McIntoshes were truly the perfect married couple.

Monday, March 19, 1990, appeared to be the same as any other day at the McIntosh residence. Dana drove his Mercedes to his office. A couple of hours later, he elicited a co-worker's assistance in driving one of his cars from his home to a service station for repair. He and his colleague drove out together to pick up the vehicle.

Dana opened his garage door and recoiled in horror. Lying on the floor in a pool of blood was the body of his wife. Susan had been horribly slashed across the throat. Dana, believing she was still alive, insisted they place her in his Mercedes and rush her to hospital. At the nearest hospital, doctors counted 25 stab wounds all over Susan's body. When told his wife had been pronounced dead, Dana collapsed.

Detectives were soon made aware of the pertinent facts surrounding the murder. Some of these facts were strange. Susan's hair and underclothing were wet, yet her outer garments were dry. After examining the McIntosh home, police reported no sign of forced entry. When found, Susan had been fully clothed and had not been sexually interfered with. From an examination of the body and the crime scene, police ascertained that Susan had put up a desperate struggle for her life. She had incurred several defensive wounds to her arms and hands.

The initial investigation was dominated by one circumstance that caused detectives to seriously question Dana McIntosh. He had several scratches about his face, which had obviously been recently inflicted. Dana, rather shocked that police would even insinuate he was involved, told them that the family collie had scratched him. Neighbours verified that Dana often played with the collie in the backyard, but none of them could remember his ever having been scratched before.

Scrapings were taken from underneath Susan's fingernails, but results of these tests were unsatisfactory. In fact, lab reports indicated that Susan's fingernails were uncharacteristically clean for someone who might very well have scratched her assailant. A scientific search of the McIntosh home revealed traces of blood in the master bedroom, the bathroom sink and on the shower-stall floor.

Neighbours, friends and employees at Dana's company were interrogated by the police. They were unanimous in their opinion that Dana McIntosh was not the type of man who would murder his wife. In most cases, they had known him for well over 10 years and believed him to be a loving husband and father.

Police were beginning to doubt the avenue their investigation had taken, when a new element entered the case. McIntosh's office was burglarized. Documents were strewn about the office and photographs of Susan were spread across Dana's desk. Detectives noted that nothing of value was removed from the office. Was there someone out there warning Dana he would be the next to go, or was the break-in an attempt to lead police away from suspecting Dana himself?

As so often happens in murder investigations, the backgrounds of the principals held many answers not apparent at first glance. Detectives delved into Dana McIntosh's business activities. They learned his enterprises had been in deep financial difficulties for years. His computer company had been sued by banks and suppliers on several occasions. Each time, Dana had managed to come up with enough cash to avoid bankruptcy. Throughout the financial storms, his and Susan's lifestyle had remained stable.

Looking still further into Dana's affairs, detectives found out that Susan had often come to the company's rescue with her own money. Employees of the McIntosh computer company were questioned confidentially. In this way police learned that Susan had helped out her husband in the past year to the tune of $200,000. Moreover, employees had witnessed Dana and Susan arguing over finances at the office. All was definitely not as copacetic as it appeared to neighbours and social acquaintances.

The trouble started way back in 1981 when Susan had mortgaged several hundred acres of land she had inherited from her father to raise money to finance one of her husband's emergencies. When Dana was unable to keep up the payments, the bank took the land. Susan was furious at losing property that had been in her family for generations. Shortly after this fiasco, the couple had visited a marriage counsellor.

When police discovered that Susan's life was insured for $250,000 and the balance of her estate amounted to another $250,000, all of which would be Dana's upon her death, they charged him with murder.

On April 8, 1991, Dana stood trial for his wife's murder. The state's case was strictly circumstantial. They contended that Dana killed his wife before he left for work and then saw to it that he had a colleague with him when he found her body in the garage. After the vicious attack, which may have occurred in the master bedroom, he removed his wife's outer garments and washed blood from her wounds in the shower stall. He then dressed Susan and placed her body in the garage. One thing he didn't count on was his wife's struggle for her life, during which he suffered telltale scratches to his face.

The prosecution produced one witness, a nurse, who

gave the most startling evidence of the entire trial. When Susan was being examined at the hospital in her husband's presence, she noticed he was sucking her fingers. When she asked him to release Susan's fingers, he did so, but moments later she observed him doing the same thing. This time he snapped at the nurse that he was kissing his wife's fingers. The inference was clear. Realizing Susan had scratched him, Dana knew her fingernail scrapings would be retrieved by police. He was attempting to destroy the evidence.

The Texas jury took only 45 minutes to agree with the state's theory of how Susan McIntosh met her death. They found Dana McIntosh guilty of her murder. He was sentenced to 75 years' imprisonment, a sentence he is still serving.

Bill McIntyre

(Canada)

SOMEONE HATED Bill McIntyre enough to kill him, but no one knows the identity of the killer.

The obvious suspects, those individuals who found themselves facing criminal charges as a result of Bill McIntyre's relentless determination, have been exonerated of involvement in his murder. You see, Bill McIntyre was an undercover police officer with the Ontario Provincial Police (OPP). He wasn't killed in a shootout. He wasn't murdered while undercover. He was shot to death in his own luxurious apartment at 1300 Marlborough Court in Oakville, Ontario.

When his family moved from Winona to Oakville, Bill was enrolled in school. In 1969, he graduated from White Oaks Secondary School. After graduation he immediately applied for a position with the OPP, but was rejected because he was too young to join the force. In 1972, he reapplied, was accepted and stationed in Goderich.

Over the years, working out of Goderich, Exeter and Mount Forest, Bill McIntyre took part in many undercover operations. He often worked in conjunction with other police forces. His colleagues, as well as his superiors, speak highly of him. In fact, his tireless efforts won him several commendations. By 1981, he was employed in Hamilton under the direction of the Special Services Branch of the OPP. A year later, he sold a home he owned near Exeter and purchased the condominium in Oakville.

During his 11 years on the force, Bill had become a highly qualified officer. He graduated from the Ontario Police College in Aylmer in 1973. A year later, he completed a marine course, followed by a criminal investigation course, and a physical surveillance course. Finally, in the fall of 1983, Bill successfully completed an analysis and intelligence course. In 1983, Bill McIntyre, career police officer, was promoted to the rank of corporal and assigned to be team leader in the physical surveillance section of the OPP. Six months later, he was found dead on the floor of his condominium.

On Thursday, April 19, 1984, Bill and a colleague were working as a surveillance team in Toronto. Later that day, they visited Grant Brown Motors to look at cars. Bill was interested in a Trans Am. They checked in at OPP headquarters on Harbour Street, after which they joined other officers for a beer at a bar in Burlington. The exact times of Bill's activities that Thursday are well documented.

Subsequent investigation revealed that while Bill was in the bar in Burlington, his neighbours in the condo in Oakville heard strange noises emanating from his apartment. Three neighbours, questioned separately, later told police that they heard doors slamming, and thought they heard two males shouting at each other. Unfortunately, they could not hear the actual conversation.

The next day, Friday, Bill McIntyre worked as usual. In hindsight, some officers who came in contact with him thought he was acting strangely. At a meeting in Bowmanville, Bill left his colleagues in an office and made phone calls in private. In the past, he had always called members of his team in front of the other officers.

That evening at 7 p.m., Bill showed up for a dinner date with his long-time friend, Bill Truax. McIntyre and Truax had known each other since both attended Grade 3 in Oakville. A half-hour later, the two men were digging into the prime-rib special at the Executive Tavern in Burlington. After the meal, the friends parted. Bill McIntyre had less than a day to live.

Bill had promised to help Acting Sergeant Nelson Kincaid move some furniture the next day, Saturday. Bill didn't show up, nor did he answer his pager. Kincaid phoned McIntyre around 2 p.m., but received no response.

The day wore on. Two other officers attempted to contact McIntyre, but no one answered their knock on the apartment door. When McIntyre failed to arrive at a scheduled meeting in Bowmanville, Sergeant Kincaid became concerned. McIntyre was not the type of officer who would fail to show up for an appointment without notifying his superiors. Something had to be wrong.

Kincaid phoned Corporal Ken Allen and advised him of the ominous situation. Allen was ordered to pick the lock of the McIntyre apartment. Together with Acting Corporal Dave Crane, he proceeded to 1300 Marlborough Court. McIntyre's two vehicles were in the underground parking lot. The officers listened at the apartment door. They could hear McIntyre's pager beeping inside.

When the officers gained entrance to the unit, they found McIntyre's body on the floor in the hallway leading to the bedroom. An autopsy performed at the Centre of Forensic Sciences in Toronto indicated that Bill McIntyre had been killed as a result of a single wound to the head from a .22-calibre bullet.

Naturally, when an undercover police officer is murdered, it is most logical to look for the culprit among those he had helped apprehend. Investigators checked McIntyre's previous cases. Although they came up with several suspects, all their investigative efforts indicated that none of these individuals was involved in Bill's death.

Investigative probes into Bill's work life indicated that he was an exceptional police officer. Some described him as a workaholic. His personal life was surprisingly private. Officers who had worked with him for months didn't really get to know him. Many never realized how very little Bill McIntyre related to them of his family or his private life.

Who had been in Bill's apartment that Thursday? Evidently, there was more than one individual present. Why were they there? Why did they shout and slam doors? There was no evidence of forced entry.

The door to McIntyre's apartment could only be locked with a key from the outside. Since Bill McIntyre's keys were found intact in the apartment, it is logical to assume that Bill had given a spare key to his killer, who was cool enough to shoot Bill and calmly lock the door behind him as he left the condo.

Police assure me that they found "physical evidence in the apartment that could help identify the killer if and when he is apprehended." However, it is one thing to conjecture about the whys and hows and quite another to trace the killer.

Here matters stood for almost a year, until a woman, whose identity would serve no useful purpose here, came forward with her story. She was visiting her father, who lived in the same condominium complex as Bill, on the day Bill McIntyre was murdered. That morning she was walking the dog at approximately 10:00 a.m. She noticed a man looking up, talking to someone on a fifth-floor balcony. The woman looked up and later was able to identify Bill McIntyre as the man on the balcony. He was wearing jeans and no shirt, the same way he was dressed when his body was found that evening.

As the woman walked by, the man on the street stopped talking. Inside the condo, her father nonchalantly glanced out the window. He too saw the man talking upward toward the balcony.

What were the two men saying to each other? The woman can't be sure, but she thought she heard the man say, "What are you going to do today?" The reply might have been, "I don't know, maybe nothing."

The woman, who may have been the last person, other than his killer, to see Bill McIntyre alive, was alarmed when she learned that the man on the balcony had been murdered. When she discovered he was a police officer, she and her husband thought the killing might be a gangland slaying. What would prevent the killer or killers from coming after her if she came forward? As a result, she remained silent for almost a year before revealing what she had witnessed on the day of the murder.

The woman's memory was less than perfect after such a lengthy period of time. However, under hypnosis, she gave the following description. The man on the sidewalk that day was a white male, wearing a white shirt, blue jeans, white running shoes and beige jacket. He was holding a motorcycle helmet in his hand. The man, who w approximately 5 feet 9 inches tall, was in his twenties or early thirties. He was clean-shaven, had a light complexion and straight blond hair.

It is now over fifteen years since Bill McIntyre was gunned down in his own apartment. Despite the best efforts of investigating officers, many of them McIntyre's own colleagues, his killer has never been apprehended.

Charlotte Miller
(Australia)

FOR MORE THAN 15 years, Hilda Miller had a terrific relationship with her common-law husband, 40-year-old Arthur Houdson.

Life hadn't always been good to Hilda. She had taken her lumps along the rocky road of romance before she met Art. Not the least of her problems had been her first husband, Steve Miller, who went out one day for a pack of cigarettes and never returned. He left Hilda and their three-year-old daughter, Charlotte, high and dry.

Hilda attempted to locate Steve, but to no avail. As a result, she was unable to obtain a divorce and marry Art. Still, the present arrangement was not half bad. Art had been a good provider for both mother and daughter. He treated the now 18-year-old Charlotte as if she were his own flesh and blood.

The Houdson menagerie lived in Melbourne, Australia, in apparent harmony until October 15, 1979. That was the day 41-year-old Hilda took ill. She was admitted to hospital with a mild case of kidney stones, but was soon released. From the outset of her illness she was convinced that she had cancer of the liver. Doctors told her she was totally mistaken. Art attempted to talk some sense into the distraught woman, but nothing could convince her that she was in fine health. At home she wallowed in a state of severe depression.

Hilda remained in bed about 90 percent of the time and

in her own psychosomatic way suffered from the ravages of cancer. The family physician, Dr. John Fuller, prescribed tranquilizers and barbiturates to ease Hilda's imagined pain. For three months, Hilda lay in bed. By now her health had deteriorated to the point where Art and Charlotte were seriously concerned for her welfare. They had good cause to be worried.

On January 10, 1980, Charlotte frantically called Dr. Fuller. Her mother was lying motionless in bed and couldn't be roused. When Dr. Fuller arrived at his patient's bedside, he immediately realized that Hilda had been dead for several hours. He noticed an empty glass on the bedside table, the dregs of orange juice adhering to its bottom and sides. Alongside the glass were two empty plastic tubes, each of which had contained 25 barbiturate tablets. It was obvious to the doctor that his patient had committed suicide. Dr. Fuller took care of Charlotte, who had become hysterical when she was told that her mother was dead. Then he called the police and the coroner's office.

A postmortem revealed that Hilda died from a dose of 50 barbiturate tablets dissolved in orange juice. The death was officially labelled a suicide. Hilda was laid to rest.

To all intents and purposes, that was that, except for one fact that came to the attention of one police officer, Inspector Thomas Hunt. It was the inspector's job to rubber-stamp Hilda's file officially closed. In due course the evidence of the suicide case would be destroyed. Hunt was puzzled. When he examined the glass, there were no fingerprints on it, nor was there any information in the file that there had ever been fingerprints on the glass. The inspector questioned Dr. Fuller and the first officer at the scene. The doctor swore that he had never touched the glass. The officer told his superior that he had carefully placed the glass in a plastic evidence bag. When Charlotte was questioned, she couldn't recall whether she had touched the glass, nor could she remember whether she had wiped the glass clean.

Inspector Hunt was convinced that all things being equal, Hilda's fingerprints should have been on that glass. Who had wiped it clean and why?

The inspector dug in like a pit bull. A few months after Hilda's death, he decided to have Art followed. Much to his surprise, he learned that Art and Charlotte were still living in the same flat where Hilda had ended her life. The inspector thought it was unusual for an 18-year-old girl to stay in the same residence where her mother had so recently committed suicide.

Perish the thought—was there hanky-panky going on? Neighbours were discreetly questioned. Sure enough, they thought that Art and Charlotte were behaving more like husband and wife than father and daughter. The inspector had to sit back and think this one through. If Hilda had committed suicide, and if Art and Charlotte were lovers, no crime had been committed by the two occupants of the flat. After all, Art was not legally or biologically Charlotte's father. Perhaps nature had simply taken its course. After all, Charlotte was an extremely attractive young woman.

On the other hand, had Art killed Hilda and wiped his fingerprints off the glass so that he could claim her daughter? Inspector Hunt was a bit disappointed to learn that Art had been 50 miles away in Geelong on the day of the murder. However, it would have been possible for him to make the return trip without being noticed.

A couple of things bothered the investigating officer. Art Houdson had been faithful to Hilda for more than 15 years. He had been a kind, caring father to Charlotte for the same period of time. It was only after Hilda's death that neighbours noted the change in his attitude towards Charlotte. The same could be said for Charlotte. She had been a respectful daughter and had never caused her mother one moment's aggravation in her entire life. In addition, Hilda, convinced that she had cancer, had often talked of committing suicide rather than endure the painful death she firmly believed awaited her. She had even mentioned suicide to Dr. Fuller.

Perhaps suicide was the answer after all. Yet, according to the neighbourhood gossips, Art and Charlotte were living as husband and wife. Had Art managed to commit the perfect murder, and in so doing, traded in the 41-year-old mother for her 18-year-old daughter? Maybe.

As the months passed, detectives, keeping Art under surveillance, reported that his appearance had changed since Hilda's death. Where he had once been a rather dapper dresser, he now looked slovenly. He even walked hunched over, as if he had a great deal on his mind.

Surprise of surprises, one day Art walked into a police station of his own volition with a story to tell. He started at the beginning. When Hilda was in hospital, he and Charlotte were thrown together alone in their flat. The furthest thing from Art's mind was romance. After all, he had brought up Charlotte since she was three years old. But Charlotte had naughty thoughts on her mind. One night, she turned off the lights, lit the candles, poured the wine and seduced Art. According to Art, he was weak and simply couldn't resist her charms.

When Hilda returned home from hospital, the surreptitious affair continued. A week before Hilda's death, Charlotte came up with the super idea of murdering her mother. Charlotte explained that Hilda wanted to die anyway. Everyone would be happy all the way around. Art said that he had admonished Charlotte for suggesting such a thing and told her never to bring up the subject again. After Hilda's death, he asked Charlotte point-blank if she had killed her mother. She didn't say yes, but she didn't say no, either. Art was beside himself with guilty knowledge. When he couldn't stand it any longer, he decided to report the entire matter to the police.

Charlotte was taken into custody and questioned. She confessed immediately. Her motive was crystal clear. She wanted Art for herself and her mother stood in the way. It had been easy. She had fed Hilda the barbiturate-laced orange juice. Of course, it was she who had wiped her fingerprints off the glass. Charlotte added that she had no remorse for what she had done.

Charlotte Miller was examined by psychiatrists and judged to be too ill to stand trial. She was confined to a mental institution for an indefinite period.

William Mothershed

(United States)

ON THE DAY before Christmas 1980, 30-year-old Officer Dennis Webb was patrolling in his black-and-white along the relatively peaceful streets of San Fernando, California. It was close to 4 a.m. when his radio crackled with information about the robbery of a 7-Eleven convenience store. The robber was described as a small male Caucasian, 90 pounds, five feet five inches, with blond hair.

Within minutes, Webb spotted a young man who fit the description walking down a deserted street. Webb pulled up beside his suspect, got out of the car and shouted, "Freeze!" In response, the young man drew a handgun from his pocket and poured three slugs into the officer. Webb fell to the ground. The gunman stood over the fallen policeman and fired three more shots into his body. He then jumped into Webb's police car and drove away.

Three minutes later, Dennis Webb, a veteran of six years on the San Fernando Police Force, was found dead by a fellow policeman. His own weapon was still in its holster.

Meanwhile, the killer was listening to the details of the shooting on the police radio. When he learned that detectives were looking for Webb's police car, he decided to ditch the vehicle. He drove the car into a field adjacent to a golf course, turned off the ignition and made his way on foot out of the area. It was approaching daylight when Nancy Webb was informed that her husband of two years had been killed in the line of duty.

A massive investigation was immediately organized. It was learned that another 7-Eleven store had been robbed two days before Webb's murder. The clerks in both stores gave detectives roughly the same description of the undersized suspect. It was reasonable to assume that one man was responsible for both hold-ups and Webb's murder.

Precious few clues were garnered by investigating officers. The police car was found with the driver's door still open, but the vehicle yielded nothing that would lead to the killer. Six 9mm automatic pistol cartridge casings were recovered at the scene of the crime. The casings were reloads—ones that had been used before and loaded again by hand, a practice sometimes followed by gun enthusiasts. By mid-January, rewards totalling $34,000 were being offered for information leading to the policeman's killer.

Bob Berndt was a 26-year-old drifter who had been in and out of jails and mental institutions since age 17. His father, a career police officer, had died of cancer. After his father's death, Bob fell apart. He fantasized about being a Vietnam veteran and sometimes claimed to work for the CIA. Bob was fascinated with Webb's murder. He kept clippings of every scrap of information concerning the case.

Bob stood five feet five inches tall and weighed 125 pounds, with a crop of thick blond hair. It was uncanny how closely he fit the description of the killer. He even bragged to his roommate, 35-year-old Robert Hensley, that he had killed the police officer. It made him a big man in Hensley's eyes. Sometimes Bob lent Hensley his Colt .357 Magnum, even though he didn't trust Hensley as far as he could throw him.

In mid-January, the two drifters, Berndt and Hensley, left L.A. by bus and roamed the country, finally landing in Phoenix, Arizona, where Hensley had a friend named Dick. Because they were running out of money, the three decided to rob the Tinhorn Bar. The robbery didn't go well. Hensley acted like a madman, waving Bob's Colt at the lone female employee and a young couple seated at the bar. Once he had the three occupants of the Tinhorn lying face down on the floor, Hensley bent over and deliberately shot each one in the head. His two companions begged him to leave the bar, but Hensley wouldn't go until he had shot all three. The two customers died where they lay, while the barmaid survived the senseless attack.

Back in their motel room, the three robbers counted their loot: $100. When Dick lectured Hensley on the folly of killing people for such a paltry sum, Hensley unceremoniously shot him in the chest. Rushed to hospital, Dick survived the spontaneous shooting. Bob and Hensley were taken into custody. Bob was released, Hensley detained.

Bob Berndt took off. In Clinton, Oklahoma, he was picked up as a suspicious character. When his belongings were searched, police found an unmailed letter written to Bob's priest back in San Fernando. The letter contained the incriminating sentence, "I also killed a police officer, Dennis Webb, in San Fernando Valley."

Oklahoma police contacted San Fernando police. Detectives quickly ascertained that Bob had been in the San Fernando area at Christmas time. Besides, he owned a .357 Magnum pistol and had purchased hand-loaded ammunition from a friend. Detectives flew to Clinton to question Bob. Under interrogation, he fell apart. He told detectives about the wild shootout at the Tinhorn Bar and confessed to the murder of Officer Dennis Webb, as well as the robberies of the two convenience stores.

Bob was brought back to San Fernando. He was taken to the street where Webb had been gunned down and immediately pointed out the spot where the killing had taken place. He claimed he had sold the murder weapon. Bob led authorities to the area where the police car had been abandoned. He was pleased with his performance and seemed to delight in co-operating with detectives. About the only flaw in the case was that both convenience store operators failed to positively identify him as the man who had robbed them.

On February 17, 1981, Bob Berndt was charged with the murder of Officer Dennis Webb. While in jail, he continually told guards and fellow inmates how sorry he was that he had killed a police officer. Psychiatrists stated that by murdering Webb, Bob was in reality killing his policeman father.

That's where matters stood when the Los Angeles police received a phone call from the FBI in Hobbs, New Mexico. Some students at New Mexico Tech had come forward with information about a fellow student, 18-year-old William Mothershed. Evidently, Mothershed had spent his Christmas vacation at his home in San Fernando. Although he was a top student with no criminal record, his description fit the convenience store robber in every detail.

New Mexico officers interviewed a student who was an avid gun collector and who had sold Mothershed a 9mm Smith & Wesson before the Christmas break. He had also provided Mothershed with 200 rounds of hand-loaded ammunition. Before selling the weapon, the student had fired off 10 rounds to make sure the gun was in perfect order. He still had the shell casings of those 10 rounds. The casings were flown to Los Angeles, where they were microscopically compared to the shell casings found at the scene of Webb's murder. They matched. Mothershed's 9-mm was the murder weapon.

William Mothershed, a studious young man, had never been in trouble in his life. He was picked up and immediately confessed to robbing the two convenience stores and murdering the police officer. He told police that he had taken apart the Smith & Wesson and had disposed of it piece by piece while driving through the desert. He and his friends at New Mexico Tech had often discussed a life of crime. He had decided it was the easiest way to make money. It was Dennis Webb's misfortune to cross his path.

When told of Mothershed's confession and proof of his guilt, Bob Berndt burst out laughing. He admitted he had lied to show how clever he was. It hadn't been that difficult. He had studied the newspapers and pretty well knew the locations of the murder and the abandoned police car.

Bob wasn't that clever. Although the charge of murdering Officer Webb was dropped, he was found guilty of murder in the two killings in the Tinhorn Bar in Phoenix. For these crimes he received a total of 37 years' imprisonment.

Robert Hensley was found guilty of the same double murder and was sentenced to death.

William Mothershed was found guilty of the murder of Officer Dennis Webb. He was sentenced to life imprisonment and is presently serving that sentence.

Roderick Newell

(England)

LET ME introduce you to the Newall family. Nicholas met and married Elizabeth in 1963. Both were teachers. Both came from wealthy British families, which afforded them private personal incomes exclusive of their teaching salaries. A son, Roderick, was born in 1965. A second son, Mark, arrived a year later.

Because of their privileged financial situation, Nicholas and Elizabeth resigned from teaching in 1968 and purchased a yacht, the *Chanson du Lecq*. They would do what so many of us dream of doing. They would find their paradise in the West Indies. The couple were experienced sailors.

On the way to their new life, the Newalls stopped in Jersey, one of the Channel Islands. Once there, they became enamoured with the place. It wasn't the West Indies, but it had a rugged beauty and favourable tax laws. Nicholas and Elizabeth decided to seek their Shangri-La no further.

The family settled into island life. Both Nicholas and Elizabeth obtained part-time teaching jobs, and they purchased a home, the Crow's Nest, which had one of the finest views on Jersey. The two boys were sent to boarding schools in England. From the ages of six until their teens, they were separated from their parents for long periods. Those who knew the family felt there was a coldness between sons and parents. Nicholas was strict, one might even say arrogant. Still, the two lads had all the creature comforts.

The Newalls led an active social life. Their best friends were David and Maureen Ellam, whom they saw at least once a week. To add to their comfortable lifestyle, Nicholas and Elizabeth bought a villa in Spain. Their eldest boy, Roderick, chose the army as a career and rose to the rank of lieutenant. Mark became a financial fund manager. Both parents were proud of their two successful, strapping sons.

If there was any flaw in the portrait of domestic tranquillity, it was the lack of love flowing from parents to offspring. Nicholas adored Elizabeth; Elizabeth adored Nicholas. Neither seemed to express the same affection toward their sons.

In 1987, with their boys away pursuing careers, the Newalls sold the Crow's Nest and moved to a smaller dwelling at 9 Close de l'Atlantique. On October 9, the Newall boys flew to Jersey on a visit. They stayed at a home Mark was building. The boys made a date to take their parents to dinner the next evening at the Sea Crest Restaurant. It was their mother's forty-eighth birthday.

Roderick and Mark arrived at their parents' home at 8 p.m. Everyone appeared to be in good spirits. They knocked back two bottles of champagne. Mark, a moderate drinker, volunteered to drive to the Sea Crest. The party arrived after 9 p.m. and stayed until after midnight. During the meal, more champagne and wine were consumed, followed by liqueurs. After dinner, back at 9 Close de l'Atlantique, the Newalls opened a bottle of Scotch. Tongues loosened, voices rose, and an argument ensued. Roderick was thinking of abandoning his army career. His father objected. Other subjects came under scrutiny. Roderick and his father didn't see eye to eye on anything. Finally,

Mark, who had often heard such bickering, tired of the discussion and went home.

The dispute between father and son grew more intense. According to a statement given much later by Roderick, his father gave him a push. He fell to the floor. Within arm's reach were a pair of rice flails, which is a weapon used in martial arts. Roderick clubbed his father to death. Initially, Elizabeth tried to separate the two men. Then she ran into the bedroom in fear for her life. Roderick raced after her and clubbed her until she too was dead.

Hours later, Roderick contacted Mark and told him what he had done, adding that he was contemplating suicide. Mark told his brother to do nothing; he would be there in minutes. Mark arrived and calmed his brother down. He claims to have found some tarpaulins and tools in the garage. The boys wrapped their parents in the tarps and carried them outside to Mark's rented van. They drove to a field near the sea, where they used the tools taken from the garage to bury Nicholas and Elizabeth.

The brothers returned to their parents' home and cleaned up evidence of the murder, most particularly the blood that was everywhere. It was quite a job. In order to dry rugs and walls, they turned up the heat and left. Roderick took some of his parents' possessions and the materials used to wash up the blood. He burned these in a nearby field. Next day, Roderick and Mark left Jersey.

Two days passed. The Ellams figured that their friends had left the island to visit relatives. When they received no word from the Newalls, David Ellam went over to investigate. He found five days' of unopened mail and a hole in the roof of the house from a recent storm. Strangely, the heat was intense in the house. David turned it down. The Ellams contacted Roderick and Mark, who flew to Jersey and inspected the house with their parents' friends. They too appeared to be mystified. Elizabeth and Nicholas Newall had vanished. Police were notified.

Under questioning by police, Roderick and Mark told straightforward stories. They said they had returned to their parents' home the morning after the birthday party. They had breakfast and lunch, before leaving at around 3 p.m. While they were there, Elizabeth's friend, Maureen Ellam, brought over flowers for their mother. Since Elizabeth was asleep at the time, Roderick took the flowers to her. Everything was normal when the boys left. That evening, taking separate flights, the brothers had left Jersey.

Forensic scientists spent four days examining the interior of the house. Bloodstains were found in the lounge and in the bedroom. Both areas revealed signs of having been washed. J-cloth fibres, identical to those stored in the kitchen, were found adhering to a rug. Specks of blood were analyzed. The samples taken from the lounge were the same type as Nicholas's, while the bedroom samples matched Elizabeth's blood. Officials concluded that Nicholas had been attacked in front of the fireplace in the lounge, and Elizabeth had been accosted in the bedroom. The disappearances were now being treated as murders.

Hundreds of volunteers joined police to search for the bodies of the victims. Helicopters, dogs and radar were used, to no avail. Because Roderick and Mark were the last known individuals to have seen their parents alive, they were questioned extensively. They reiterated that they had left their parents alive and well.

The disappearance of the missing pair was the main topic of conversation on the island. The Ellams insisted that the search continue, but as months turned into years the hunt diminished. Roderick resigned from the army and spent much of his time aboard the family yacht in the Mediterranean. The intensive police investigation revealed the cold relationship that had existed between the Newall brothers and their parents. Both were suspected of involvement in the disappearance, but police uncovered nothing concrete to connect them to the crime.

On January 3, 1991, the Newalls were declared officially dead. Their sons inherited their entire estate. Mark became a huge success in the financial world. Roderick continued to roam the world in his yacht. No one knew Roderick's innermost feelings. He was racked by guilt. Each day he relived the blows landing on his parents' skulls, the blood spattering on the floor, the bodies being placed unceremoniously in the shallow grave.

In June 1992, Roderick visited relatives in England. He constantly brought up the subject of his missing parents and seemed to be on the verge of confessing. He planned to visit Stephen Newall, his father's twin brother, in Scotland. When a relative informed Maureen Ellam in Jersey that Roderick seemed near the breaking point, she called police. They in turn notified Scottish authorities, who asked Stephen Newall to wear a wire during conversations with his nephew. Stephen agreed and arranged to have tea with his nephew in a private room at the Dunkeld House Hotel.

During the dramatic meeting, Roderick broke down and described how he had unmercifully beaten his parent to death. He stated that Mark wasn't present during the killings, but had assisted in the burial of the bodies. At the end of the confession, Stephen asked his nephew the obvious question, "Why?" Roderick replied, "You wouldn't understand, because I don't understand."

Because the confession had been procured in an unorthodox manner, police sought legal opinions as to its admissibility. The process took days. In the meantime, Roderick left in his yacht. On August 7, 1992, the yacht was intercepted by a Royal Navy frigate. Roderick was arrested and incarcerated in Gibraltar. Although he fought extradition, he was eventually returned to Jersey. Mark was picked up in Paris.

Once back in Jersey, Roderick gave authorities a map indicating the location of his parents' grave. With the use of the map and Roderick's personal direction at the site, police recovered the Newalls' bodies.

The murder charges against Mark were dropped. Roderick stood trial for the murders of his parents. Because there was proof that he had purchased tools, tarpaulins and plastic sheets before the killings, he was convicted of premeditated murder. Roderick Newall was sentenced to two concurrent life terms in prison. Mark Newall was convicted of assisting his brother after the fact of murder. He was sentenced to two concurrent six-year terms.

Stella Nickell
(United States)

I HAVE ALWAYS claimed that, as a group, poisoners are the most reprehensible of all murderers. Among these cowardly individuals are a select few who not only kill their intended victim, but care not one iota if they murder others.

Stella Nickell was one such individual.

In 1986, we find Stella well into her second marriage. Ten years earlier she had tied the knot with second husband Bruce Nickell, who was employed as a part-time heavy-equipment operator with the state of Washington. Stella had brought her daughter, Cynthia, to the union. Cynthia was a striking 20-year-old redhead in 1986. Stella, on the other hand, would never see forty again. Years of drinking and carousing were beginning to take their toll. Stella discerned crow's feet and other nasty signs of aging when she gazed into the mirror of her home in the Seattle suburb of Auburn.

It is difficult to pinpoint exactly when Stella decided she didn't want to take a position on the proverbial shelf. Bruce, a recovered alcoholic with a bad back, only worked a few days each week and would never earn more than a bare living. Life was drab, dull, boring. To Stella's way of thinking, cold hard cash would deliver her out of her predicament. Of course, Bruce, a definite encumbrance, would have to go.

Stella formulated a plan. She studied the effects of th

foxglove plant and decided its deadly poison was just what the doctor ordered. She cultivated foxglove plants, harvested her crop of deadly seeds and fed some to the unsuspecting Bruce. The diabolical plan didn't work. In fact, Bruce seemed to be extraordinarily chipper after digesting what should have been his last meal. Cynthia, observing her mother's sudden obsession with foxglove, couldn't help but be curious. When Cynthia asked her about it, Stella insinuated that they would both be better off without Bruce.

The arithmetic worked out fine. The state of Washington had insured Bruce's life for $31,000 with an additional $105,000 payoff if he left this mortal coil due to an accident. To sweeten the pie, Stella took out two additional policies on Bruce's life for $20,000 each. Let's see now, our Stella had a potential $176,000 at stake. She decided to try again.

Scheming Stella remembered the horrendous Tylenol murders that had taken place in the Chicago area in 1982. Someone had placed cyanide into Tylenol capsules and had returned the capsules to store shelves. In that instance, seven people had died. No one was ever convicted of the crimes. Stella saw some merit in the diabolical scheme. There was one drawback—Bruce didn't use Tylenol. He preferred Excedrin.

Stella purchased cyanide-laced rat poison and put some in the Excedrin capsules Bruce kept in a bottle in a kitchen cabinet. On June 5, 1986, Bruce took four capsules and muttered, "I think I'm going to pass out." He fell unconscious to the floor. After being helicoptered to Harborview Medical Center in Seattle, he died several hours later without regaining consciousness.

Cynthia immediately thought her mother was responsible for Bruce's death. Before she could utter an accusatory word, Stella said, "I know what you're thinking and the answer is no."

Neither the attending physician at Harborview nor the coroner detected cyanide in Bruce's body. Death was attributed to pulmonary emphysema. Stella was home free. As matters stood, she would collect $71,000, a tidy little sum, but $105,000 short of what the payoff would have been if her husband's death had been declared accidental.

Stella felt cheated. There had to be a way she could get her hands on that money. Her mind raced back to the Tylenol tragedies. If she planted cyanide in more Excedrin bottles and placed them back on a store shelf, another death would surely take place. With a little help, Bruce's death would be coupled with that of the latest victim. No tight-fisted insurance company could then claim that Bruce had died a natural death.

Stella proceeded with her unbelievable plot. She purchased several boxed bottles of extra-strength Excedrin. Despite improvements in drug packaging since the Tylenol incidents, Stella managed to empty some of the capsules and refill them with cyanide. Her work at repairing boxes and bottles was amateurish, but she was successful in placing the lethal packages back on the shelves of three different stores.

Forty-year-old Susan Snow, the mother of one adult daughter and one teenager, had risen to the position of assistant vice-president of the Puget Sound National Bank. Every morning, Susan and her husband, Paul, each took two extra strength Excedrin to start the day. June 11, 198 was no exception. Paul rose early, took two Excedrin out of a new bottle Susan had recently purchased and, by the luck of the draw, ingested two bona fide painkillers.

Later, Susan took her usual two capsules. Within minutes, her 15-year-old daughter, Hayley, found her unconscious on the bathroom floor. Susan was rushed to the hospital, where she lived for six hours before her husband agreed to disconnect life-support equipment. Medical examination revealed the presence of cyanide in the Excedrin Susan had taken. Naturally, the unusual death and its horrific ramifications received wide publicity.

Displaying a keen sense of public responsibility, Stella Nickell came forward with the suggestion that her husband might also have been a victim of the tainted medication. Tissue tests proved that Stella's suspicions were correct. Bruce Nickell had been poisoned. Now the Seattle poisoning case received nationwide publicity. Health officials, as well as Bristol-Meyers, the manufacturers of Excedrin, instructed stores to remove all painkillers from their shelves. Two bottles of cyanide-laced Excedrin were uncovered in this manner.

Detectives confiscated bottles of Excedrin from Stella's home. Two of the bottles were found to contain cyanide. Soon, almost a hundred investigators, including FBI agents, were employed to track down the demented person who had taken two lives. Laboratory analysis revealed that the cyanide found in the two bodies and the unused recovered capsules had come from a single source.

Susan Snow's husband, Paul, came under mild suspicion s someone who stood to gain financially from his wife's ath. He agreed to take a polygraph test, which indicated he knew nothing whatever about the murders.

Stella was questioned for the same reason. In addition to Washington State's policy on Bruce's life, detectives learned that Stella had taken out other life insurance policies totalling $40,000 shortly before her husband's death. Although Stella was a strong suspect, there was no hard evidence pointing to her guilt.

In conjunction with other drug manufacturers, Bristol-Meyers put up a reward of $300,000 for the arrest and conviction of the poisoner. Whether it was the 300,000 big ones that enticed Stella's daughter, Cynthia, to come forward or whether it was, to quote her own words, "the right thing for me to do," we will never know. Cynthia told authorities of her mother's first attempt to kill hubby Bruce with foxglove and of their many conversations regarding poisons.

In 1988, Stella was taken into custody and charged with "causing death by product tampering." She has the distinction of being the first person ever convicted of this charge. Stella Nickell has never collected one penny of her husband's life insurance money. She was sentenced to 90 years' imprisonment and will be eligible for parole in the year 2018, when she will be 74 years old.

Sam Parslow & Cordelia Poirier

(Canada)

THE QUAINT villages with their large churches and hard-working farm folk that make up rural Quebec are a strange backdrop for murder most foul. Yet, even here, the passions that simmer, boil and erupt into bloody murder have found their way.

Back before the turn of the century, the tiny village of St. Canute was a remote community. The God-fearing French farmers led a hearty, healthy and, for the most part, happy existence. But not Cordelia Poirier.

You see, Cordelia was unhappily married to Isidore Poirier. Now, Isidore wasn't a bad fellow, really. It was just that he was about as exciting as maple sap dripping into a bucket. Isidore worked hard, was a respected member of the community and attended church regularly. But he was oh so very colourless. Isidore made love as though it was a duty rather than a pleasure. Besides, he was well into his forties, while Cordelia had not yet celebrated her thirtieth birthday.

Sam Parslow, the Poiriers' young hired hand, had none of Isidore's finer qualities, but what he lacked in stability, he more than made up for in bed. Many a chilly winter night, when Isidore was away for one reason or another, Sam would dim the lantern in Cordelia's bedroom and partake of the forbidden fruit which lay within. Some nights

Sam attempted to harvest the entire orchard, so eager was Cordelia for his substantial charms.

In 1895, as luck would have it, Isidore received an opportunity to work in California for several months. He jumped at the chance. Cordelia practically pushed him out the door. Sam and Cordelia's sack time increased dramatically.

Mon Dieu, could this go on in a quaint French-Canadian village without tongues wagging? Of course not. The lovers sometimes went out together. They held hands and occasionally stole a kiss in public. Mind you, all the while that Cordelia was performing between the sheets with Sam, she was attending Mass regularly. In fact, both she and Sam sang in the choir. Cordelia also played the organ during Mass.

Can't you just hear the whispers? "A disgrace, and poor Issie in California"; "They should be horsewhipped for carrying on so." It couldn't go on.

Finally, Sam's mother, who felt that her son was being led away from the straight and narrow by the wicked Mrs. Poirier, went to the parish priest, Father Pinault, and asked him to save her boy. The good father, obviously a man of few words, sent a note to Isidore in California. "Come back at once, or else take away your wife."

In response, Isidore wrote a scorching letter to Father Pinault, telling him in no uncertain terms that he had the utmost faith in his wife. Isidore, never one to keep a secret, wrote dear Cordelia about the priest's ridiculous accusations. Cordelia replied that he was right—they were ridiculous.

In due course, Isidore returned to his home in St. Canute. We can only assume that Sam moved out of the master bedroom and into the hired hand's quarters. The gossip grew to a crescendo. Cordelia, by far the most dominant personality in our triangle, knew she had to do something. It didn't take her that long to come up with a murder plan that would turn a dishonest dollar at the same time. She would insure her husband's life before she and Sam killed him.

After paying her insurance agent a brief visit, Cordelia wrote the man a letter. The letter is so incriminating we reproduce it here:

> *"I told my husband that I had been to see you with regard to our policy. I forgot to ask you for books in French. My husband wants to understand the thing before disbursing too much money. He is well decided to continue, but he wants first to understand whether if he should die by any means—by being killed or by accident, or by poison or by railway accident—your company would pay, because he has spoken to several people and they say you would not. It seems to me you told me I would be paid no matter what death my husband would meet. My husband today is in perfect health. Reply and I will arrange with you."*

The agent assured Cordelia that his company would pay off no matter how Issie might meet his death. In due course, Isidore Poirier's life was insured for $2,000.

With financial matters in place, Cordelia proceeded to cajole, urge and otherwise convince Sam that the only proper thing to do was to kill Isidore. They would allow a decent interval to pass before marrying. Sam didn't need much persuading. He thought it was a great idea.

On November 21, 1898, Isidore attended Mass as usual.

Cordelia and Sam filled the church with ecclesiastical melodies. After the service, Isidore stopped off at the blacksmith shop, where he and Smitty Bouvrette had a few blasts out of a whisky bottle the blacksmith kept handy for just such occasions.

Cordelia knew that Isidore would take a nap when he arrived home. The opportunity she and Sam had been waiting for was at hand. Sam hid in the house, fingering the new butcher knife he had purchased in Montreal. Isidore went to bed. In minutes, Sam and Cordelia could hear Isidore snoring. Sam sneaked up to the bed. He was scared stiff. He aimed the knife at the sleeping man's throat, thrust forward, but failed to inflict a fatal wound. Isidore woke up. The two men struggled. Cordelia shouted, "Kill him, kill him!" Thus encouraged, Sam stabbed Isidore in the neck and about the face. Finally, Isidore was dead.

The conspirators lifted the body onto the bed and placed the butcher knife in the dead man's hand. They put a half-empty bottle of whisky beside the body. Then Cordelia slipped out of her blood-soaked dress and burned it in the stove. If you didn't look closely, the gory mess might have passed for a suicide.

Cordelia put on her Sunday best and returned to church, where she played the organ as usual. After services she travelled to her father's home in St. Jerome and spent the night. Next morning she returned to St. Canute to play the organ for a wedding at the church. Cool as a cucumber, Cordelia conversed with several villagers, her parents and the parish priest without giving any sign that her husband had lain dead for more than 24 hours, his head almost severed from his neck.

On the way home from church, Cordelia told blacksmith Bouvrette to walk through the house with her. We all know what they found in the bedroom. The parish priest was the first one called. Father Pinault reluctantly announced that it looked like suicide to him. Cordelia smiled.

A nosy farmer noted that the ashes in the stove didn't look like residue left from wood. He scooped out the ashes and discovered a number of hooks and eyes. Of course, we know they were all that remained of the bloody dress Cordelia had been wearing.

Someone thought a more experienced individual should be brought in to ascertain the cause of Isidore's death. Detective K.P. McCaskill was dispatched from Montreal. He took one look at the bloody footprints on the floor and knew he was investigating murder. One of the prints matched Cordelia's shoe, another matched Sam's. The jig was up. Cordelia and Sam were taken into custody. Cordelia, by far the stronger personality, immediately confessed, claiming that Sam was the instigator of the plot and the actual killer. No one believed her. Both she and Sam were found guilty and were sentenced to hang.

On March 10, 1899, eight hundred screaming ticket holders were allowed into the prison yard at St. Scholastique to witness the execution. It was a gala affair. They sang songs and even took a few shots at the scaffold.

Sam Parslow had to be practically carried to the noose. Cordelia walked with head erect. When she saw Sam's condition she shouted in disgust, "Stand up!" Then she and her lover plunged into eternity.

Alan Poole

(England)

CONSTABLE ALAN BAXTER, age 33, woke up on the morning of Monday June 5, 1951, firmly believing that things had to get better. Alan wasn't asking for much. A week earlier, his father had suffered a stroke and died. His wife was still in Chatham, at England's All Saints Hospital, where she had given birth to a stillborn baby. Alan's series of misfortunes would continue. This would be the second to last day of his life.

Alan Poole, 20, woke up that day convinced he was one tough guy. Poole read gangster comic books and never missed a gangster movie. For as long as he could remember, he had attempted to emulate the fictional heroics of bad men. His parents, local God-fearing citizens, couldn't handle their son, who was always in trouble. In 1946 he was incarcerated after being found guilty of no fewer than 19 burglaries.

Sentenced to a term in prison, Alan escaped long enough to rob a sports shop. Once again behind bars, he developed a deep hatred for police. Like his comic-book characters, he knew he was smarter than the coppers and could beat the system. In 1949 he escaped a second time and attacked the first police officer he encountered. Back to prison he went.

On a pleasant spring evening, these two men, Alan Baxter and Alan Poole, born in the same area of England to middle-class families, were destined to cross paths. Their lives and the lives of their families would never be the same.

The Chatham police station received a call that someone in the Luton section of the city was threatening citizens with a Sten gun. Constable Alan Baxter, Sergeant William Langford and Constable John Brown responded to the call in a patrol car. With Baxter behind the wheel, they made their way to a large garbage dump surrounded by a number of shacks. They were told that the gunman was in the area.

Unarmed, Langford and Brown proceeded to check each shack. As Langford approached one of the buildings, the gunman appeared and, without hesitation, opened fire. It was Langford's good fortune that the man was a poor shot. Bullets whizzed past his head as he threw himself to the ground.

The assailant walked directly to the patrol car where Constable Baxter was seated. A hail of bullets shattered the windshield. Baxter was able to open the door and get out before a second fusillade ripped into his body. Langford rushed to his fallen comrade's aid. Baxter could only say, "He's got me in the guts, Sarge. I've had it."

Langford managed to place Baxter back in the patrol car and rush him to St. Bartholomew's Hospital.

Within minutes, surgeons were frantically trying to save Baxter's life. He survived the operation and was able to see his wife, who was brought to his side from All Saints Hospital in an ambulance. From a trolley, Mrs. Baxter spoke briefly with her husband. He died 18 hours after being shot.

A massive search was instituted for the gunman. Roadblocks were set up. Army and navy personnel stationed nearby were pressed into the hunt. At the time, authorities had no idea as to the identity of the shooter. They soon found out from witnesses who had seen the man with the Sten gun. It was local bad boy Alan Poole.

Poole's most recent brush with authority was his desertion from the army. He had enlisted, but promptly went Absent Without Leave. Police learned that Poole's parents lived at 114 Symons Avenue, approximately a mile from where Constable Baxter had been murdered. Evidently Poole had never before solicited assistance from his parents. He chose to live by stealing from local shops and hiding out wherever he could find shelter. Now, with the heat on, police felt Poole would somehow make his way to his parents' house. They dispatched a number of armed officers to stake out the Symons Avenue address.

The night passed uneventfully. Early next morning, police were surprised to hear a burst of gunfire from the rear of the home. Poole, behaving like the gangsters he loved to emulate, had fired his Sten gun just for fun. He had obviously made his way to the house before it was surrounded by police.

Inside the house, Poole's parents were terrified by the unfolding events. Poole's 11-year-old sister, Doreen, sobbed as her brother fired off his weapon through an upstairs window. Finally, Poole came downstairs and faced his parents, "Get your hats and coats on and get out. I'm going to shoot it out with the cops." Albert Poole attempted to reason with his son, "Good God, son, where have you been! The police are after you."

There was no reasoning with Alan. "I'm going to shoot it out with them," he repeated. "They'll never take me alive.

I've plenty of ammunition and I'm going to kill some more of the bastards." The ex-convict, army deserter and murderer, turned to his little sister, "Good-bye. You won't see me again," he said.

Later, Albert Poole would state that he thought about staying and reasoning with his son, but he could tell that Poole was crazed with the all-consuming idea of shooting it out with the police. Alan Poole had seen the action too often in American movies and had voraciously read gangster comic books where the anti-hero went down in a hail of bullets. He had cast himself in the real-life role of gangster and there was no turning back. Albert saw the look in his son's eyes, shook his head and calmly escorted his family from the house.

Alan went to an upstairs bedroom. He peered out the window and opened fire. Police scurried for cover. Some returned fire with their single-shot .303 rifles. They realized they had surrounded a madman, armed with an automatic weapon, who had no intention of surrendering. The army and navy threw equipment and manpower into the siege. Scores of police evacuated the inhabitants of nearby homes. Eventually, more than 200 personnel surrounded the house on Symons Avenue.

Realizing the standoff could last indefinitely, police were able to obtain tear-gas grenades from a nearby army base. Due to the danger of fire breaking out in the house, the fire department was brought in to direct streams of water through shattered windows. A volunteer officer dashed to the side of the house and lobbed in the tear-gas grenades.

Alan Poole witnessed the scene he had helped orchestrate. Just like in the movies, he was holed up with no chance of escape. He fired sporadically at any movement, while outside, police returned fire as hoses poured water into the house. Gas billowed up to the bedrooms from the first floor.

In the midst of the siege, the gunfire from the house abruptly ceased. All was silent. For two hours police waited. Finally, they decided to enter the house, not knowing whether the demented man was setting a trap or not. There was grave fear that he was cunning enough to hold his fire in anticipation of killing as many officers as he could when they entered.

Officers broke down the front door and rushed inside. Alan Poole lay dead in his own blood. He had not taken his own life, but had been hit by the last return fire.

On June 11 and 12, there were two funerals in Chatham. Two local men had been killed less than a week earlier. Constable Alan Baxter was afforded a hero's funeral by the police department. Hundreds of citizens lined the streets to pay their last respects. Next day, only Alan Poole's immediate family and a clergyman were present when the boy who wanted to be a gangster was laid to rest.

Jerry Rosenberg

(United States)

TOUGH LITTLE Jerry Rosenberg walked toward me with the aid of a cane. He has had a rough life. You see, Jerry has been imprisoned for 34 years. Those three decades are indelibly etched in the lines of his face. The Wende Correctional Facility guard who accompanied him to meet with me in this maximum-security institution didn't take his eyes off us as Jerry shook my hand.

Jerry Rosenberg was a small-time Brooklyn thief who dabbled in cons, scams and armed robbery back in the late fifties and early sixties. By the time he was 24 years old he had been arrested 26 times, but with the aid of a protective father he beat all the raps with the exception of one. He was convicted of armed robbery and spent four years in prison.

It was just another job for Jerry that May 18, 1962, when he and a buddy, Anthony Portelli, 26, planned to rob the Boro Park Tobacco Co., a wholesale/retail candy and tobacco outlet on New York's 48th Street. The decision to commit the robbery would change Jerry's life forever.

Jerry and Portelli charged into the Boro Park premises. Both men were armed and masked. They demanded money, scooping up whatever loose bills they could find. Waving weapons, they herded seven employees to the rear of the store, shouting at David Goldberg, president of the business, that they wanted more money. Goldberg was shoved into an office, where he produced more bills. Still the men weren't satisfied. One said, "If I don't get some more dough, somebody's going to get hurt." Either by accident or to make a point, one of the robbers discharged his weapon into the ceiling.

Outside, Detective Luke Fallon, 56, a police officer for 25 years, and his partner, John Finnegan, 29, the father of three children and a veteran of six years on the force, had just made a purchase in the Boro Park store. Fallon had bought a box of candy for his wife's birthday. As they were leaving the area, they heard a shot emanating from the Boro Park outlet. Fallon re-entered the premises. He didn't have a chance. Portelli got off three shots, one of which entered the officer's chest. He died in the doorway. Finnegan rushed in. He managed to fire six shots, but missed with every one. Portelli fired twice more, killing Finnegan in a matter of minutes.

The bandits, now frantic to get out of the store, paid little attention to their masks, which had fallen from their faces. Outside, the third member of the robbery party, whose job it was to drive the getaway car, panicked and sped off. The two desperate men got away clean, but dropped their hats and weapons as they fled the crime scene.

All three men were quickly identified. David Goldberg, who claimed to have seen the thinner of the two men in the warehouse when his mask slipped from his face, identified him as Jerome Rosenberg from police mug shots.

Three days after the murder, Portelli, a bachelor, was arrested in the Lido Motel in Chicago. When he wasn't robbing stores, he worked hustling gas at his father's station in Auburn, New York. Anthony Dellernia, the alleged driver of the getaway car, was the father of two children. He was employed at the Navy Submarine Base in New London, Connecticut. Dellernia's wife, Jean, talked him into giving himself up to police the day after Portelli was apprehended.

That left Jerry Rosenberg at large. Jerry worked as a novelty salesman for General Sales Associates, his father's firm. Two days after Dellernia gave himself up, Jerry contacted two *New York Daily News* reporters and had them drive him to the newspaper's office at 220 E. 42nd Street, where they handed him over to the police. The day before had been his twenty-fifth birthday.

On January 14, 1963, the three men stood trial for the murder of the two officers. The mood in the courtroom was tense. Publicity concerning the cold-blooded murder of two of New York's finest had the public in an uproar. Presiding over the trial was famed judge Samuel Leibowitz.

In the case of Anthony Dellernia, a mistrial was ordered on a technicality. Three months later he was retried. The jury deliberated for ten hours before returning a not guilty verdict. Dellernia walked out of the courtroom a free man and has led an exemplary life ever since his close brush with the law.

Jerry Rosenberg and Anthony Portelli didn't fare as well. David Goldberg positively identified them as the two bandits who had been in his premises, Portelli being the trigger-man. The jury found both men "guilty with no recommendation for mercy." A month later, Judge Leibowitz, in the preamble before sentencing, said, "The evidence against Rosenberg was so overwhelming it was a moving picture case." Leibowitz followed Jerry's assertion that he didn't get a fair trial with, "I hereby sentence you to be executed in accordance with the law during the week of March 31, 1963." When Jerry shouted back, the judge added, "Get this killer out of my sight."

Jerry and Portelli were lodged in the death house at Sing Sing. Appeals delayed the execution, but it appeared that nothing on this earth could save these two men from the electric chair housed down the hall at the end of death row.

Jerry's entry into the world of the legal profession was initiated by his lack of confidence in his own lawyer. In frustration, he borrowed a law book from a fellow inhabitant of the death house. Painfully, the Grade 8 dropout struggled over the legal terminology with the aid of a law dictionary. Eventually, Jerry enrolled in a correspondence course, seeking more knowledge. After two years of study, he realized that he was understanding the law and how to manipulate it to his advantage.

Ironically, during the incarceration of Jerry and Portelli, the death penalty was abolished in New York State for all inmates except cop killers. Jerry and Portelli could only watch as death house occupants were transferred to other prisons, their sentences commuted to life imprisonment.

Jerry, now something of a legal beagle, obtained a copy of the bill abolishing capital punishment. There, in black and white, was the description of the circumstances that excluded him and his buddy from having their sentence commuted to life imprisonment. The bill referred to "premeditated murder of police officers." He and his friend had been convicted of "felony murder" and felony murder was punishable only by life imprisonment. Their crime had been committed during the course of a robbery. Jerry had discovered a bona fide loophole. He appealed to Governor Nelson Rockefeller's office and made headlines when he received executive clemency from the governor, having his and Portelli's sentences commuted to life imprisonment. He had spent more than three years on death row.

Portelli was sent to Dannemora; Jerry to infamous Attica State Prison, where he chafed under the inhumane conditions that existed in the institution. The rules were strict and stringently adhered to. Food was substandard and scarce. For example, at that time, the total food cost per prisoner per day was 63 cents. Unlike life on death row, Jerry was put to hard work in Attica. Despite this, he managed to study law at night, receiving his LLB degree in December 1967.

Jerry's career as a jailhouse lawyer was now fully launched. He was well known as the man to see if you wanted your legal rights to get to the attention of the proper authorities.

In September 1971, a portion of the prison population revolted against the harsh treatment meted out by prison authorities. Guards were taken as hostages. Prisoners demanded to be heard. Jerry was chosen by the leaders of the uprising to be a member of their negotiating team. When Governor Nelson Rockefeller refused to come to the prison, negotiations broke down. State troopers opened fire on inmates. Ten minutes later, 39 individuals—some hostages, some prisoners—lay dead. Eighty-nine others suffered serious gunshot wounds. It was the largest massacre ever to take place in a U.S. prison.

After the Attica riot, Jerry was shipped back to his old alma mater, Sing Sing, where he was eventually put in charge of the newly installed law library. Soon Jerry was handling complicated appeals, winning most of them. Frivolous cases were not his style, nor did he represent sex offenders. He took only those cases in which he felt a prisoner's rights had been violated. His reputation as the nation's top-rated jailhouse lawyer grew.

During the intervening years, Jerry resided in what amounts to a list of New York State's more infamous correctional facilities—Sing Sing, Dannemora, Greenhaven, Auburn, Sullivan, and finally Wende.

Over the years he has, in addition to his LLB degree, earned a Doctorate of Law, qualifying him to teach in law school. More than three hundred former prisoners owe their freedom to his legal endeavours. Occasionally Jerry receives dispensation to appear in court. Usually heavily guarded and handcuffed, he is released from his restraints outside the courtroom. Judges and opposing counsel all agree he is a formidable foe, well prepared in all aspects of the law.

In October 1985, Jerry was rushed to the Upstate Medical Center in Syracuse with arterial cardiac disease. During the ensuing bypass surgery, Jerry's heart stopped for more than 90 seconds. He was declared dead by the attending physicians. However, they managed to revive him, and in so doing gave Jerry the foundation for one of the most unusual actions ever brought before the courts. He appealed for immediate release, claiming that he had been sentenced to life and that his life had been terminated when he was declared dead. Jerry lost that one.

Although Jerry's forte has been his indefatigable determination to assist his fellow prisoners, he has the distinction of being the only American convict allowed to appear in a federal court in defence of a non-prisoner.

It is now 37 years since that day in 1962 when two police officers were shot down in cold blood. Anthony Portelli, who fired the fatal shots, died in prison in 1975 after suffering a brain hemorrhage. Jerry is the longest-serving prisoner in New York State. The average sentence served in the United States for murder is 15 years. Many serve far less. He has come up for parole seven times in the last 14 years, but despite his best efforts he has been denied parole each time.

Probably Jerry's most memorable case involved the appeal of Mafia don Carmine Galante. It was Jerry Rosenberg, self-educated jailhouse lawyer, who was instrumental in gaining the release of the notorious mobster. Jerry apologizes with a suppressed smile, "It wasn't my fault he was murdered after he got out."

Jerry has achieved a degree of fame while serving his prison term. A book, *Doing Life*, by Stephen Bello, reviewing Rosenberg's remarkable life, was published in 1982. This was followed by a TV movie on the same subject. Still, there are those who disagree with the acclaim Jerry has received. They are quick to point out that Luke Fallon and John Finnegan were deprived of their lives more than three decades ago.

As we parted, I alluded to the two officers' deaths and the devastation their murders caused their families. Jerry nodded his head in agreement and said, "Remember, Max, I didn't kill anyone."

Pierre & Bernadette Rouaux

(Belgium)

PHILIPPE ROUAUX had a few reversals in his young life. At age 20, he attempted to take his own life when a girlfriend broke off their relationship. Two years later, the quiet philosophy student was madly in love with 20-year-old Pascale Iserbiet. The attractive couple were engaged to marry when, for reasons of her own, Pascale broke off the engagement.

Philippe didn't take the rejection well. On December 6, 1982, while sitting in his car in his hometown of Assesse, Belgium, he pointed a .22-calibre rifle at his head, pulled the trigger and ended his life.

Detectives investigating the apparent suicide found Philippe's rifle lying in his lap. His right index fingerprint was on the trigger. They also learned that he'd attempted suicide before and that three members of his mother's family had taken their own lives. Case closed. At least for the time being.

On November 5, 1983, an unrelated incident took place in Assesse when Dr. Michel Delescaille was reported missing by his wife, Jacqueline. She stated that her husband, a 33-year-old general practitioner and psychiatrist, had received a phone call the previous evening and had rushed out of their home, shouting over his shoulder that someone had broken their ankle.

When he didn't return home, Jacqueline went looking for Michel throughout the village, but could find no trace of him or his Opel Kadett car.

Next morning, she notified police. Dr. Delescaille's fate wasn't a mystery for long. Within hours, a jogger, Marie Angares, came across the doctor's car. Marie observed that the door of the vehicle was wide open and thought the scene looked suspicious. She walked around the vehicle and saw Michel's body lying in the mud some thirty feet from the car. Marie ran to a nearby town and alerted police. Soon detectives from Namur, the closest large city, took over the investigation.

A physician examining the body found multiple wounds to the head. In the mud near the body, detectives recovered two large bloody hammers with hair adhering to both. They theorized that when the good doctor got out of his car, he had been struck an initial blow from one of his attackers. Two individuals then hit him continually as he crawled in the mud in a futile attempt to get away from his assailants.

There were faint tire tracks beside the Opel which indicated that the murderers had driven away in their own vehicle. No doubt the phone call to the doctor's house had been a ruse to lure him to this lonely spot and to his death.

Who would have committed such a crime? Jacqueline and Michel were happily married. Detectives made discreet inquiries. Jacqueline was totally devoted to her husband and their two children. There were no lovers lurking in the wings. Likewise, Michel was not involved with any women. There was absolutely no flaw in the couple's married life.

When the investigation wound down, police decided to

interview each of Dr. Delescaille's psychiatric patients in case one of them had nurtured a real or imagined grudge against the physician.

It turned out that Michel didn't have many seriously ill mental patients. All were interviewed and proved to have airtight alibis for the time of the murder. Only one was not interviewed, for the simple reason that he was dead. As luck would have it, Philippe Rouaux had been one of Michel's patients.

The doctor had diagnosed Philippe as a manic depressive, which was more or less confirmed when the poor boy shot himself after being rejected by his fiancée.

By nature, police are curious. They took another hard look at Philippe's suicide and turned up some startling discrepancies. Philippe had been left-handed. You may recall that the fingerprint on the trigger was from his right index finger. Strangely, the investigative report indicated that although Philippe had killed himself inside a vehicle, no empty shell had been recovered from the weapon's chamber. At the time, the missing empty shell was attributed to mishandling by investigators.

Detectives interviewed one of Philippe's friends, who said Philippe had confided that he hated his father and was going to kill himself so that his father would have a guilty conscience. At the time of the apparent suicide, it was believed that Philippe had taken his life because of the termination of his engagement. All this served to reopen the Philippe Rouaux case.

Three years had passed since Philippe's death. Police were surprised when they received an anonymous note accusing Philippe's ex-fiancée, Pascale Iserbiet, and her current boyfriend, Georges Landry, of murdering Philippe. Pascale was hurt, and at the same time, insulted that anyone would believe she had anything to do with the tragedy.

She had an airtight alibi for the time of Philippe's death. As for Georges, he wasn't even in the area, nor did he know Pascale at the time. Police wrote them off as suspects, but actively attempted to find out who would send such an incriminating letter.

Because the letter was mailed in Assesse, police showed the envelope to post office clerks. Sure enough, one of the clerks recalled having seen the handwriting before, but couldn't remember where.

Police made photocopies of the envelope and gave a copy to each employee. In this way, they could compare the writing to any other similar mail that passed through their hands. Three days later, letters turned up at the post office with handwriting matching that on the photocopied envelope. The letter accusing Pascale and Georges had been written by Pierre Rouaux, Philippe's father.

When Pierre was questioned, he admitted sending the anonymous letter to police stating that Pascale was responsible for his son's death when she broke off their engagement. Police explained that Pascale may have been indirectly responsible, but that was not a criminal offence. Besides, suicide ran in the Rouaux family, and Philippe had attempted suicide before he ever met Pascale.

The elderly Rouaux underwent extensive questioning. Finally, both he and his wife, Bernadette, broke down. They blamed Dr. Delescaille, their son's psychiatrist, for Philippe's death. It was they who had made the phone call about the broken ankle. Michel had agreed to meet them along the road, believing they would lead him to the patient. Both had rained blows to the physician's head with the big hammers as he crawled in the mud.

On March 29, 1988, Bernadette and Pierre Rouaux were found guilty of murder and sentenced to 20 years' imprisonment. The suspicious death of Philippe Rouaux has never been solved. Had Pierre Rouaux not written the anonymous letter to police, he and his wife would never have been suspected of murdering Dr. Michel Delescaille.

Norman "Red" Ryan

(Canada)

CAN YOU name two infamous Canadian bank robbers? If you are over fifty, you might remember Edmond Alonzo Boyd and his notorious gang. It's tough to recall another of his ilk. But of course there was one such desperado. Indeed, Norman "Red" Ryan not only robbed banks, he also hoodwinked the judicial system of an entire country.

Red was born in July 1895 on Markham Street in Toronto and managed to stay squeaky clean until he attained the ripe old age of 12. That's when he was caught stealing a bicycle and was charged with theft. A kindly magistrate looked down at the freckle-faced, red-haired youngster and gave him a suspended sentence. When Red was caught stealing chickens a year later, he was hustled off to St. John's Reform School, but good behaviour had him back on the streets in a matter of months.

In 1912, Red wrecked a motorcycle in what is now Mississauga. When a local man refused to help him, Red pulled a revolver and fired several shots over the man's head. Police apprehended the impetuous youth and found stolen property on his person. Even the motorcycle had been stolen. A realistic magistrate figured this young man was about to become an habitual criminal. He sentenced Red to four terms of three and a half years each, to run concurrently. Red Ryan entered Kingston Penitentiary. He was 17 years old.

Even today, Kingston is not the Holiday Inn. In 1912 it was hell. Red hated eating his meals alone in his cell and despised the isolation—hour upon hour of solitude. He managed to keep his nose clean, did his assigned tasks without complaint and gained parole after two years, on condition that he stay under the supervision of his father.

It should be pointed out that the Ryans were a hard-working, God-fearing family. Red's dad operated a tin shop and was forever urging his son to enter the business and give up his criminal ways. Red promised his father that he would be a good boy.

Within months, Red, along with a buddy whom he had met in Kingston Pen, held up the Dominion Express Co. in Parkdale. This operation was soon followed by a daring armed robbery of the Toronto Piano Factory. The pair's good fortune didn't last long. In June 1915, they were spotted in Owen Sound. A shoot-out ensued before Red was taken into custody.

For the Owen Sound caper, he was sentenced to eight years in Kingston. For the two previous robberies, he received 12 years' imprisonment on each charge. The cold grey walls of Kingston Penitentiary closed in on Red Ryan for the second time. He celebrated his twentieth birthday in the pen, but the redhead with the lengthy sentence to serve had a visit from Lady Luck.

In 1918, with the war in Europe depleting this country's manpower, the Canadian government took unusual steps to fill army ranks. Simply put, penitentiary prisoners were offered their freedom in return for overseas duty. Red jumped at the chance. He was shipped to England, where he deserted and stole from army stores. He was apprehended, convicted and sentenced to six weeks in the lockup. Red escaped, joined the merchant navy under an assumed name, and in 1921, managed to make his way back to Toronto. All in all, it had been quite a three-year adventure.

Red Ryan was back in town looking for banks to rob. He even took time off to get married. Times were tough in Toronto, so Red went down the road to Hamilton and knocked off the Union Bank at the corner of Main and Locke Streets. The take was a cool $5,000. Other banks fell to Ryan and his partner, George McVittie. They relieved the Bank of Hamilton of nearly $4,000 before moving to Montreal, where shots were fired when they attempted a withdrawal from the downtown branch of the Bank of Commerce. No one was hurt. The two men were later apprehended, holed up at the YMCA on Drummond Street

On December 9, 1921, Red received a sentence of 40 lashes and seven years' imprisonment in St. Vincent de Paul Penitentiary. Later he was taken from prison to stand trial in Hamilton. He was found guilty of several charges and received sentences totalling 25 years, to be served at his old home, Kingston Penitentiary.

From the moment Red entered the pen, he thought of little else but escape. He gathered ruthless, desperate men around him—Arthur "Curly" Sullivan, an armed robbery specialist serving a 10-year sentence; Thomas "Runty" Bryans, a Sault Ste. Marie native serving time for manslaughter; habitual criminal Edward "Wyoming" McMullen, serving 20 years; and Gordon Simpson, an armed robber.

On September 10, 1923, these men set fire to a large

straw stack. Under cover of smoke, the five men made their way over the twenty-foot stone wall. Ryan, the last man up the homemade ladder, was grabbed by guard Matt Walsh. But Red, the natural leader of the gang, had prepared for this eventuality. A pitchfork lay beside the ladder. Red clubbed the officer to the ground and quickly joined the other members of his gang.

The men were able to steal an old Chevy from a home near the prison. Guards were hard on their heels and opened fire. A wild car chase took place through the streets of Kingston, in which McMullen was shot in the hand. When the gang abandoned the vehicle a few miles outside Kingston, McMullen, weak from loss of blood, couldn't keep up. He was taken into custody, but the other four members of the gang managed to make it to Toronto, where underworld contacts outfitted them with clothing and a few dollars until they could get on their feet, which literally meant until they could rob banks.

Twelve days after the daring escape, while newspapers featured their photos on the front pages, the gang brazenly knocked off the Bank of Nova Scotia, getting away with $3,000 in cash. The stolen Overland they used in the robbery was found abandoned in the parking lot of the Granite Club on Church Street

The gang decided to split up. Simpson and Bryans went their own ways and both managed to stay at large for some time. Simpson was captured in New York in 1925, while Bryans wasn't picked up until 1927 in Chicago.

Meanwhile, Red and Sullivan travelled to Minneapolis, where acquaintances knew them as the Miller brothers. The boys kept in pin money doing what they did best, robbing banks. Their undoing was Red's penchant for keeping in touch with friends back in Toronto. It became known to police that he picked up his general delivery mail at a certain post office in Minneapolis.

Red and his sidekick Sullivan were the most wanted men in Canada. No less than R.H. Tucker, deputy warden of Kingston Penitentiary, and Walter Duncan, of the Federal Department of Justice, travelled to the U.S. city to be in on the capture with the local police.

On December 15, 1923, while the city was in a festive Christmas mood, police staked out the post office. Sure enough, Red showed up. A Minneapolis police officer named Maxon opened fire just as Red spotted him. Red pulled out his own weapon and both men fired at the same time, but only Maxon's bullet found its mark. Red was wounded in the right shoulder and was taken into custody.

As he was being ushered away by police, he shouted a warning to Sullivan, who was waiting in a nearby car. Sullivan opened fire and wounded an officer and a bystander. The police returned Sullivan's fire, inflicting only a superficial wound to his nose. He got away clean. However, police learned of his friendship with one Irene Adams. They staked out her apartment and next day, when Sullivan came calling, police shot him dead directly through the heart.

Red Ryan was returned to Canada. Huge crowds gathered to catch a glimpse of the country's most desperate criminal. Red was a broken man when, for his accumulated crimes, he was sentenced to life imprisonment along with 30 lashes, 10 to be delivered each month for the first three months of his sentence.

Red was unceremoniously returned to his home away from home—Kingston Penitentiary. This time, extraordinary security measures were taken to prevent his escape. Red spent the first nine months of his sentence in solitary confinement.

The Roman Catholic chaplain of the penitentiary, Father Wilfred T. Kingsley, often visited the prisoner in the hole. He implored Red to leave his past behind him and embrace the straight and narrow. Red seemed to listen and learn. Father Kingsley noted the gradual change and recommended that Red be removed from solitary confinement. He was transferred to an isolation cell, where he remained for another eighteen months. It wasn't much, but it was at least a small step towards joining the regular prison population.

Red Ryan, who had always been more than willing to shoot his way out of tough scrapes, took to the Bible with a vengeance. It appeared that the notorious badman, with the support of Father Kingsley, had found the path to reformation. Warden Ponsford was impressed.

In 1926, Red was transferred to the mailbag department, a section of the institution devoted to the production of mailbags for the federal government. Red distinguished himself by inventing a theft-proof lock for the bags, a device which was adopted by the federal postal authorities.

Two years later, model prisoner Red Ryan was transferred to the prison hospital as a junior male nurse. After six years Red became head orderly nurse, which was about as high as he could go in Kingston Pen.

Red Ryan became a rare phenomenon in prison. He was admired by inmates for his past daring deeds on the outside and thought highly of by prison authorities for his obvious efforts to totally change his life even though incarcerated.

Year after year, Red continued to be a model prisoner. He quit smoking, tended the sick far into the night and, miracle of miracles, became an altar boy. His hobby was moulding images of the Virgin Mary.

As the years passed, writers visited Kingston to do feature articles on the criminal who had apparently reformed. In the early 1930s there was a groundswell movement afoot to have this intelligent man who had so much to contribute to society released from prison.

Miss Agnes MacPhail, MP for Grey-Bruce, brought the plight of Red Ryan before the House of Commons. Other prominent citizens travelled to Kingston to visit the former badman. All came away impressed. Among their number was none other than the Prime Minister of Canada, the Honourable R.B. Bennett. The two men had a long chat, which culminated with Bennett promising Red that he would take up his case with the Minister of Justice.

The wheels were now in motion. A year later, on July 24, 1935, after serving 12 years in prison, Red Ryan was released. Toronto newspapers vied for his life story. Prime Minister Bennett, Chaplain Kingsley and Warden Ponsford were commended for displaying humanitarian judgement towards a reformed man once destined to spend the rest of his life behind bars.

For weeks Red was a welcome guest at religious functions. He settled down into his brother Russell's home and obtained employment as a car salesman. Dignitaries stil' wanted to be seen with Red. He attended sporting even with politicians and entertainers. Law enforcement officials, as well as religious leaders, often invited Red to be guest speaker at various meetings.

On May 25, 1936, in an incident seemingly unrelated to the life of Red Ryan, a thief named Harry Checkley entered a Sarnia liquor store with another man. Both wore masks and dark goggles. By chance, a passerby, Geoffrey Garvey, noticed the hold-up in progress and called police. In minutes the store was surrounded.

The two trapped bandits decided to shoot it out. Sarnia Constable John Lewis was shot dead. So were the two masked robbers. When the masks and goggles were removed from their faces, one man looked strangely familiar. A driver's licence in his pocket confirmed his identity. The man was Norman "Red" Ryan.

Later it was learned that Red had led a double life since his release from prison. He had secretly and successfully robbed several banks before being killed in Sarnia. Because of his charade, in succeeding years the number of paroles granted to prisoners diminished appreciably. Red was directly responsible for changing the parole system of the entire country.

Anna Marie Sambataro
(Italy)

EVERY TIME a native of Sicily shoots a fellow citizen, it is most convenient to chalk it up to another hit by the Mafia and go on one's way.

Despite this nonchalant attitude toward the Secret Society, it is a fact that folks not connected with organized crime do, from time to time, dispose of strangers and, in selected cases, dear friends and relatives.

On May 6, 1987, the quiet small town of Aci Castello was disrupted when four bullets tore into the body of Concetto Centurino. A police doctor told investigating officers the bullets that took the life of the 45-year-old truck driver were of the 9mm variety. The medic explained that the killer had been a better-than-average marksman, who had managed to find Concetto's heart with two of the bullets and had scored near-heart misses with the other two. The police figured this was the work of a professional killer, most probably a member of the Mafia. They went about delving into Concetto's past.

Right from the start, authorities were a bit puzzled. After all, it is most unusual for someone of Concetto's humble stature to be singled out by the Mafia. There had to be some underlying reason for someone to want him out of the way. As it turned out, Concetto proved to be a most unusual truck driver. You see, he was not only a truck driver, he was a pimp. Not your ordinary run-of-the-mill pimp with a stable of prostitutes, but a pimp with feelings. For years, Concetto had managed only one girl at any given time. The proceeds from his meal tickets had provided him with a luxury car and clothing worn only by the rich and famous. Concetto took care of his regular expenses from his salary as a truck driver.

There was more to Concetto's makeup than meets the eye. Get this—he routinely got his prostitutes pregnant and was the proud daddy of two adult daughters and a 17-year-old son.

Concetto was well known and well liked in Aci Castello. In fact, all his prostitutes had thought highly of the handsome devil. When residents were interviewed, they told investigators that Concetto didn't have an enemy in the world. Of course, that was a barefaced lie. Someone had disliked him enough to pump four slugs in and around his heart.

The women in Concetto's life were questioned extensively. Let's see now: there was 56-year-old Mathilde Sambataro, who was the mother of at least one of his daughters, also named Mathilde. Both mother and daughter practised the oldest profession. Though Concetto had left Mathilde, she didn't have a bad word to say about the father of her daughter. Mathilde's other daughter, Anna Marie, denied Concetto was her biological father, although many of the townsfolk attributed Anna Marie's paternity to him. Mathilde, active as she was, couldn't be sure.

Concetto's 17-year-old son, Franco, was the offspring of Grazia Contino. To complicate matters, Grazia and Concetto had married a week before his murder. She had been his lover off and on for many years. Grazia spoke of her husband in glowing terms.

Police figured one of these women must have hired a killer to dispose of Concetto for some as-yet-unknown reason. Try as they might, detectives couldn't come up with any derogatory information about the dead man. The pimp with morals had been faithful to each prostitute while he lived with them.

Four slugs had found their mark. Someone was responsible. Officials decided that since switching prostitutes had been Concetto's lifestyle for years, this was not the motive for his murder. The only unusual occurrence in Concetto's life was his recent marriage. Somehow, his murder had to be connected to his marriage to Grazia.

During their investigation, police learned that immediately after his wedding, Concetto had been fearful for his life. Was it possible his old flame and the mother of his two daughters had been resentful of his marriage? She was the only one with an iota of a motive.

Detectives interviewed Concetto's neighbours, all of whom swore they had noticed nothing unusual about his house, with one exception. One of the neighbours noted the postman had had difficulty delivering mail to Concetto before his death. Concetto had refused to accept certain letters each day. Police checked with the local mailman, who informed them the refused mail was being returned to Anna Marie Sambataro. Now, why in the world was Concetto's daughter writing to him every day and why was he refusing to accept the letters?

Police decided to bring in both Sambataros for questioning. Mother and daughter swore they had nothing to do with the murder, just as they had sworn earlier in the investigation. This time around, their flats were searched while they were in custody. Nothing was found in Mathilde's flat, but police discovered the returned letters in Anna Marie's. It was obvious from their contents that Anna Marie didn't believe Concetto was her biological father. What's more, Anna Marie was madly in love with him. Now that Concetto had left her mother and married Grazia, she was furious and insanely jealous.

The letters were shown to Mathilde. She confirmed that her daughter was deeply in love with Concetto. Mathilde simply wasn't positive her former lover was the girl's father, but to keep peace in the loosely knit family, she had offered to give up Concetto to her daughter. He had vehemently objected because he wasn't sure the young girl who wanted him so badly wasn't his daughter.

In recent months, Anna Marie had made life miserable for her mother and Concetto. It had become so bad, Mathilde gave up Concetto who, resilient as a rubber band, married Grazia. Anna Marie went out of her head with rage.

Detectives told Anna Marie they knew of her relationship with the murdered man. She confessed she had done what any self-respecting spurned lover would do: she had hired a hit man to kill the scoundrel. In that part of Sicily, putting out a contract was not difficult. The alleged killer was 33-year-old Nunzio Ruscica, an accomplished assassin who was well known to police, but who was so efficient at his chosen profession he had never been arrested or charged with any crime.

Nunzio was taken into custody and questioned. He

denied any knowledge of the murder. Since police only had Anna Marie's word for his involvement, they were unable to charge him with any criminal act. They reluctantly released Nunzio from custody.

On September 8, 1988, Anna Marie stood trial for the murder of Concetto Centurino. She confirmed her earlier confession and threw herself on the mercy of the court. Anna Marie Sambataro was found guilty of inciting to homicide. She was sentenced to eight years in prison.

Yvonne Sleightholme

(England)

YOU WOULDN'T want to meet a nicer young fellow than William Smith. Will finished school and, following family tradition, took over Bloat's Farm in Yorkshire, England. All the while, Will was keeping steady company with Jayne Wilmore. Many thought the pair would eventually marry, but things didn't turn out that way. Jayne left the rural area to train as a registered nurse. She no longer saw Will and was soon dating other young men.

Will busied himself farming and playing rugby. It was at a rugby social club in 1979 that he met Yvonne Sleightholme. Before you could say touchdown, Will and Yvonne were going steady. Unlike Jayne, Yvonne was an aggressive young lady who knew exactly what she wanted. What she wanted was Will Smith.

A little over a year after they met, Yvonne moved into Bloat's Farm. She was soon hinting about more permanent arrangements. Yvonne suggested marriage. Will was aghast. The live-in relationship was just hunky-dory with him. Why spoil it all with an unnecessary tying of the knot? He even mentioned that if Yvonne insisted on such a drastic change in their relationship, it might be better for all concerned for them to separate now, rather than prolong the union. As a result of their disagreement, Yvonne moved out of Bloat's Farm.

A month later Yvonne informed Will that she had leukemia, which she maintained had been brought on by his ill-treatment of her. Will was devastated. He had no idea that an illness as serious as leukemia could be caused by the trauma of rejection. Under the circumstances, he invited Yvonne to move back to his farm. Yvonne, complete with bag and baggage, moved back to her rightful manipulative position at Bloat's Farm.

The change of venue did wonders for Yvonne, if she ever really had leukemia. Thereafter she never even complained of a headache.

Years passed. Yvonne brought up the subject of holy matrimony once again. This time, Will acquiesced. The blushing bride-to-be figured it would take six months to arrange the gala affair. We're talking wedding dress, showers, reception, honeymoon—in short, the works. Yvonne felt it had taken her years to wear Will down, so she planned to have a wedding with all the trimmings. For his part, Will made inquiries about a new suit.

As the fickle finger of fate would have it, Will was visiting the small town of Salton when he happened to meet his old flame, Jayne Wilmore. Jayne was as charming and beautiful as ever. She told Will that if they hadn't run into each other, she had planned to look him up. It wasn't exactly for old time's sake. Jayne explained that kind, trusting Will was in over his head and it was her duty to warn him. In brief, she told him that Yvonne was no good. Yvonne, she said, was a scheming female who had trapped him into marriage. Jayne felt Will deserved a better fate.

Will listened. Jayne made a lot of sense. He asked her what he should do to remedy his precarious situation. Jayne suggested that it wasn't too late to break off his engagement to Yvonne. In addition, there was their own future to consider. Now that they had met again, Jayne let Will know that she was not averse to continuing their long interrupted friendship.

Friendship be damned! Within weeks, Jayne and Will were spending a large portion of their time doing what comes naturally between the sheets. Both suffered from guilty consciences, but not enough to abstain.

Will attempted to broach the subject of delaying the wedding, but it wasn't easy. Yvonne was busy planning the elaborate affair. When she declared she was pregnant, Will backed off. Three weeks before the great date, Yvonne miscarried. Will decided this would be his last chance to tell his betrothed he could not go through with the wedding. He told her that he would not continue to lead a life of deception and that was that. In tears, Yvonne advised guests to ignore the wedding invitations. There would be no marriage. For the second time she moved out of Bloat's Farm.

Quick as a bunny, Jayne moved in. In May 1988, Will and Jayne married. For some time, they were supremely happy. Will farmed. Jayne continued with her nursing career. Then the threatening anonymous phone calls began. These were followed by a mysterious fire on the farm, which consumed a barn. When Will and Jayne received a funeral wreath in the mail, they advised police that they suspected Yvonne, the only one they felt was capable of such an act.

Police located Yvonne, living with her parents on their farm. She was not exactly what they expected. In fact, she was polite, co-operative, and claimed she had no idea who was harrassing the Smiths. The police believed her, particularly after she told them she was moving out of the area to a cottage on the Scottish border. They told the Smiths the results of their inquiries.

That's where matters stood in December 1989, when Yvonne drove from her cottage to the road just outside Bloat's Farm. It was a Tuesday night. Yvonne knew Will would be attending his usual rugby club function that night. She waited until she saw him leave. Then she drove her vehicle to the front door. Lugging her trusty shotgun with her, she knocked. Jayne answered the door, and found herself staring directly down the barrel of a shotgun. Yvonne marched Jayne across the farmyard in the pouring rain and, without a word, shot her in the back of the head. Jayne Smith died on the soft earth of the farmyard.

Resourceful Yvonne went about simulating a rape scene. She ripped Jayne's blouse, tore away her brassiere and scratched her breasts. She removed Jayne's panties and took them away with her.

Those close to this soap-opera murder feel Yvonne might very well have gotten away with murder if it hadn't been for the one act she performed when her emotions got the better of her. There she was in the pouring rain, tearing and pulling away the clothing of the woman who she believed had ruined her life. She had planned well, but in the heat of the moment she ripped off Jayne's wedding ring.

When Will learned of the missing wedding ring, he told police about Yvonne Sleightholme living in that cottage up near the Scottish border. Yvonne was questioned. Police learned she wasn't at home on the night of the murder.

Blood matching Jayne's blood type was recovered from Yvonne's car.

Accused of murder, Yvonne mysteriously lost the sight of both eyes. At her murder trial, she claimed Will had been keeping company with her after his marriage. He wanted to divorce Jayne, but she wouldn't hear of it, so he had hired an assassin to kill her. Thoughtful Will had even provided the assassin with Yvonne's father's shotgun. In an attempt to frame Yvonne, he had summoned her to the farm on the night of the murder.

No one believed Yvonne's fanciful tale. In May 1991, she was found guilty of murder and sentenced to life imprisonment. In 1993, she appealed her conviction, but was turned down.

Erwin Spengler
(Germany)

KATHARINA KORNAGEL lived in the small German town of Wagen im Allgaeu. The 70-year-old, overweight Katharina planned to spend the rest of her life in relative tranquillity. Things didn't work out that way for her, but that's getting ahead of our story.

In 1987, Katharina lived in a flat on the first floor of her building. She had resided there for years, ever since her mother had died and left her a small fortune. Everyone in the building liked good-natured Katharina. Maria and George Weh, who lived a couple of floors up from her, were dear friends. So was Brigitte Scherer, who often spent pleasant afternoons sipping white wine with Katharina.

For the past five years, Katharina had employed 33-year-old Erwin Spengler as her chauffeur. She had decided it was too tough walking everywhere, so she purchased a second-hand Mercedes and hired Erwin at the same time. She explained to her friends that both parties were happy with the arrangement. She now was able to take comfortable trips for a few days at a time, and Erwin, who didn't have a vehicle of his own, could use the Mercedes when he wasn't chauffeuring his boss. Within months, Erwin, who was grossly overweight himself, was not only Katharina's chauffeur, but her best friend as well.

On January 18, 1988, Erwin walked into the police station in Wagen im Allgaeu and reported Katharina Kornagel missing. According to Erwin, he had driven his boss to the train station on December 11 and hadn't heard from her since. She had left for Bremen to visit relatives and friends, but it wasn't like her to stay away so long. Police decided to take a look inside Katharina's flat. What they found added credence to Erwin's concern for his employer. There was a small brown crusty stain in the front hall, which at first glance looked ominously like dried blood. Plants in the flat had shrivelled and died during Katharina's prolonged absence. Her washing machine was full of wet clothing. The general appearance of the flat indicated the occupant had left hurriedly.

The stain in the hall turned out to be blood that had been there for well over a month. Laboratory technicians meticulously checked the flat. They found that someone had cleaned the bathroom with hydrochloric acid. The taps, sink and particularly the bathtub had been scrubbed with the acid. Pipes leading from the bathtub were taken up and examined. They were clean. Police estimated that several gallons of hydrochloric acid were used to eliminate any foreign material that might have been forced down the drain. Whoever had worked with the acid must have worn rubber gloves and a mask. Of course, the horrible thought that someone had murdered Katharina and dissolved her body parts was uppermost in the minds of the police. Was it possible that a 200-pound woman could be disposed of in such a manner? Detectives studying the scene felt it was not only possible, but that Erwin Spengler was the logical suspect.

Erwin was taken into custody and questioned. He admitted that up until that past December he had been extremely short of funds, but was flush with cash from around Christmas on. Erwin told his interrogators he had hit a lucky streak at the casino in Baden-Baden. Unfortunately, no one could recall a big winner of Erwin's conspicuous description at the time he claimed to have won at the roulette wheel.

Friends and relatives of Katharina's in Bremen had never expected a visit from her, nor had she arrived in their city. Erwin had to backtrack. He now said he had dropped Katharina off at the station and had assumed she was going to Bremen. It was always possible she had gone elsewhere.

Under pressure to account for his new and sudden supply of money, Erwin admitted his winning streak at roulette was a fabrication. He came into his money honestly enough. Katharina had given him two signed blank cheques and he had merely filled in the amounts. She had given him the money because he needed to pay off debts. Besides, he and Katharina were very good friends.

Police traced the cheques and had the signatures examined. They were disappointed when the signatures on both cheques proved authentic. Police were stymied. Katharina had signed those cheques all right. If she had been forced to sign them, she could have stopped payment if she so desired. There was also the matter of a motive. Why would Erwin want to kill Katharina? He wasn't mentioned in her will, a fact he knew very well.

While detectives were pondering how they could nail Erwin, an unsettling series of items were received in the mail by Katharina's friends. Maria and George Weh received a postcard from Bremen, apparently signed by Katharina. Brigitte Scherer received one the following week from the Canary Islands. It too appeared to be signed by the missing woman. Other occupants of the building also received cards. Police checked the signatures. They were all different and none were genuine. Who was sending postcards from different places in the world to Katharina's friends? For sure it wasn't Erwin Spengler. He was resting not so comfortably in the town jail. Detectives thought perhaps the writer was someone who had lived in Katharina's building and had moved out or gone on a long vacation, but such was not the case. The senior citizens who occupied the flats were of the staid variety. No one had moved out and no one had taken a vacation.

It was left to one officer to come up with the solution to this minor mystery. He checked out men who had been in jail with Erwin and had been released. Of the six men who fell into this category, four were traced. One lived in Bremen and one had visited the Canary Islands. Both men were taken into custody and both admitted they had sent the postcards. They explained that while they were in jail, Erwin had given them the names and addresses of people who had lived in Katharina's building. He had even provided them with a bit of personal information about Katharina and her neighbours so the cards would have an authentic ring to them.

When Erwin was faced with this evidence, he claimed he was being framed. He said he had overheard the men planning a robbery. They were telling lies about him so he would be executed and silenced forever.

Detectives were positive their man had killed Katharina Kornagel and disposed of her body down the bathtub drain with the aid of hydrochloric acid. Despite their suspicions, they had no body and no motive. To the investigators, it appeared Erwin would be better off with Katharina alive.

After all, he was gainfully employed by a generous boss, and the use of the Mercedes was a pleasant perk of the job.

Police theorized that the murder had been a spontaneous one. No doubt an argument had taken place that had culminated in murder. Erwin had had over a month to clean up the evidence before strolling into the police station. Had he concentrated so much on cleaning up the bathroom area with hydrochloric acid that he had overlooked the brown stain in the hall? Murderers have been known to make such mistakes. The unsuccessful attempt to create the impression that Katharina was alive by having his former cell mates send postcards to acquaintances was just plain stupid.

Still and all, the prosecution was going to trial with a weak case—no motive, no murder weapon, no witnesses and no body. Despite the shortcomings in the prosecution's case, the German jury brought in a guilty verdict. Erwin collapsed and had to be carried from the courtroom when he was sentenced to life imprisonment.

Michael Taylor
(England)

I HAVE NEVER been a big fan of exorcism. Does all that ranting and raving under the guise of prayer really help drive the devil from the possessed? I think not. Let's go back to the seventies and take a peek at the Taylor family who lived in Ossett, a town of twenty thousand souls in Yorkshire, England.

Michael and Christine Taylor had five sons, ranging in age from 6 to 12 years. Michael, 31, was religious to the point where he didn't feel fulfilled by attending only the Church of England. As a result, he assisted in forming a group known as the Christian Fellowship.

On September 24, 1974, the Taylors hosted the first meeting of the group at their council-house home. Everyone had a jolly good time. There was singing and bible discussion. At the height of the fervour, Michael spoke in tongues which, as you may know from observing Jimmy Swaggart, is a soliloquy of ecstatic spiritual emotion that manifests itself by the worshipper uttering strange words that no one understands, not even the speaker.

The Fellowship meetings rotated from home to home. At one of them a member of the flock demonstrated an amateur attempt at exorcism. Everyone was impressed as all get-out, particularly Michael, who was so affected by the service that he commenced to shake all over.

Five days after the meeting, Michael attended St. Thomas Church, where Father Peter Vincent conducted the service. Later the same day, the Fellowship meeting was held at Michael's home. Once again he witnessed a demonstration of exorcism and was totally enthralled.

A couple of days later, unemployed Michael was extremely depressed. He had applied for a job and had been rejected. On a visit to his mother that day he told her he had seen the devil, who had told him he was a useless bloke who should kill himself. His mother advised Michael that although he wasn't a world-beater, he was definitely not useless. She was no doubt referring to his stud-like ability to sire five offspring.

The following day, people witnessed Michael behaving irrationally on the streets of the town, dropping to his knees before total strangers and preaching to them that the world was about to end. Operating in a religious fog of sorts, Michael left his ecclesiastical street pursuits to attend a meeting of the Fellowship at the home of St. Thomas's choirmaster, Ron Smith. Father Vincent must have been slumming. He was there too.

Michael related to the assorted gathering that he had been seduced by the devil. Collective ears perked up. It was decided that Michael should describe his experience in detail. After all, it isn't every day that one is seduced by Satan himself. Michael must have poured his heart and soul into his recital, because those who met him after the meeting said he appeared pale, tired and agitated.

On Friday, October 4, Michael, in a state of frenzy, ordered Christine to remove all the religious books and crucifixes from their home. Christine did as she was told.

Other members of the community, especially members of the Fellowship, who didn't mind a tad of exorcism and the like, noticed that Michael's behaviour was well beyond the norm, as every so often he would let out a piercing scream. Once, on a drive with a friend, John Eggins, he started screaming so loudly and so often that Eggins drove directly to Father Vincent's vicarage. Michael demonstrated his appreciation by throwing the vicarage cat through a window.

Someone suggested that Michael was possessed of the devil and required exorcising in the worst way. The idea seemed like an excellent one at the time. Everyone agreed that they would call in Rev. Raymond Smith, a Methodist minister, and his good wife, Margaret, who were recognized in the area as real-life honest-to-goodness experienced exorcists. John Eggins and a Methodist lay preacher, Donald James, would complete Team Exorcism.

All was in readiness for the night-long ritual. Michael was taken to the adjoining vestry, where he was placed on his back. In turn, those is attendance asked questions and broke into prayer.

Much later, Michael related that when they told him of sins he had committed, he confessed, even if the allegations were false. He said he would have confessed to anything. Michael said that every time he exhaled, Team Exorcism would congratulate themselves on getting rid of another devil. Many weeks later, doctors stated that Michael was probably hyperventilating.

As the sun came up and poured into the vestry, the job, in the opinion of the assorted members of the group, was over. They figured they had removed about 40 demons from the exhausted subject, but that there might be a couple left. In particular, Rev. Smith felt that the one demon remaining in Michael was the murder demon, which could not be ousted. The reverend's wife, Margaret, went one step further by stating, "I have had word from God that if he goes home this morning he will murder his wife and children."

All this talk about murder made the exorcism group extremely nervous. They discussed restraining Michael from returning to his home. Several suggested they bring in a medical welfare officer, but it was Sunday and none was available. Instead, they called police, who advised them to call a doctor. Christine wouldn't hear of it. She feared Michael's wrath. This was a spiritual matter, not a medical problem.

At 9 a.m., Michael and Christine were delivered to their home. An hour later, Michael attacked his wife with his bare hands. He tore out her tongue, her eyes and ripped flesh from her face before choking her to death.

Neighbours heard the attack and called police. When the authorities arrived at the scene, they found Michael in a kneeling position, covered with blood. He was taken into custody and asked if he had killed his wife.

He replied, "No, not her. I love her. I destroyed the evil within her. It had to be done. I am relaxed. What had to be done has been done. The evil in her has been destroyed. Christine was good. The evil had been put into her by them. I had to kill it. It came through religion. They primed me for this last night."

Michael was tried for murder, but was found not guilty by reason of insanity. He was detained indefinitely at Broadmoor Hospital, an institution for the criminally insane.

William Townsend

(Canada)

IF YOU DRIVE along picturesque Highway 3 from Simcoe to Dunnville in southern Ontario, you will pass through the tiny hamlet of Nelles Corners. Just a few miles north of Lake Erie's shores, Nelles Corners is off the beaten track. In 1854 a crime took place in this community that gave rise to a series of events that made it one of the strangest murder cases in Canada's history.

John Nelles operated a general store. He and his wife lived together with his brother, Augustus, and his wife's sister, Lucy Humphreys. On the night of October 18, the family had finished supper. The early evening was no different from hundreds that had preceded it. A chill wind whistled outside as one by one the family retired for the night. John, left alone at the kitchen table, took a long last pull on his pipe before knocking the ashes against the grate of the kitchen stove. He was about to go to bed when it happened.

Four men burst through the front door. Their intent was never in doubt. Their faces were blackened with burnt cork. The desperate men demanded money. Nelles rose from the kitchen chair, but made no attempt to comply with the robbers' wishes.

A shot echoed through the once peaceful home, and John Nelles sank to the floor. The badly wounded man moved slightly, eliciting a further shot from the pistol carried by one of the men. Mrs. Nelles and her sister, Lucy, rushed into the room and ran to John's aid. The four bandits tore a watch from the wounded man. Ignoring the women, they continued to search the house for anything of value.

Augustus Nelles woke up with the first shot. Wisely, he remained in bed; not the most heroic action, but one that most certainly saved his life. As quickly as the wanton killing had taken place, the five men opened the door and disappeared into the darkness.

A few miles down the road the killers bumped into two farmers, who were relieved of the few dollars they had in their possession. Within hours the unknown assailants had boarded a train bound for Buffalo. Once in the U.S., the men separated, having left heartache and tragedy in their wake.

Despite the fact that their faces had been blackened, a good description of the wanted men was given by both the two women, and the two farmers who had been robbed. Three of the men, King, Blowes and Bryson, were quickly apprehended. They were placed in prison in Cayuga, Ontario. All three were tried, found guilty and sentenced to death. King and Blowes were hanged, but Bryson's sentence was commuted to life imprisonment. He probably saved his skin by confessing to being one of the men in the house at the time of the murder. All three men claimed that they hadn't fired the fatal shot. They stated that the trigger had actually been pulled by one William Townsend.

Meanwhile, an event took place that had a direct bearing on the shooting at Nelles Corners. Approximately a month after the murder of John Nelles, two men entered a hotel operated by a Mrs. Jordan at Port Robinson, Ontario.

While the two men were eating, other men in the hotel swore that one of the strangers looked like William Townsend, the wanted killer of John Nelles. They notified the authorities.

Several police rushed to the hotel to apprehend the wanted man. One of the policemen, Constable Charles Richards, faced the stranger, who immediately pulled a gun and shot him. The constable died a few hours later. The man known as Townsend got away.

Over two years went by, and again Townsend was recognized in the U.S. This time he was taken into custody without incident by the Cleveland, Ohio, authorities. The government of Canada immediately proceeded to have the wanted man extradited to Canada. In May 1857, he was delivered to the Canadian authorities and placed in jail in Cayuga to await trial for the murder of John Nelles.

From the moment he was taken into custody, William Townsend captured the imagination of the country. Townsend remained hostile towards the authorities, but despite this hostility, well-placed powerful men took an interest in his case. Throughout his stay in custody and his ensuing trial, Townsend claimed that he wasn't Townsend at all. He swore he was Robert J. McHenry, a Scotsman who worked as a mariner out of Cleveland. He further swore that he had been in California searching for gold at the time of John Nelles's murder.

Townsend's unusual trial began on September 27, 1857. The Cayuga courthouse had never seen such an array of legal talent. The Crown was represented by Henry Smith, the Solicitor General of Canada. S.B. Freeman, Q.C., one of the finest orators of his time, represented Townsend. The accused pleaded not guilty. From the beginning, the trial boiled down to the question of whether the accused man was Townsend or McHenry.

Lucy Humphreys identified the prisoner as the robber who had fired the shots that killed her brother-in-law. William Bryson was brought from Kingston Penitentiary to testify, and identified the accused as the murderer Townsend. Sometime previous to the murder of Nelles, Townsend had been employed as a cooper in the neighbouring community of Dunnville. A number of former neighbours of the man in the dock took the stand, and all identified him as William Townsend.

Although this should have been enough to convict the prisoner, such was not the case. Freeman paraded close to a hundred witnesses to the stand, all of whom swore that they knew Townsend well, and that the prisoner was not William Townsend. Townsend's brother-in-law, Ezra Smith, said the man in the dock was a stranger to him. Benjamin Diffin, who worked with Townsend one whole winter, said the accused was unknown to him. No expense was spared to place witnesses in the stand who swore the accused was not William Townsend.

After six hours of deliberation, the jury returned and informed the court that they were undecided. They were dismissed. The accused man was about to be returned to his cell when the deputy sheriff of Welland County read a warrant charging the prisoner with the murder of Constable Charles Richards of Port Robinson.

William Townsend, or whoever he was, was taken from Cayuga and lodged in the Welland (then called Merrittsville) jail.

On March 26, 1858, he again stood trial for murder. Again his case rested on his claim that a terrible mistake had been made. He was not the murderer William Townsend. All the same witnesses were heard again. This time the foreman of the jury spoke out loud and clear, "The prisoner is McHenry, and is not guilty." That night the taverns of old Merrittsville rocked with celebrations held by McHenry's friends.

Townsend-McHenry was returned to Cayuga, for he was still in custody for the Nelles murder. Within a few days, however, he heard that the Crown had no intention of trying him again. He was released on bail with the understanding that he would make himself available if the Crown ever decided to place him on trial once more. This never happened. The strange, silent, hostile prisoner walked out of the Cayuga jail a free man.

For some time after, Robert McHenry was in great demand as a speaker at clubs and fairs throughout the country. Later, he dropped from sight and was never heard from again.

To some, he was a killer named Townsend, who got away with murder. To others he was a harassed, innocent man named McHenry. Who was he? This question remains unanswered.

Rev. John Selby Watson
(Ireland)

THERE WAS no great mystery about it. Rev. John Selby Watson had bludgeoned his wife to death. The dastardly deed was performed with an old pistol that the man of the cloth kept stored in a display box. Hate was involved in the slaying, which took place well over a hundred years ago. Anne Watson had received a total of eight blows to the head, any one of which could have killed her.

The reverend's history gave no hint of the violence that was to erupt on that pleasant fall day of October 8, 1871. You see, Rev. Watson had never committed as much as a teeny-weeny indiscretion in his entire life.

John Watson was born into abject poverty in London, England, at the wrong time. In those long-ago days, a higher education was a privilege enjoyed only by the wealthy. But Watson wasn't to be denied. By the sweat of his brow and dogged determination, he managed, at age 34, to obtain his bachelor of arts from Trinity College in Dublin.

Nothing came easy for Watson. He met a young woman he fancied while still a student, but with no money and few prospects, it took him seven years to ask Anne to marry him. During those seven years, the scholarly Watson joined the Church of England and rose slowly through the ranks, becoming a curate at age 37. Three years later he was appointed headmaster of Stockwell Grammar School in Surrey. Only then did he ask Anne for her hand in marriage. She accepted, and the respectable, staid pair were married at St. Mark's Church in Dublin.

You would never call the Rev. John a lightweight in the academic world. In his spare time he translated the works of Xenophon, the ancient Greek historian, as well as various materials written by Cicero, Lucretius and Justinian. Many of the reverend's translations were published. He also wrote a book on the life of Scottish patriot William Wallace, recently the subject of the Academy Award–winning movie *Braveheart.*

When Rev. John wasn't attending to his religious duties or teaching, he found time to pick up a Master of Arts degree from Oxford University and a Fellowship of the Royal Society of Literature.

Throughout his career, Rev. John was beloved by pupils and parents, but his sterling efforts were not financially rewarding. For twenty-five years he laboured diligently, but even in those days downsizing was the practice when times got tough. In 1867, enrollment fell off dramatically. The governors of his school gave him three months' notice and the boot. There was no early-retirement package or compensation of any kind. The reverend simply gathered up his pens and left the school, a disillusioned man.

From the time of his dismissal, Rev. John operated in a daze. Those who knew him later stated that he was so depressed he appeared to be disoriented. Anne, his dutiful wife of so many years, had a difficult time adjusting to her husband's personality change. Some say she became a cranky, annoying woman who constantly criticized him for allowing himself to be manipulated into such an unenviable position.

On Sunday, October 8, 1871, the Watsons attended morning prayer at St. Andrew's Church. Ironically, the sermon that day concerned the punishment of those in high office who misused their power.

That afternoon, former employees of the Stockwell Grammar School paid a social call on the Watsons. Mr. and Mrs. Tully found the reverend rather tense. At one point Mrs. Watson confided, "I am so frightened. I am afraid of anybody getting into the house by the back over the garden wall." Shortly after hearing this strange statement, the Tullys left.

At 9 p.m., Ellen Mary Payne, the Watsons' only servant, returned from her afternoon off. When she entered the house, Rev. John told her, "Your mistress won't be home for two or three days." He told Ellen that Mrs. Watson had gone out of town. Ellen thought it strange that her mistress had not mentioned the trip to her that morning. Rev. John accompanied Ellen up the stairs, leading the way with a lit candle. He pointed out some discolouration on the floor near the library door. "This stain on the floor; it is port wine which your mistress has spilt. I have told you in case you might wonder what it was."

The following day was uneventful for Ellen. That night, when the reverend returned, he told Ellen, "If you find anything wrong with me in the morning, go for Dr. Rugg." Somewhat startled, Ellen inquired if he was ill. Rev. John would only say, "I may require medicine in the morning."

Next day there was still no sign of Anne Watson. The

reverend was up and about with the birds and passed up breakfast. He dashed down to a hardware shop, where he ordered a packing case to be made to the specific measurements he provided. He then returned home and retired to his bedroom.

Around noon, Ellen thought she heard noises emanating from the bedroom. She went up to investigate and found the reverend spread out on his bed, unconscious and nude. There were four letters and a glass on a night table beside his still form. Ellen picked up the letters. One was addressed to her and included a five-pound note. It read, "*For the servant, Ellen Payne, exclusive of her wages. Let no suspicion fall upon the servant, whom I believe to be a good girl.*"

Another letter was addressed to Dr. George Rugg. Ellen ran to the doctor's house and gave him the letter, which read,

> *To the surgeon. I have killed my wife in a fit of rage. Often she has provoked me and I have endeavoured to restrain myself, but rage overcame me and I struck her. Her body will be found in the little room off the library. The key is in a letter on the table. I hope she will be buried as becomes a lady of birth and position.*

Dr. Rugg rushed to the Watson residence. Using the key, he opened the small room. There lay Anne Watson. The doctor could see at a glance there was nothing he could do for Anne. He hurried to Rev. John's room. The good man of the cloth was not in bad shape. Dr. Rugg recognized the smell of bitter almonds about his mouth and knew that he had taken prussic acid. He quickly procured an antidote, which he gave to the cleric. Rev. John recovered rather speedily. It occurred to the doctor that he was at the scene of a half-hearted suicide attempt. He felt that Rev. John might have spat out the prussic acid rather than swallowing any great quantity.

Police were summoned. In a display case they found five old pistols, four of which had not been touched for years. The fifth one was damaged. The wooden stock had been split and there was dried blood on it. This pistol proved to be the murder weapon.

Rev. John was charged with his wife's murder. On January 10, 1872, he stood trial at London's Old Bailey. He was able to explain away the ordered shipping case, stating it was to be used to store his literary works. Besides, he had not even bothered to pick it up. His attorney pleaded insanity. There didn't seem to be much of a motive for the murder. Despite admitting to the killing, Rev. John would not reveal why he had murdered his wife.

Rev. John was found guilty and sentenced to death, a sentence later commuted to life imprisonment at Parkhurst Prison on the Isle of Wight. He stayed in prison for 12 years, until he suffered a fall in his cell and died at the age of 80.

That should have been the end of the Rev. John Selby Watson and his infamous crime, but that's not the case. Remember those letters found in his bedroom? The fourth letter was written in Latin. It is believed that it reveals the real motive for the crime.

The mystery letter reads:

"*Felix in omnibus fere rebus praeterquam quod ad sexu*

attinet foemineum. Saepe olin amanti amare semper nocuit."

For more than a hundred years, Latin scholars have been attempting to translate the message and solve the motive for Anne Watson's murder. Here a few of their efforts:

"To one who has often loved, it has always been harmful to love."

How about, "Many men have found that it is a mistake to be too true to the object of a boyish passion."

Or: "It is often injurious or fatal to a man who once loved to go on forever loving."

There are other interpretations of the vexing letter, but so far no one has come up with a satisfactory explanation as to why an educated religious teacher who had never committed a violent act in his life took it upon himself to bludgeon his wife to death and hide her body for three days.

James White & Betty Wilson

(United States)

DR. JACK WILSON was a beloved ophthalmologist with a flourishing practice in Huntsville, Alabama. His road to the good life in Huntsville had been a rocky one. Jack had to struggle financially to obtain his education, which was followed by a stint in France and Germany with the U.S. army. After his discharge, he married, but the union ended in divorce. Jack and his first wife had three sons—Perry, Scott and Steven.

After the breakup of his 15-year marriage, Jack met and married Betty Woods, an attractive nurse and the mother of three sons from a previous marriage. None of the couple's six children were implicated in the murder that took place on that Friday in May 1992.

Both Jack and Betty had medical problems. Jack suffered from Crohn's disease, which had grown progressively worse since his days in medical school, necessitating an operation known as an ileostomy, in which a portion of his large intestine was removed. From the date of the operation, more Jack wore an ostomy bag. Betty hated that bag. Over the years, she started drinking heavily, until she realized that her social drinking had evolved into a way of life. Betty joined Alcoholics Anonymous, became a devoted follower of the organization and quit drinking.

Meanwhile, slim, short Dr. Jack was one of the leadi

eye doctors in the area. He had amassed an estate of more than $8 million and had an annual income in 1991 of slightly more than $1 million. He and Betty were recognized as leading members of Huntsville's medical and scientific community. If Betty had ever been in love with Jack, that love had ceased to exist. She confided to many of her affluent friends that she no longer cared for her husband. To confirm her feelings, she entered into several affairs with local men. It was generally agreed among their mutual friends that Jack must have known his wife was playing the field. Maybe he didn't care.

At nine-thirty on the evening of May 22, Betty returned to her home at 2700 Boulder Circle after attending an AA meeting with a girlfriend. She told her friend that the next day she and Jack would be starting their vacation, which they intended to spend in New Mexico. Betty walked into her home, took one look and ran hysterically from the residence. She rang a neighbour's doorbell, screaming that Jack had been attacked by a burglar. The neighbour dialled 911.

Detectives at the scene came across Jack's body at the top of the stairs, just as Betty had minutes before. Jack had been beaten about the head with what they speculated was a metal baseball bat, and had been stabbed twice in the chest and stomach, most probably after death had occurred. Despite Betty's assertion that a burglar must have been responsible, the investigating officers didn't think so. Nothing had been taken from the house, nor was anything disturbed.

A few hours later, the investigation into the murder of the prominent doctor took a strange turn. The day before

Jack's murder, a detective in Columbiana, Alabama, received a visit from Janine Russell. Ms. Russell had a strange tale to tell. A friend of hers, James White, an unemployed handyman, had told her, while drinking, that he had been hired to kill a doctor in Huntsville. He had been approached by a respectable schoolteacher, Peggy Lowe, who said she was acting for her twin sister in Huntsville. Janine didn't know the name of Peggy Lowe's sister.

The conversation about the contract killing had taken place over a period of weeks. At one point, White, who was usually broke, had flashed a sizable amount of money. He told Janine that he had received a down payment for the proposed murder and would soon complete the contract. Badly frightened, Janine decided to share her knowledge with the police.

The detective listening to her story called his counterpart in Huntsville and passed along the information. The lawmen figured they could be dealing with a hoax, but agreed to run a check on James White. They learned White had once been arrested on a drug charge and had escaped from a local jail, remaining at large for five years before being apprehended. He was released from prison on May 27, 1982, after having been incarcerated for almost a year. Since that time he had committed no infractions. His record certainly didn't indicate he was a contract killer.

Within 24 hours of Janine Russell's visit to the police, Dr. Jack Wilson was murdered in Huntsville. His wife, Betty, had a twin sister. Her name was Peggy Lowe. Was it possible that a respectable churchgoing schoolteacher had hired a killer to dispose of her twin sister's unwanted husband? Police thought it was more than possible. They believed that was exactly what had happened.

Unaware that he was being sought by authoriti
White was easily located. Under intense interrogatio
admitted he had killed the doctor. "Betty Wilson paid m
to do it." With that sentence, White placed himself in jeopardy of ending his life in the state's electric chair. Eventually, he told how he had made the acquaintance of Peggy Lowe. He said they had become intimate, an accusation denied by Peggy. White professed that he had been in love with Peggy. When asked to do a favour for her twin sister, Betty, he had agreed. To sweeten the pie, he was offered a payment of $5,000 to do the job.

White may not have been the cleverest man in the world, but when it came to saving his own skin, he was cunning enough. He realized the state required his testimony in order to convict the twins. His lawyer made a deal. White would testify against Betty and Peggy in return for a guarantee that he wouldn't be put to death.

White met Peggy when he was doing some work at the school where she taught. They became good friends and chatted on the phone a few times each week. The subject of murdering Betty's husband had been broached gradually. Peggy put White in touch with her sister. He received an advance of $2,500 from Betty for the impending murder.

The date of the murder was set for the day before Betty and Jack were to leave on vacation. Two days before the murder, Betty had provided White with a loaded .38-calibre pistol to do the job. The pistol was found in White's room. It was loaded with distinctive bullets, a box of which were later found in Betty's home. White never used the weapon because he simply didn't like guns.

On the day of the murder, Betty picked up White at the Ramada Inn in Huntsville and drove him to her home in her BMW. He lay in wait for Jack to return from his office. White killed the ophthalmologist with the baseball bat and, to make certain he was dead, stabbed him twice in the chest and stomach. As agreed, he waited in the house until Betty came back and drove him to his waiting pickup truck in a parking lot.

White's story was checked and rechecked. Times, places and circumstances were all authenticated. The three conspirators were sent to trial separately. James White was found guilty of murder and sentenced to life imprisonment. He will be eligible for parole in the year 2001. Betty Wilson was found guilty of capital murder. The state agreed to waive the death penalty and sentenced her to life imprisonment without possibility of parole. She has appealed her conviction. She resides in the Julia Tutwiler Women's Prison in Wetumpka, Alabama, where she is employed in the laundry.

After a nine-day trial, Peggy Lowe was inexplicably found not guilty. Because of her notoriety, she refused to resume her teaching position. She is now employed in administration at her old school.

Robert Wood

(England)

ON SEPTEMBER 12, 1907, when Bert Shaw boarded the 7:20 a.m. train at Sheffield, England, for his home in Camden Town, London, he had no idea he was taking part in the first act of what was to become one of England's most infamous murder cases.

Upon arrival at his apartment, Bert was greeted by his landlady, Mrs. Stocks, and his mother, who had picked that precise moment to visit. It was 11:30 a.m. and the two women were mildly concerned that Bert's wife, Phyllis, had not left her apartment all morning. Bert went directly to his quarters and found the door locked. Mrs. Stocks provided a duplicate key. Bert walked into his parlour. Drawers had been opened, their contents strewn over the floor. When Bert found the bedroom door locked, he broke it down. Phyllis's nude body lay on the bed. She had been stabbed in the throat.

Phyllis had been an avid collector of postcards, which she kept in the front room. Bert noticed one of her albums in the bedroom. It was open and several postcards were scattered on the floor. A subsequent check of the apartment revealed that a silver cigarette case, a gold watch and a glass charm were missing. A bloody basin bore evidence that the killer had washed up after the murder. In the parlour, a meal for two had obviously been consumed. Quite possibly Phyllis's dinner guest had been her killer.

Murder investigations uncover embarrassing facts about

the participants. In the Camden Town murder, almost everyone involved had a secret. Bert's wife wasn't legally his wife at all. Her name was Phyllis Dimmock and, shame to tell, she was a prostitute. She and Bert had known each other for two years. About nine months earlier, Bert had agreed to have Phyllis move in with him on condition that she never ply her trade again. He had told everyone, including his mother, that he and Phyllis had married.

That was subterfuge number one. There was more. Phyllis hadn't given up her old ways one little bit. Most nights she sold her body, seeking out customers in the many watering holes in Camden Town. She had no difficulty bringing her customers to her apartment. Mrs. Stocks was always sound asleep in her own quarters and Bert worked nights in Sheffield.

Bert learned of Phyllis's deception from the police. He was investigated as a suspect and was able to prove without a doubt that he was miles away at the time of the crime and could not have been the killer.

Police checked out the pubs frequented by Phyllis. They discovered that her favourite hangout was the Rising Sun in Camden Town. In this way they came in contact with Robert Roberts, a ship's cook with a wad of money to blow before accepting his next berth. He had spent three consecutive nights, Sunday, Monday and Tuesday, with Phyllis, leaving early each morning. On Wednesday night, the night of the murder, he had wanted to visit Phyllis for the fourth time, but she told him she already had a date for that night.

Although it was an unlikely story, every word Roberts told police proved to be true. He had more to tell. On

Wednesday morning, before he left the apartment for the last time, there was a knock on the door. Two pieces of mail were pushed under the door. Roberts picked them up. One was an advertisement. The other was a letter, which Phyllis read before handing it over to Roberts. He remembered the contents. *"Dear Phyllis, Will you meet me at the Eagle, Camden Town, 8:30 tonight, Wednesday?—Bert."*

After Phyllis showed the letter to Roberts, she went to a bureau and pulled out a postcard. It read, *"Phyllis darling, If it pleases you, meet me, 8:15 p.m. at the* [a drawing of the Rising Sun]. *Yours to a cinder, Alice."*

Roberts had noticed that the letter and the postcard were written by the same hand. Phyllis threw the letter into the fire and returned the postcard to the bureau drawer. It appeared to detectives that Phyllis's killer had desperately searched for the incriminating postcard, which they could not find in the apartment.

The investigation was winding down when Bert Shaw called police with the startling news that he had found the missing postcard. It was under some newspaper lining the bureau drawer. Scotland Yard released copies of the postcard to major newspapers, asking anyone who recognized the writing to come forward

Out of the millions who saw the reproduction of the postcard, two individuals recognized the writing. Ruby Young had every intention of passing along her information to police, but before she could do so, her friend Robert Wood, whom she knew had written the postcard, called on her. Ruby accused Robert of the being the writer. He didn't deny it, but had a ready explanation as to how his card had ended up in a murdered woman's apartment.

Robert told Ruby that he had met a woman named Phyllis in the Rising Sun. They had a few drinks. When Phyllis told him she collected postcards, he produced one. Phyllis was delighted and asked him to write something nice on it. He wrote the note as a sort of an appointment, but when he went to sign it, Phyllis instructed him to sign it "Alice." He told Phyllis he would mail it, and placed it in his pocket. Next day, strictly by coincidence, he met Phyllis on the street. They talked a bit and separated. The day after that, he mailed the postcard. A day later, he dropped into the Rising Sun and bumped into Phyllis once more, but she left without him and he never saw her again. Ruby believed Robert's story and didn't pass her information on to Scotland Yard. After all, she had known Robert off and on for three years. For two of those years, the pair had been intimate.

The other person who recognized the writing on the postcard was a Mr. Tinkham, who worked with Robert Wood at a fancy glassware manufacturing company. Tinkham told Robert of his suspicions and Robert gave him the same basic story he'd given Ruby Young. He too believed Robert and did nothing. It should be pointed out that Robert Wood was a respected artist and executive with his company. He had been employed by the firm for 14 years, had no criminal record and was considered to be a fine upstanding citizen.

During the height of the investigation, Robert met with his old flame Ruby on several occasions and urged her to tell anyone who asked that he had been with her on the night of Phyllis's murder. Sometimes Ruby wavered, but always agreed to lie for Robert. He also looked up a Mr.

Lambert, whom he knew had seen him with Phyllis at a pub about a week before the murder. He implored Lambert not to reveal what he knew. Robert explained that he wasn't guilty of any wrongdoing. He just didn't want to get involved in a murder case as it would be an embarrassment to his father. Lambert agreed that there was no reason for him to tell anyone what he knew.

Robert had effectively stifled those people who could connect him to Phyllis's murder, except for one thing—human nature. Ruby Young couldn't resist telling a friend the whole story. The friend told a newspaperman, who in turn informed Scotland Yard. On October 4, 1907, Robert Wood was taken into custody. Two days later he was charged with Phyllis Dimmock's murder.

In December 1907, Robert stood trial for Phyllis's murder. The Crown produced a witness, Mac Cowan. Although Cowan could not identify Robert by sight as the man he had seen leaving Phyllis's apartment on the morning after the murder, he was able to identify him by his distinctive walk.

Robert Wood was represented by the finest English defence lawyer of his time, Sir Edward Marshall Hall. He pointed out that Robert had no motive for killing Phyllis. None of the articles missing from Phyllis's home were ever traced to Robert, nor was the murder weapon found in his home. As for Robert's attempts to have friends and colleagues lie to protect him, Marshall Hall claimed that he went to such trouble because he didn't want his family to find out that he often associated with prostitutes. Marshall Hall further asserted that despite Robert's suspicious behaviour, there was nothing to connect him to the crime other than he had admittedly known the victim. He dismissed Cowan's eyewitness identification as an honest mistake.

The English jury returned a verdict of not guilty, after which the courtroom crowd gave Robert Wood a standing ovation.

Karen Anne Woodcock
(Canada)

CRIMINAL INVESTIGATION Branch File #621100540/73 is dog-eared. The thick file at the Ontario Provincial Police headquarters has been handled repeatedly. Stark black letters identify the documents inside: KAREN ANNE WOODCOCK—HOMICIDE

Floyd and Karen Woodcock were married in Peterborough, Ontario, on May 15, 1958. By the summer of 1973, the couple lived in their own home in the village of Villiers in Otonabee Township, a few miles from Peterborough. They had seven children, ranging in age from 4 to 15. Floyd was employed as a welder with the Outboard Marine Co. in Peterborough.

Karen had decided to go back to work. In the fall of 1972, she had enrolled in a commercial stenographic course at Sir Sandford Fleming Community College in Peterborough. Karen was a better than average student. She was active in the school paper and was well liked by both teachers and students. The forty weeks flew by; June 29 was to be Karen's graduation. Certainly a happy day by anyone's standards, but particularly for a woman returning to school after raising seven children.

The Woodcocks' story seems to portray a contented, industrious couple forging their way ahead in the world. This may have been so, but their marriage did have one flaw. Both were heavy drinkers, but not on a day-to-day basis. Every four months or so, Karen would go on a binge.

Sometimes with her husband, and sometimes alone, she would stay drunk for three or four days.

Karen was well known in the beverage rooms of Peterborough. Regulars took her to their homes, where all-night drinking bouts would only be interrupted when someone passed out. Karen's drinking habits in no way were a reflection on her morals. No one has ever insinuated that she did anything but drink with her male companions. Usually these periodic bouts ended with Karen sleeping if off at her father's home. Floyd often picked her up there to take her home.

Floyd drove into Peterborough on June 29 to attend his wife's graduation. Quite by chance he ran into Daniel Robert Smith, a co-worker at Outboard Marine. Together they went to the McGillis Hotel. After only one beer they moved to the Grand Hotel. Floyd later excused himself to attend his wife's graduation. Still later, both he and Karen joined Smith at the McGillis. The three of them drank away the rest of the afternoon. At around 6:30 p.m. they left the beverage room to continue the party at Smith's residence. In the meantime, Karen Woodcock took a taxi to a liquor store where she picked up three bottles of gin and two bottles of wine. Smith paid for the two bottles of gin, and the Woodcocks paid the balance.

At around 8:30 p.m., Floyd suggested that it was time to call an end to the party. Karen would hear none of it. Floyd had often left his wife at parties before, and this was one of those times. He left and she remained, drinking with Smith until about 10:30 p.m. Then the pair went hotel hopping, visiting the King George Hotel and Queen Hotel in Peterborough. At the Queen, Smith left Karen for a fev moments to say hello to some friends. When he returned she was gone.

Karen left the hotel and contacted another friend, Daniel Johnson. She slept overnight at Johnson's residence on Reid Street. The next day, Saturday, June 30, Karen and Johnson drank all day, consuming three bottles of wine. They had nothing to eat.

At 1:30 a.m. on Sunday, July 1, Mrs. Woodcock showed up at the home of her father, Edwin Mitchell, at 617 Ludgate Street in Peterborough. Mr. Mitchell, who was having a few drinks himself, can only remember that his daughter made a phone call and then left.

Percy Johnson was the father of Mrs. Woodcock's drinking buddy, Daniel Johnson. At 3:15 a.m. his phone rang. A female voice asked for his son. He quite naturally replied that his son was sleeping, and he hung up. It is believed that this is the call Karen made from her father's home.

Unable to reach Daniel Johnson, Karen left her father's house. At 3:30 a.m. Ronald Baldwin had just driven his babysitter home. He was returning to his own home when he spotted Karen. She wanted a lift. Ronald Baldwin drove her to the corner of Parkhill Road and Reid Street. He was back in his own home at 4 a.m.

At 4:20 a.m. Harold Morton, an employee of Canadian Pittsburgh Glass, was on his way to install a window at Minacola's Furniture Store. He noticed a woman hitchhiking about twenty feet south of the Parkhill Road intersection. He thought she was drunk. It was Karen. Other than her killer, Harold Morton was the last person to see Karen Woodcock alive.

At 7:20 a.m. Fred Simmond was driving to work. Beside the road, but plainly visible from his car, Fred spotted the nude body of Karen Woodcock. The exact spot was about two miles north of the Woodcock residence at Villiers, just south of Highway 7. Simmond never got out of his car. Instead, he continued to the home of Grant Elmhairst. The two men viewed the body together. They returned to the Elmhairst residence and called the OPP detachment in Peterborough.

Beside the nude body the police found an indentation in the soil where a rock had been dislodged. Karen had obviously been beaten about the head with the rock. An autopsy revealed that her death had been caused by a fractured skull. She had firmly held on to her purse strap with her left hand. The purse was open and the contents, which included $32.02, appeared intact. Karen had not been sexually interfered with. None of her clothing was ever found.

Between the hours of 4:20 a.m. and 7:02 a.m. on the first day of July, someone picked up Karen Woodcock and rained blows to her head with a rock until she was dead. Who and why?

Every movement made by Karen Woodcock from the time she started partying after her graduation has been gone over moment by moment by the Ontario Provincial Police. They think they know the identity of her killer.

Many months before the murder, a drinking companion attempted to sexually attack Mrs. Woodcock while her husband was asleep upstairs in their home. No charges were ever brought against the man. Two days after the murder, the same man came forward voluntarily to the OPP in Peterborough. He had information which tended to support his claim that he was so drunk the early morning hours of July 1 that he didn't know where he was. Upon investigating this man, police believe he went out of his way to establish his movements as far away from the scene of the murder as possible.

The police succeeded in having this suspect submit to a polygraph test. Partway through the test the man changed his mind and refused to continue. From the amount of testing done, an expert in this field feels that this man had knowledge concerning the death of Karen Woodcock.

Despite this incriminating piece of information, there is no direct link between the murdered woman and the suspect. He is at large and refuses to discuss the case with investigating officers.

Peter Woodcock
(Canada)

IT WAS ANOTHER era, another world, really, almost 43 years ago that January 15, 1957, when it happened. Under the byline of a young *Toronto Telegram* reporter named Douglas Creighton, Torontonians first heard of the disappearance of four-year-old Carol Voyce.

Six hours after the youngster disappeared, her body was found, beaten and sexually assaulted, under an archway of the Prince Edward viaduct in Toronto's East End.

On that fateful January day, Mrs. Bernadette Voyce decided to visit her friend Mrs. William Auld, who lived only a few blocks from the Voyce residence. Bernadette gathered up Carol and together they set off for the Auld home at 1066 Danforth Avenue. When they arrived, they met four-year-old Johnny Auld. Carol stayed outside to play with Johnny.

A few minutes later, Peter Woodcock, 18, rode up on his distinctive cream-and-red bicycle and struck up a conversation with the two children. He asked the pair if they wanted to go for a ride on his crossbar. Both said yes. Peter chose Carol. That choice was to preordain that Johnny Auld would live and Carol Voyce would die.

As Johnny watched, the nice older boy pedalled away down the road with Carol. Johnny then ran into the house and told his mother that Carol had taken a ride with a boy on a bicycle. The two women, sensing that something was amiss, ran outside. Carol was nowhere to be found. They met Constable Earl Newman, who reported Carol missing. The search for the little girl was on.

Hours later, her body was discovered near the Prince Edward viaduct. Her blood-smeared snowsuit, along with other clothing, was found nearby. Carol had been attacked and mauled by some sadistic monster. The child's face had been pressed down into mud. An autopsy revealed that the cause of death was asphyxiation.

Several children had been attacked during the previous eighteen months, and scores of teenagers had been questioned in the course of these investigations. Now police had a description of the wanted boy and his bicycle, provided by little Johnny Auld. They also had impressions of bicycle-tire tracks leading from the scene of the murder. The tracks indicated that the killer had left the little girl's body and had proceeded by way of nearby railroad tracks. He had walked along the tracks with his bicycle, then remounted and pedalled until he reached a paved road, where all traces of the killer disappeared.

The *Toronto Telegram* featured a composite sketch of the wanted boy. North York Constable George Douglas couldn't get the description of the boy out of his mind. Months earlier, while investigating another sex crime, he had questioned a youth named Peter Woodcock. Douglas was sure that the drawing matched Woodcock's appearance in every detail. He passed along his hunch to detectives James Crawford and Edward Blakeley.

The two detectives picked up Woodcock at Bloordale College, a private school he had been attending for three years. At his home, they confiscated a cream-and-red bicycle. Impressions of the tire treads of the bicycle matched those found at the murder scene.

Woodcock appeared to be delighted to be taken to police headquarters. He basked in his new-found importance. When questioned by detectives George Sellers and Dick Gibson, Woodcock admitted being near the murder scene at the time the murder must have taken place. Initially, he described a boy he had seen on a CCM bicycle. The description of the boy and the bicycle was quite unlike his own.

Detectives then informed him of the mounting evidence, such as the bicycle tracks, pointing to him as the killer. Faced with these facts, Woodcock confessed in detail to the mad-dog-type murder of Carol Voyce. He related a tale of horror that placed him as one of the most diabolical killers in Canadian history.

Detective James Crawford, who picked up Woodcock so many years ago, remembers well the slightly built teenager with the horn-rimmed glasses. Crawford recalls, "Woodcock was responsible for the deaths of three children and several other attacks. Some of his victims were sexually attacked, strangled and left for dead, but regained consciousness and lived."

A 14-year-old youngster, who has never been identified, had been committed to the Toronto Psychiatric Hospital for the murder of seven-year-old Wayne Mallette. Woodcock proved without a doubt that it was he who had killed the Mallette child. The boy who had been incarcerated for six months was released.

Peter Woodcock stood trial for the murder of Carol Voyce. There was no doubt that he had committed the murder. The tire tracks, teeth marks on the body that matched an impression made of Woodcock's teeth, as well as his confession, left only his sanity in question. Woodcock was found not guilty by reason of insanity and incarcerated at Oak Ridges, the maximum security unit of the Penetanguishene Mental Health Centre.

It has been almost 43 years since this monster disguised as a human was incarcerated. Wars have been fought since that day when Peter Woodcock snuffed out the life of little Carol Voyce. Detective Jim Crawford rose in the police force to head the homicide squad before retiring. Constable George Douglas left the police force, went into private business and still lives in the greater Toronto area. Detective Edward Blakeley suffered a fatal stroke at age 59. Reporter Douglas Creighton went on to co-found the *Toronto Sun.*

But what of the slightly built boy with the horn-rimmed glasses sent away to the Penetanguishene Mental Health Centre? A few years ago, Woodcock had his name legally changed to David Michael Krueger. The man who terrorized Toronto as an 18-year-old youth is now 61 years old. He was successful in obtaining a transfer from the maximum security unit in Penetang to the medium security unit of the Brockville Psychiatric Hospital.

On July 15, 1991, David Michael Krueger, once known as Peter Woodcock, and former Penetang patient Bruce Hamill were charged with the murder of patient Dennis Kerr. Kerr had been beaten to death in what may have been a homosexual love triangle.

Peter Woodcock has again been charged with murder, just as he was 42 years ago. As you read this, he is back in the Penetanguishene Mental Health Centre, which will no doubt be his home for the rest of his life.

Celebrity Murders
and Other Nefarious Deeds

For the last twenty-five years, Max Haines has been feeding the public's undying fascination for true crime with his captivating stories of devious deeds, cons, and murders.

From Martin Luther King to Nicole Brown Simpson; from Marilyn Monroe to Errol Flynn; from John F. Kennedy to Charlie Chaplin: the most celebrated personalities in the annals of true crime are featured in this exciting new volume from Max Haines, Canada's master of mayhem.

Whether perpetrator, victim, or suspect, celebrities have been involved in some of the most mysterious and shocking crimes ever committed—crimes of sex, violence, passion, stupidity, debauchery, deception and greed.

So lock the doors, pull up the covers, and get ready to enter the fascinating world of celebrity crime.

Murders Strange
but True

FROM A MODERN-DAY GREEK TRAGEDY complete with a murderous mother-in-law, and backyard bonfire, to lesbian lovers who allow nothing—and nobody—to stand in the way of their affection, MURDERS STRANGE BUT TRUE sets the stage for murder most foul. Impeccably researched and filled with the meticulous attention to detail that has become Max Haines's trademark, his sparkling talent as a storyteller adds life, drama, and even humour to some of the most shocking and baffling criminal investigations of all time.

Meet Michael Sams who, after holding Stephanie Slater prisoner in a tight-fitting wooden coffin for seven days,. released his hostage with these parting words, "Get back to your normal life as soon as possible. You may need some counseling. I'm sorry it had to be you."

No one spins a murderous yarn quite like Max Haines. Encompassing the genres of suspense-thriller and murder-mystery, MURDERS STRANGE BUT TRUE depicts real people, in incredible situations, who commit unbelievable crimes, and is a haunting reminder that truth is definitely stranger than fiction.

Canadian Crimes

FROM 1890, WHEN BALLADS were sung and poems were written about Reg Birchall and his scheme to become financially secure by means of murder, to the horror of the abhorrent indignities endured by the victims of Paul Bernardo and Karla Homolka, CANADIAN CRIMES provokes a heightened awareness of the deviant figures who live among us, and makes it impossible to deny their grisly existence.

Impeccably researched and filled with the meticulous attention to detail that has become Max Haines's trademark, CANADIAN CRIMES showcases his sparkling talent as a storyteller. True to form, Max adds life, drama, and even humour to some of he most shocking and baffling criminal investigations in Canadian history.